# Notes from the Green Room

*Coping with Stress and Anxiety
in Musical Performance*

Paul G. Salmon
Robert G. Meyer

LEXINGTON BOOKS
*An Imprint of Macmillan, Inc.*
NEW YORK
Maxwell Macmillan Canada
TORONTO
Maxwell Macmillan International
NEW YORK • OXFORD • SINGAPORE • SYDNEY

*To Susan*
—*P.G.S.*

*To Peggy*
—*R.G.M.*

*The music of our lives*

———

*Library of Congress Cataloging-in-Publication Data*

Salmon, Paul
Notes from the green room : coping with stress and anxiety in
musical performance / Paul G. Salmon, Robert G. Meyer.
p. cm.
Includes bibliographical references and index.
ISBN 0-669-25010-4
1. Music—Performance—Psychological aspects. 2. Stress
(Psychology)—Prevention. 3. Anxiety—Prevention. 4. Stress
management. I. Meyer, Robert G. II. Title.
ML3830.S148 1992
781.4′ 3111—dc20 91-48193
CIP
MN

Lexington Books
An Imprint of Macmillan, Inc.
866 Third Avenue, New York, N.Y. 10022

Maxwell Macmillan Canada, Inc.
1200 Eglinton Avenue East
Suite 200
Don Mills, Ontario M3C 3N1

Macmillan, Inc. is part of the Maxwell Communication
Group of Companies.

Printed in the United States of America

printing number
1 2 3 4 5 6 7 8 9 10

# Contents

# Preface

The "green room" is well known to performers. It is where they traditionally await their entrance onstage and is a place that many associate with anxiety and tension. The stressful experiences that many musicians have shared with us—memories of the green room and other aspects of performing—led to the realization that there is a pressing need for psychological resources to be made available to performers to help alleviate these stressors.

Recent years have seen the awakening of marked interest in both psychological and medical aspects of musical performance skills. Although music and the fine arts have always played a prominent role in Western culture and society, the aesthetic aspects of the arts frequently have tended to capture our attention more than the personalities, skills, and traits of those with artistic skills. Granted, there is no lack of information about the lives of persons with notable artistic talents and their personal accomplishments, but until recently relatively little attention has been paid to psychological aspects of performance skills that underlie the many levels of musical performance ability, ranging from that of relative novices to highly professional musicians.

Musical skills exceed many other skills in terms of complexity, potential level of refinement, capacity for expressiveness, and preparatory rigor. It is well known that relatively few performing musicians rise to prominent levels of professional accomplishment, so arduous and demanding is the pathway leading to this plateau. Becoming a performer is not for the faint of heart. Not only does one have to persist through years of rigorous training, but the intense competition any young performer must face is sufficient to discourage all but a persistent few.

Many musicians, possessed of marvelous skills and highly attuned musical sensitivities, flounder during their training for any of a variety of reasons. Some become discouraged by the sheer amount of work, in return for which only the most tenuous promise of subsequent reward is offered. Some, because of practice regimens that leave little time to eat or sleep, experience burn out or incur physical injuries during their formative years of development. Still others fall victim to psychological vulnerabilities associated with performing, chief among these being prolonged stress and anxiety that can markedly detract from the expressive capabilities of even the most skilled performer.

In recent years, musicians, physicians, and other professionals have begun to respond to the obvious need of performers for resources that can help them adapt to chronic stress, intense competition, and prolonged training and preparation. It has become clear that the development of even modest levels of achievement as a performer can be aided by access to educational, medical, and psychological resources that, while no substitute for ability and practice, can help performers refine their skills, cope with stress more effectively, and perhaps make the likelihood of disabling physical or psychological impairments less likely to occur. The recent establishment of medical and psychological clinical treatment centers for performing musicians signals a clear awareness of the physical and mental health needs of performing musicians. With increasing frequency, books, articles, manuscripts, and other resources are beginning to appear devoted to various aspects of musical performance skills, and there is increasing evidence of significant scientific interest in the exploration and refinement of musical performance skills as well. The past five years have seen a real awakening of interest in the characteristics and needs of performers that has stimulated work in a variety of health- and education-related fields.

This book has developed out of the several years of work that led to the establishment of the Performance Skills Program at the University of Louisville, under the direction of the first author. It is intended to help address the psychological needs of performing musicians, particularly as they can be related to problems of stress, anxiety, and tension. This book also represents an attempt to merge contemporary psychological theories of stress and anxiety with a consideration of several pragmatic aspects of becoming an effective performer. Clearly, the advice offered here is not intended to supplant musical instruction, but rather to serve as a source of information to broaden the perspectives of musical performers on factors related to personal identity, stress-handling capabilities, practice and work habits, and coping skills. Many of the ideas and techniques described throughout the book were developed in conjunction with clients who participated (and continue to participate) in the Performance Skills Program. One of the basic tenets of this book is that therapeutic assistance is successful to the degree that it enables performers to effectively analyze and remedy their own performing skills. One of the clearest conclusions to emerge from work with performing musicians is that there is a pressing need to integrate more effectively the disciplines of musical pedagogy, psychology, and medicine. In particular, it is becoming increasingly evident that the *prevention* of psychological and medical impairments in performers, rather than just their alleviation, should be the focus of collaborative, interdisciplinary activity.

Contemporary work on anxiety and stress in the field of psychology increasingly has emphasized the need for a consideration of the roles that mental, physical, and behavioral factors play in the evolution of skills—musical or otherwise. This dynamic relationship has been embodied in a variety of psychological therapy techniques collectively referred to as *cognitive-behavioral* and is firmly rooted in contemporary scientific investigations that have left little doubt that few behaviors can be adequately explained in simple, straightforward terms. Thus, the antidote to stage fright is not simply to think positively, any more than the attainment of musical perfection is simply to practice. Central to this perspective is the idea that behavior is governed by the confluence of a variety of factors reflecting both our psychological and biological makeup.

Much of our work with performing musicians aims to help them become effective evaluators of their own musical expressions so that they can make better use of learning, practice, and rehearsal time. The techniques described throughout the book, while helpful in their own right, are especially important because they have resulted from thoughtful analyses of performance-related issues by performers attempting to grapple effectively with a variety of roadblocks to musical expressiveness. We offer no predetermined solutions for alleviating the many sources of stress and anxiety that affect performers and make no claims as to the efficacy of the techniques described here in the absence of basic skill, preparation, and motivation. What we do offer are some ideas and suggestions that, if applied thoughfully and carefully, can make perceptible differences in both objective assessments of performance skills and personal appraisals of one's own capabilities. The ultimate goal of our approach is to help performers become liberated from unnecessary feelings of stress and anxiety so that they can become more directly focused on the effective expression of their music.

Many people and organizations have contributed to the development of this book. We are especially grateful to Joel Elkes, M.D., Leah Dickstein, M.D., and our colleagues in the Arts in Medicine Program at the University of Louisville. This innovative program integrates the arts into medical education, practice, and research. It owes its existence to the generosity and steadfast support of a number of persons and institutions. We most gratefully acknowledge the following: Mrs. Mary Bingham, Mr. and Mrs. Barry Bingham, Jr., Mr. and Mrs. Edward Bonnie, Mr. and Mrs. Fritz Drybrough, Mrs. Nana Lampton, Mr. Laurance Rockefeller, Mr. and Mrs. Henry Rolfs, Mrs. Stuart Sales, Mrs. Mary Shands, Mr. and Mrs. Bosworth Todd, Lucy Waletzky, M.D., Ms. Marion Weber, The L. U. Whittier Foundation, The George W. Norton Foundation, The Nathan Cummings Foundation, The Fetzer Institute, the Humana Foundation, and The Institute of Noetic Sciences.

A number of colleagues and friends, through their stimulating ideas, have contributed both directly and indirectly. Among these are Gail Berenson, Alice Brandfonbrener, Janet Borden, David Casey, Melvin and Margaret Dickinson, Allan Grishman, Jeffrey Jamner, Judith Kupersmith, Paul and Phyllis Lehrer, Susan Matarese, Peter McHugh, Jonathan Newmark, Naomi Oliphant, Robert Parris, Dallas Tidwell, Jesse Wright, and others too numerous to mention. The administrative staff of the Arts in Medicine Program provided typing and secretarial support through many drafts and revisions of the manuscript. The assistance of our editors at Lexington Books, Paul O'Connell, Margaret Zusky, and Carol Mayhew throughout the preparation of this manuscript, is gratefully acknowledged. We feel that the development of this book has been a truly collaborative undertaking and hope that the final product adequately represents the considerable assistance and support provided by our colleagues.

Finally, we thank those performers who have so openly shared with us their experiences in the "green room," on stage, and in practice studies. They give so much to others through their music, often at great personal cost. We hope that this book in some small way repays these and other performers for so enriching our lives.

*Note:* Names and other identifying information concerning performers mentioned throughout this book have been altered to ensure confidentiality.

# The Performer

**B**etsy: *By the time she was a high school student, Betsy had decided on a career in music. A talented pianist, she had studied since age six with a variety of teachers, all of whom agreed that she possessed the necessary skills to "make it." Her parents were supportive as well, investing their time and money on lessons, music camps, concert appearances, and on an expensive instrument for Betsy to play. Betsy was a serious student and a seasoned performer who practiced for hours each day; she had already won a number of important competitions and auditions by the time she was fifteen. To an outsider, conditions appeared ideal for the advancement of a very promising career, and upon graduation she was accepted as a student at a prestigious conservatory affiliated with a good university. By the end of her first year at college, however, Betsy's family was shocked to find her doing poorly in school and on the verge of leaving music altogether.*

What happened? Stories like Betsy's are not uncommon, and almost everyone can think of friends, colleagues, or classmates whose apparently promising careers in the performing arts have been derailed for one reason or another. Even so, Betsy's situation might seem difficult to understand because of the favorable circumstances that surrounded her early development. Gaining a clearer understanding of the factors that led to the surprising turn of events in Betsy's life requires that we adopt a broad psychological vantage point and consider what is entailed in the process of becoming a successful musical performer.

It was not until comparatively recently that the practice of performing what might be referred to as "classical" music in public became widespread, and only quite recently that the idea of having a career as a professional musician became feasible. Music is a very social activity, and for centuries it was performed extensively in settings where people convened for specific purposes, such as religious services and secular ceremonies. In these contexts, performers played a somewhat subsidiary role to the central figures, and there was relatively little emphasis on the importance of individualized musical skills. Musical virtuosity for its own sake was not stressed.

From time to time, individual musicians were recognized for their unique performance skills. It is interesting that many were composers, adept at playing their own music, which was often beyond the capabilities of less gifted musicians. J. S. Bach, for example, had such extraordinary musical gifts that his performances—particularly as an organist—became legendary. Likewise, Mozart was recognized early as much for his precocious performance skills as for his gifts as a composer. Paganini's reputation for virtuosity as a violinist rested largely on his ability to play his own works, which were beyond the comprehension of most of his contemporaries. Likewise, Franz Liszt's astonishing pianistic skills attracted crowds, who came to hear him play his own piano works. Many of his performances had a theatrical quality, which was allegedly heightened by Liszt's penchant for casually tossing his gloves to the swooning audience when he first appeared onstage.

Not all—in fact, not many—composers are gifted performers. The converse appears to be equally true, particularly because the rigorous demands of a performing career leave little time for more comtemplative activities such as composing. These observations imply that a distinction between the tasks of composing and performing music, and thus an increasing specialization of labor, have gradually developed. A good example is the German composer Max Reger, who, though a competent organist, could not play many of his own works. Instead, he relied on an organist who was allegedly able to play the composer's works on first sight, despite their dense, complex musical structure.

Today's performer faces a very different world from that of the nineteenth-century concert artist. For one thing, there are far more skillful and highly trained performers than ever before. Competition for playing engagements is intense, and the process of winnowing out promising performers begins very early. Children in grade schools frequently are exposed to the rigors of competitions, auditions, and performances, which begin a process of identifying an increasingly select group of musically gifted individuals. Those who survive this selection process must deal with intense competition for admission to a conservatory or university, where they are suddenly thrust into the limelight of an arena shared by other equally, if not more, gifted individuals. The survivors of this winnowing then face a comparatively limited number of jobs and, frequently, the prospect of economic hardship. It is little wonder, then, that many otherwise extremely capable performers find the physical and psychological stresses associated with becoming a professional musician to be more than they can handle.

The capacity to adapt to the rigors of life in the world of the musical performer is not something acquired overnight. Rather, several identifiable stages in the psychological development of the individual appear to have a cumulative effect on the ability to cope with the demands of a musical career. These are discussed elsewhere in greater detail.[1] For the time being, suffice it to say that the process sometimes goes awry, as once-promising careers seems to founder unaccountably.

To explore this problem a bit further, let's return to Betsy's situation. Although extremely musically gifted, she was also a rather shy and sensitive child. She seemed to make friends relatively easily, but she spent a great deal of time by herself, absorbed in a variety of solitary pursuits. Her musical aptitude became apparent at an early age, when she spontaneously learned to play tunes she had heard on the radio on the piano. Her father, a part-time violinist, became convinced that Betsy was highly gifted and decided to seek every opportunity to advance her musical development. Convinced that an early start was vital, he began what turned into an endless quest for the perfect teacher to work with his daughter. As it turned out, no one proved suitable, with the result that, by the time she was twelve, Betsy had studied with five different teachers over a five-year period.

Betsy approached each new teacher with great enthusiasm and

interest and would practice diligently for a few months. Her parents, buoyed by these signs of progress, relaxed a bit, but nonetheless continued to keep a close eye on her practicing and playing. Eventually, her motivation would begin to diminish noticeably, to her parents' great consternation. A conference with the teacher would be held and things would improve again for a while. Eventually, however, Betsy's parents would decide that she wasn't making enough progress and switch to a new teacher.

Betsy's teachers were uniformly impressed with her musical aptitude and felt that she had the abilities needed to succeed in a professional career. Nevertheless, all of them commented to her parents that she seemed to be a somewhat anxious, self-absorbed child and that she didn't seem to derive much pleasure from music. This feedback was not well received by Betsy's parents, who felt that it was the responsibility of a good teacher to motivate musically gifted children, whatever their degree of interest at the outset.

Betsy continued her piano studies and, despite erratic motivation, made substantial progress overall. In the eighth grade, she also successfully auditioned for a local community orchestra in the second violin section. Gradually, she began to attract the attention of the local music community as a rising star. As a high school senior, she narrowly missed winning a competition to play Mozart's *Coronation* concerto with a nearby college orchestra, finishing second to a student a year younger than herself. A good student as well, Betsy gained admission to a college music conservatory some distance from home and was awarded a partial scholarship.

In this new environment, Betsy seemed to be at a loss. Without the structure provided by her parents and last teacher, she found it difficult to either study or practice. As a performance major, she was only one of many talented musicians, many of whom had established enviable credentials in the musical world as soloists or ensemble players. She was both astonished and intimidated by the work habits of many of her peers, who disappeared into practice rooms for hours at a stretch, emerging only for a trip to the Coke machine or the bathroom. Performances suddenly acquired greater significance than she could have imagined. Playing before her peers and the faculty at weekly convocations, she became increasingly self-conscious, and she even experienced occasional inexplicable spasms of panic. Confused, depressed, anxious over her inability to cope with this situation, and convinced that she was a failure, she made plans to leave school and return home. Only a chance encounter with one of her teachers, who sensed her dilemma, led to a reassessment of the situation and, ultimately, to her decision to seek help at the university's psychology clinic.

Betsy's struggle to pursue a career in musical performance was handicapped by problems involving motivation, personal relationships, and her musical background. With respect to the first of these, her motivation to perform was based largely on the support and encouragement of others, including her parents, teachers, and the audiences, whose applause she took as a sign of acceptance and validation. Yet she herself had never come to terms with what it means to pursue a career in the performing arts. She was attracted to the image of being a performer, but she had not articulated to herself how success is related to the process needed to achieve it. Betsy could easily visualize herself at the center of everyone's attention on the concert stage, but she didn't link this concept to the music she practiced every day. Her image of performing was based more on sight than on sound, more on a picture of herself than on an impression of the music she could make.

What little personal motivation she possessed was largely negative and involved feelings of guilt. Betsy felt almost morally obligated to make good use of her musical talents because of all the time and money that other people had invested in her musical development. She felt compelled to practice and perform partly because doing otherwise would greatly disappoint her parents and teachers, whose sense of well-being she believed to be largely dependent on her own behavior.

A second factor that seriously impeded Betsy's development as a musician concerned her relationships with her parents and teachers. Betsy was a conduit through whom the others communicated. Her parents judged the quality of her instruction on how well they believed she played and how much time she spent practicing. Accustomed to taking an active role in their childrens' development, they felt obligated to assess her progress nearly every day. This task was difficult for them, however, because neither parent had a clear idea of what was reasonable to expect of Betsy. Her father, a violinist of modest talent and even more modest accomplishment, saw in his daughter a chance to redeem himself. He expected a great deal of her, and expressed considerable impatience at teachers whom he felt were not pushing her hard enough. Betsy's mother was an intuitive, emotionally expressive individual who shared her daughter's sensitive temperament and whose own motivations varied with her many moods. An accomplished writer, Betsy's mother believed in the idea that artistic accomplishment is not something that can be forced; as a result, she was inclined to be very tolerant of Betsy's intermittent progress. Likewise, with Betsy's teachers, she tended to adopt a hands-off approach, feeling that active involvement with her daughter's musical training would be an uninvited intrusion. The differences in attitude between Betsy's parents created a number of conflicts, which diminished in intensity whenever she was in one of her more musically productive phases.

Betsy's relationship with her teachers over the years varied markedly. Her first, a kindly, elderly woman who played several instruments including the piano, was the one she remembered best and liked the most. She introduced Betsy to the piano and provided her with elementary instruction. She actively encouraged Betsy's curiosity about the sounds the piano could produce and spent a great deal of time with her exploring the properties of the instrument. Never one to demand too much of a student, she stressed the importance of enjoying music and exploring it in creative ways. Unfortunately, failing health caused her to give up teaching a year after Betsy had begun lessons.

Her next teacher was a high school music instructor who gave private lessons to supplement his income. A forceful and dynamic individual, he was an enthusiastic teacher who expected much of his students. Betsy was somewhat overwhelmed by him at the outset, but later found his enthusiasm infectious. Things went well for the first few months, as Betsy began to progress steadily through the timeless, color-coded series of *John Thompson* instructional books. During this time it became apparent that she could not only read simple tunes, but also play by ear and even harmonize some of the pieces she knew. Her teacher, a former nightclub jazz pianist, encouraged this tendency, much to the consternation of her father. And so, after less than a year, it was time for a new new teacher.

Teacher number three was a somewhat haughty descendent of the old school, who stressed discipline and rigid adherence to musical scores. A perfectionist, she had the habit of rapping her students' knuckles with a steel-edged ruler when they made mistakes, and she had little tolerance for those who didn't practice assiduously. Betsy worked diligently at first—mostly from fear—and by all objective accounts progressed quite rapidly. During this time, she participated in her first official recital, a formal affair held on a Sunday afternoon with the other students and their parents in attendance. Betsy—or, rather, her teacher—had selected the piece to be played, and she performed it in a dutiful, calculated manner. Subsequent recitals, held precisely at six-month intervals, were very much like the first one in being formal occasions where a premium was placed on proper decorum, note-for-note accuracy, and *serious* music.

Betsy's parents had differing opinions about this teacher. Her father felt that the highly disciplined approach would be helpful in the long run, while her mother believed that her daughter's playing, while technically impeccable, was devoid of life or artistry. To avoid a protracted debate, they switched teachers again, this time to a young woman who had recently joined the faculty of a nearby college with a good music program. A recent graduate of a conservatory and an active recitalist, she seemed to embody the strengths of most of Betsy's previous teachers without their liabilities. Within this relationship, which endured for two years, Betsy's interest in music really seemed to take root. She began to practice more consistently than before, and her playing became more lively. With her teacher's encouragement, she played in several auditions and various local piano competitions, nearly always finishing somewhere near the top. Although her teacher encouraged her participation in these events, Betsy increasingly resisted such frequent ordeals. Although she was technically quite skilled, Betsy had little sense of how to communicate her musicianship effectively to audiences and ajudicators. As a result, she received equivocal feedback, with many lukewarm comments. When her teacher began to promote the idea that Betsy begin work on a concerto for a regional competition, she rebelled and refused to continue her studies. This impasse, when Betsy was a sophomore in high school, was resolved only with another change of teachers. Having nearly decided to give up the piano altogether, Betsy agreed to take lessons only on a trial basis with a local teacher recommended by the university. An experienced performer and teacher, he was aware from the start that playing the piano for Betsy was laden with psychological conflicts and emotional distress accumulated during the years she had wandered from one teacher to the next. Known for his skill in working with young musicians, he spent much time during Betsy's early lessons simply encouraging her to talk about her experiences as a musician. This novel experience proved somewhat threatening at first, because Betsy had learned to use her music as a means of protecting herself from encounters with other people. Moreover, she had never thought much about *why* she performed; she had merely presumed that she was obligated to do so, whatever the cost in psychological or physical terms. Having a teacher who elicited her opinions about music, sought to understand her personal motivations for playing, and made her aware that she had the freedom to choose whether or not to play, was both confusing and exhilarating.

The process of self-discovery triggered by her last teacher carried over into her first year in college. Having begun to see her musical development in terms of options rather than obligations, Betsy suddenly found herself with greater freedom than she was accustomed to. Already doubting the sincerity of her motivation to become a performer, she found it difficult to cope with the realization that she was only one of many students competitively pursuing a musical career. Stunned by the intensity with which many of her peers pursued their musical training, she looked for ways to justify her own shortcomings and thereby minimize threats to her brittle self-esteem.

She had never established a stable, effective student–teacher relationship with any of her instructors, whose markedly contrasting styles of teaching and personalities further disoriented her. Neither, when she entered college, had Betsy established a clear sense of how to practice and prepare her music for performance. Like many other talented youngsters, she had been able to play well enough to impress the people who were important to her as she grew up, and even those who were aware of her limitations assumed that they would somehow be worked out once she began her university studies. Although she had played a number of auditions and competitions, she had done little or no performing under less stressful, more enjoyable, circumstances. Every performance had been important in some way, and she had had little time to relax with music and simply enjoy it.

The third aspect of Betsy's problem, alluded to earlier, involved her basic pianistic skills. She was at something of a disadvantage when she began college because of somewhat faulty technique. Because she had been capable, as a child, of playing music that sounded impressive to the naive listener, she had tended to forego the rigors of learning études and other technique-building exercises. Much of the time her practice consisted of playing through pieces in a perfunctory manner, as if repetition alone could ensure adequate assimilation. Possessed of both a good memory and an intuitive awareness of musical structure, she tended to spend comparatively little time working out the technical details of pieces. Although she was able to absorb a great deal of music in this manner, her approach to learning and practicing ultimately proved to be a liability when she was faced with stressful performance situations such as concerts and auditions.

Her teachers had approached this problem in a number of ways, none of which had been entirely successful. They were caught between wanting to cultivate her significant musical aptitude and demanding the systematic practice they knew to be necessary for anyone contemplating a career in music. Betsy's motivation was as mercurial as her moods, a trait that she shared with her mother. Consequently, she found it difficult to maintain a systematic pattern of practicing, and she was more likely to work during periods of intense energy.

A question that Betsy ultimately came to pose to herself, and one that is important for any musician to consider, was "Why perform?" There's no simple answer to this question, although it's easy to get musicians to volunteer plausible responses. Betsy's reasons were many and varied. She performed partly to please her parents and teachers. She performed because she was interested in the communicative aspects of music and how it can be shared with other people. At times, she performed to get a good grade, or to win the respect of her peers. It is less certain, however, whether she performed as the result of any deep-seated love of music itself.

If one were to make a list of some of the conscious or unconscious motives that drive performers, it might look something like this:[2]

For self-expression
As a form of sharing

To express a composer's intentions
To please or impress others—peers, teachers, parents
To impress others with your skills
To make money
To pass a course, or exam, or to graduate from music school
To provide a new interpretation of a piece of music
As a test of your confidence and abilities
For pleasure and enjoyment
To forget, at least temporarily, other problems
To get back at someone who said you'd never amount to
    anything
As a means of structuring a part of your life
Because you have nothing else to do
As a means of avoiding things you'd rather not deal with

Just as conscious motives differ from one person to another, they can shift markedly within any one person as his or her circumstances change. However, it is possible to discern in this array of possibilities a pattern of development that may be related to a performer's maturation.

It's unlikely that most performers, as children, are deeply analytical about their music and how they perform it. For one thing, their cognitive capabilities have not matured enough to fully appreciate the structural and artistic aspects of a piece of music. Nor are they likely, at least at the outset, to be highly self-conscious about playing music for themselves or others. Many begin to play because they are encouraged by parents, or because they are incidentally discovered to possess certain sensitivities that adults around them interpret as musical talent. Much of the reinforcement for playing and, later, performing comes from the praise and approval children receive for doing it. Often, it is long after a child has learned to play well enough to gain approval from parents and teachers that the importance of the medium itself—the music—begins to have any intrinsic meaning. This observation is not meant to deny that children possess an innate affinity for music, because there is ample evidence that they do. Rather, the social context in which music is normally performed becomes the focus of children's attention. It's difficult to divorce music from a network of powerful social forces comprised of parents, teachers, and peers. No only to children learn to play music, but they also come to associate musical performing with social circumstances.

Although playing to earn recognition can continue to be a powerful motivator throughout a performer's career, other factors inevitably come into play. In general, motivation becomes increasingly internalized as one's musical development progresses. If we are initially drawn to play music because of the positive reactions it evokes in other people, our interest is likely to deepen only when we find more intrinsic sources of pleasure. One such satisfaction centers in the sense of mastery and pleasure derived from the ability to perform complex tasks, musical or otherwise. Playing and performing on a musical instrument can be intrinsically rewarding because of the challenging complexities involved. Mastery, in turn, is associated with feelings of pleasure and a sense of well-being.

And what of the music itself? At what point does a Mozart sonata, for instance, evoke personal responses linked to factors other than social acceptance or a generalized sense of mastery? There are indications that performers can gain the skills necessary to master highly complex musical works without necessarily learning to appreciate their artistic value. A frequent comment about many current performers is that they possess remarkable technical skills, but their capacity to use them to express music, rather than as an end in themselves, is notably lacking.

From a psychological vantage point, what may be lacking here is a progression from being self-absorbed to being captivated by music itself. Self-absorption is a characteristic response to two rather different situations. First, it involves a tendency to be preoccupied with oneself and is often linked to worry or anxiety.[3] Some people are self-absorbed because they have little else to focus on. Depression, for example, includes a sense of self-absorption. In this sense, self-absorption is a form of deprivation in which the individual is isolated from people and activities that are normally a source of interest and pleasure.

Second, self-absorption can result from a need for self-protection. When we feel threatened, we naturally tend to protect ourselves from the perceived source of danger. When physically threatened, for example, we become preoccupied with protecting ourselves and escaping. Sometimes, however, the perceived threat is to our sense of psychological well-being. For example, situations like taking tests or performing in public, in which, we're likely to be evaluated by other people, can cause considerable self-focused evaluation. The heightened self-consciousness and anxiety that many performers—among them seasoned veterans—report experiencing often stems at least partly from becoming too focused on oneself, rather than on the music, during a performance. Many performers make good progress in developing their technical skill, but persist in playing in a self-absorbed manner. They find it difficult to go beyond this point to a stage where their personal preoccupations are replaced by feeling caught up in the flow of the music.[4]

As far as Betsy is concerned, the story had a bittersweet ending. She eventually decided to stay in college, but changed her plans for becoming a professional performer. She switched her major from one that emphasized performing to music education and decided upon graduation to return home and begin a career as a music teacher. She performed locally with a chamber music group and eventually developed a thriving studio. Nonetheless, from time to time she wondered wistfully what it would have been like if she had become a professional concert artist. Betsy sensed that she had reached a limit in her own psychological development that would have prevented this accomplishment, and she realized that long-standing unresolved anxieties about her capabilities significantly impeded a career as a performer.

Becoming a skilled musician is a daunting prospect. Aside from the discipline and practice involved in learning an instrument, the performer must contend with other factors. Many of these obstacles were evident in Betsy's situation, where we saw how motivation, personal relationships, and issues concerning her musical skills and training all significantly affected her development as a musician. But other issues need to be considered as well, the most important of which concern the nature of performing skills themselves. Opinions vary considerably about both the nature and importance of performance skills. Some musicians, for instance, tend to assume that learning and memorizing a piece of music are sufficient to make it "performance ready." According to this viewpoint, the effectiveness of a performance rests largely on how carefully one has made preliminary preparations. Another perspective is held by those who emphasize the importance of practicing performing. Many college teachers, for example, have performance classes, in which students play their music for others in advance of a more formal performance such as a recital. Depending on how these classes are conducted, the effects may or may not be beneficial.

Effective performance skills are based on a combination of both the above approaches. There's no reason to assume that learning, or even memorizing, a piece of music ensures its readiness for a performance, any more than does exposure to performance situations without meticulous prior preparation. Let's examine how some of these ideas are related to the cultivation of musical performance skills. In subsequent chapters, we will deal with these issues from a broader perspective, but for now lets consider briefly the process of learning a piece of music.[5]

What does it mean to practice and learn a piece of music? Every musician has been told that "practice makes perfect," but this concept is elusive. A young musician is not likely to question the logic of this assertion because for the beginner practice and perfection are relatively easy to define. Practice essentially entails repeating a piece until the notes are all played correctly at a particular tempo— the basic working definition of perfection. It's an idea that obviously has some validity, and its simplicity is appealing both to students and parents who are not well versed in the complexities of music.

Rather than accept this phrase as a statement of fact, we prefer to view it as an assumption that many people accept uncritically. Moreover, we believe that it reflects attitudes toward music that many aspiring performers unquestioningly carry with them into adulthood. Let's look at some of the implications of this view.

There are many different ways of practicing a piece of music. What little evidence there is about how musicians practice tells us that practice strategies vary as a function of the musician's overall level of training. Novices often play pieces through in their entirety without taking much time to analyze what they are doing. They tend to equate repetition with learning and assume, for instance, that playing a particular piece through twenty (or fifty, or one hundred) times will ensure its mastery. A variant of this idea is to judge one's mastery of music based on the amount of time spent practicing—once again without much reference to more musical performance criteria. "I played this through thirty-five times!," a student might protest in response to a teacher's criticism that a piece is not progressing well.

Part of the problem with this approach to learning music is that the performer relies on what he or she feels ought to be the case, rather than on an accurate evaluation of what is happening while the music is being learned or performed. Young children, whether musically inclined or not, are given to counting rituals and ascribe important properties to the most arbitrary of numbers. Counting and other ritualistic behaviors are interesting because, as it turns out, they play a role in learning new skills *and* in helping alleviate feelings of anxiety. Depending on the manner in which it is used, repetition can be either adaptive or maladaptive.

*Adaptive aspects of repetition:* Observations of young children reveal that much of their behavior is highly repetitive. Early behavioral reflexes, such as sucking or grasping, are predictably repetitive in nature and comprise one of the main ways in which an infant first learns about the world. Repetition is evident in the grooming behavior of many species of animals, where it often has a ritualistic quality. Rituals in general are based on cycles of repetition, which vary in length and complexity. Much intentional behavior is repetitive as well, particularly behavior grounded in our capacity to learn. First, repetition underlies the gradual coordination of the components of complex responses, which can range from actions as simple as flipping on a light switch to playing a piece of music at sight. Second, it aids the process of exploring and manipulating objects in one's environment and is an essential part of forming one's inner representations of the world. This function is demonstrated by the exploratory behavior of infants, which is characterized by endless repetitions of simple actions. Piaget has termed such behaviors "circular reactions" and has written extensively about their role in early learning. Third, we learn about cause-and-effect relationships through repetition, as when a child first learns that striking a piano key produces a sound and then repeats the action as if to verify its effect. Fourth, repetition serves to preserve a sense of continuity and provides a way of organizing one's behavior over time. Rituals and ceremonies provide a certain comfort that stems from their effect of maintaining a sense of stability or perhaps timelessness in the face of rapid change so characteristic of modern life.

*Maladaptive aspects of repetition:* Repetition can be a vital aspect of development and learning, but it can also signal the psychological distress usually associated with anxiety. The relationship between anxiety and repetition is complex, but in general repetition is a device used to try to manage or, in some cases, reduce anxiety. Anxiety is a state of acute subjective distress that simultaneously motivates behavior aimed at reducing the distress. Our usual natural response to fear or anxiety is to escape from the situation or avoid it altogether. There are several kinds of responses. If the focus of anxiety is a specific object, simply avoiding contact with it helps minimize anxiety. However, anxiety may often arise from situations that are not easy to avoid. It is difficult, for example, for a child to avoid contact with a parent who evokes anxiety. Troublesome or anxiety-provoking thoughts, too, are difficult to escape because they stem from within the individual. Reducing the anxiety generated by troublesome thoughts requires coping strategies other than physical avoidance.

Repetition may serve as a response to the anxiety associated with high levels of uncertainty. For example, a child instructed to practice a piece of music may desperately want to please the teacher but may not understand how to practice. Given a piece of music to prepare, he or she may play it repeatedly and never really learn it, but at least the child is doing something to counteract the ambiguity in the teacher's instructions.

This consideration of a seemingly simple aspect of the process of learning music—repetition—reveals that there is far more to it than meets the eye. This is true about virtually every aspect of musical performance skills involved in moving from the practice room to the stage. Subsequent chapters of this book explore the psychological aspects of performance skills, with particular consideration given to those that promote tension and anxiety. We are convinced that performance-related stress, whether expressed in muscular tension, psychological distress, or behavior that is counterproductive to effective preparation, almost always reflects a range of contributory influences rather than a simple, single cause. We also believe that learning about these contributory factors requires a careful evaluation of the performer's overall approach to music, whether the presenting problem is defined as specifically as "overuse syndrome" or as broadly as lack of self-confidence.

Becoming a skilled and confident performer obviously does not occur overnight, even though it is tempting to cite stories of young virtuosi with seemingly limitless talent and skill. While it's true that people differ markedly in their aptitude for music, in particular, and more generally in their ability to learn, it is the norm, rather than the exception, for accomplished musicians to spend years developing and progressively refining their performance skills. Despite claims that might be made to the contrary, no psychological techniques can magically improve musical performance skills. The primary reason for this is that psychologically based techniques, including relaxation training, mental imagery and cognitive restructuring involve skills that require time to learn and use effectively. Not only do such techniques entail developing certain skills, but they involve as well adopting a psychological perspective that may initially seem quite foreign to a performer. As a result, it may be necessary to examine and perhaps change one's ideas about performing in order to make effective use of techniques that may not be especially helpful when taken out of context.

Let's look at one example. Suppose that you are preparing for an important performance and are aware that you are becoming very tense. You begin to worry about the tension, which is expressed primarily through a feeling of tightness across the back of your shoulders and neck. It's an unpleasant, sometimes even painful, sensation, and it is made more significant because you find the discomfort distracting and anxiety-provoking. Deciding to do something about the problem, you request an appointment at a clinic that specializes in biofeedback training and other techniques designed to promote muscle relaxation. "I need to relax," you tell the therapist, "because I have an important performance coming up in the near future and I'm really worried abou it." Perhaps, from your perspective, you expect the therapist, on short notice, will be able to teach you to relax in time for the performance, so that you can keep your mind focused on your vital concern—preparing your music to performance-level standards.

Under such circumstances, there is probably very little that could be done to significantly relieve your tension. Certainly, in the course of several visits, you might learn some techniques for reducing muscle tension that would provide temporary relief. But, at a deeper level, such an approach is akin to "band-aid therapy," a procedure that brings temporary, symptomatic relief without dealing with the substance of the problem. Such an approach may prove helpful in certain circumstances, as when excessive muscle tension gets in the way of effective practice, but it does not address the deeper issues that may have led to the development of the problem. To derive more benefit from psychologically oriented treatment, you may find it necessary to examine your approach to music from a broader perspective in order to better understand the factors that contribute to your muscle tension. What might some of these factors be? Let's consider a few possibilities. To begin with, your concept of preparing for a performance may call for hours of unremitting daily practice in which you play each piece through in its entirety as rapidly as you can. You feel somewhat reassured by being able to do so, provided that you make an acceptably small number of mistakes. However, you do not experience an increased confidence in your ability to play well when facing the demands of a performance situation. To counteract the resultant anxiety (or, perhaps, to distract yourself from anxiety), you increase the number of hours devoted to practice, a response that not only makes you more vulnerable to physical strain and even injury, but also does little to increase your confidence.

In a situation of this kind, you've responded to feelings of physical and psychological tension in a way that tends to make the problem worse. Although a common enough response to anxiety, such behavior has the paradoxical effect of either repeating or increasing the frequency of behaviors that gave rise to the problem in the first place. Seen from this vantage point, muscle relaxation training may simply *temporarily* relieve the tension, thereby allowing you to resume the style of practice that caused the tension to begin with. This illustrates how the efforts we make to deal with our problems often compound them instead. It occurs because our problem-solving strategies are often short sighted, focusing on avoiding anxiety rather than real change in behavior or attitudes. It's important to adopt a perspective that allows us to step back from the immediate situation and look at the broader picture.

If you were to do so, here are some of the questions you might ask yourself: What are some of the factors that can give rise to a problem as specific as muscle tension? Could my practice techniques be a contributory factor? How about the ways in which I think about playing and performing? Even though muscle tension is the most apparent symptom of my distress, can I discern other factors that contribute to how I feel? What about the other, more subtle feelings of tension elsewhere in my body that tend to escape notice when the tension in my neck and shoulders is especially prominent? How about other unpleasant, but perhaps more muted physical sensations, such as fatigue or restlessness? How did I come to experience such pressure and tension to begin with? What personal meaning may I have attributed to this performance that might be partly responsible for how I feel physically? What other feelings and sensations do I associate with practicing, playing, and performing? Are these basically enjoyable activities? Are they associated with enjoyment and personal fulfillment? In short, why perform?

If you examine issues such as these, you may feel at first that you are getting sidetracked, or making a mountain out of a molehill, or perhaps becoming too introspective. You may open yourself up to the anxiety that almost always occurs when we question our most deeply held beliefs. In the long run, however, this approach can help you establish a balanced perspective on performance skills and help you come to terms with the realities of the experience of performing.[6]

# 2

# The Psychology of Coping
# with Performance Stress

**M**usicians who spend years developing the abilities needed to become skilled performers frequently are unprepared, in a psychological sense, for the stresses they encounter as they pursue their careers. Years of devotion to the development and refinement of musical skills may prepare an aspiring performer to play a concerto or sing an aria to exacting artistic standards, but such ability by no means ensures success in the highly competitive world of the musical performer.[1] Even for those who choose music as a source of enjoyment rather than as a professional career, performing can be an obstacle that discourages them from exploring this avenue of self-development.

There is no denying the highly competitive nature of music as a profession, particularly with respect to performing. Success, an ephemeral concept at best, is successively defined in terms of whether one studies with the "best" teachers, is admitted to the "best" conservatories, and ultimately secures a position with a prestigious orchestra or embarks on a solo career. Yet experience shows that this path is followed by very few, at most a minuscule proportion, of those with musical training. The situation is somewhat analogous to that of professional athletics; of the vast number of high school and college students who participate in sports, only a very small percentage ever succeed in professional careers.

Nevertheless, college conservatories continue to promote training in musical performance skills, and there is no lack of aspiring musicians willing to undergo the rigors of such training, even though they have no guarantee of securing eventual employment. And even for those who succeed, a career in the performing arts is neither particularly secure nor financially remunerative.

In recent years, increasing attention has been paid to the unique needs of performing musicians and to the medical and psychological stressors associated with this career. There are now a number of clinics around the country where one may seek help for physical injuries or the psychological problems—such as drug abuse, anxiety, and depression—experienced by many performers.[2] With regard to physical problems, increasing evidence shows that the rigors of practicing and performing required for a professional career can lead to serious injury. There are well-documented reports of highly skilled performers who have suffered disabling injuries—which in some instances have ended their careers—as a result of gruelling practicing and performing regimens. Among the best known of these were the pianists Gary Graffman and Leon Fleischer, who developed hand injuries that severely curtailed their careers. Each initially sought medical assistance when little was known about the nature of such injuries, and even less about treatment. Their experiences, however, provoked an interest in the problems by the medical profession and resulted in the establishment of a number of professional organizations and treatment clinics where performers can seek the assistance of clinicians who specialize in performance-related injuries.

Until recently, psychological resources for performers have been comparatively lacking, mainly because the stresses of a career in the performing arts were largely unappreciated. In recent years, however, active interest has focused on such topics as stress management, performance skills, performance anxiety, and the whole process of developing a career in the performing arts.

The interaction between physical and psychological well-being needs to be harmonized in order for performers to cope effectively with the rigors of their discipline. We believe that the successful cultivation of highly refined musical performance skills requires a balance between the requisite physical capabilities and healthy psychological attitudes. Of the necessary prerequisites for healthy psychological adjustment, none is more important than the ability to handle the stresses that are an inevitable part of every performer's life.

Like skilled athletes who single-mindedly refine their abilities, many performers who attain mastery of the craft do so at great personal cost. No more or less human than anyone else, musicians are not exempt from the stresses that everyone has to deal with. They experience problems with relationships, go through identity crises, have financial difficulties, and become ill, all the while having to cope with the stresses of securing and maintaining employment in one of the most fiercely competitive of all professions.

Added to these more-or-less normal forms of stress are the particular difficulties with which many musicians must contend. Gaining admission to and graduating from a noteworthy conservatory requires remarkable perseverance, as well as the ability to tolerate and even flourish in an atmosphere of intense competition. There always seems to be someone who can perform a piece of music you have just learned more expressively, with greater technical facility, or at a much earlier age; this awareness contributes to the psychological one-upmanship many performers describe. Those who master such challenges soon face others that also test their resources. Relationships with teachers, family members, and other students are often critical in determining whether or not an aspiring musician will continue to pursue a career in the performing arts. The challenge of auditions and competitions, where one is brought face to face with others who are equally, if not more skilled, requires highly developed coping skills. Some performers who have successfully dealt with these hurdles find themselves unaccountably seized by uncontrollable stage fright, which sometimes, paradoxically, seems to *increase* as their career takes off. By any definition, the life of a performing musician is highly stressful. Musicians are generally well aware of many of these potential problems, but they don't necessarily receive much sympathy from those outside the profession. For many of us, music is a pleasant diversion that we attend to in our leisure time. From such a vantage point, it can be difficult to conceive how music could be anything but a form of relaxation or entertainment. "How lucky you are to be a musician" is something that virtually every performer has heard, along with statements like, "I wish I had talent like you!" which seems to imply that the cultivation of musical performance skills grants a certain immunity to the stresses of life.

The prevelance of stress today has been acknowledged for years by psychologists and other professionals, but devising a good definition of the concept is rather difficult.[3] Applying the concept of a "stressful event" to auditions and recitals seems appropriate, because they involve the obvious pressures of performing in public, where success or failure can have major implications for one's career. To talk about such events as stressful would seem to be a virtual given, but it is very difficult to define any single event as inherently stressful. Psychological research has shown that people react very differently to events that seem to be inherently stressful, such as divorce or the loss of a job. In the field of music, many performers can handle auditions with aplomb and enjoy confronting the challenges they pose. Similarly, a graduate recital may be anticipated with dread by one performer and with eager anticipation by another.

We see examples of this principle in many aspects of day-to-day life as people respond differently to the challenges in their lives. From this point of view, the term stress is better used to refer to how people respond to events, rather than to the events themselves. An event may be stressful, not because it is inherently dangerous, challenging, or taxing, but because it makes demands that we are not well equipped to handle. As an example of how stress can affect performers, consider two conservatory students, Carla and Tom. Carla, a violinist, was preparing to play her senior recital in the spring. During the preceding fall term, she had selected a group of pieces from which the recital selections would be chosen and had performed them every few weeks in a series of practice performances before audiences of different sizes and levels of musical sophistication. A skilled musician to begin with, Carla progressively fine tuned her repertoire in the months preceding the recital. In the process, she found that her musical tastes had sharpened, leading her to keep a portion of the original repertoire while selecting some new music as well. By being able to refine each piece after playing it during practice performances, she had become increasingly comfortable with her instrument and the music in a variety of performance contexts. Her senior recital, rather than looming as a "do or die" obstacle, simply become another opportunity for Carla to express her deepening musical insights. She had become adept at both playing *and* performing music, a distinction that is often missed by many aspiring musicians.

Tom, a precocious pianist capable of great musical achievements, was a "streak" performer. He was also faced with the prospect of a graduation recital. A skillful and intuitive musician who performed chiefly when inspired to do so, he absorbed music easily by ear and tended to view musical scores as rather burdensome constraints. He imagined himself to be an exciting performer who could captivate audiences with his technical skills and interpretive sensitivity. Convinced that his flashes of brilliance would assure success, he avoided systematic preparation for the recital and waited until just a few weeks before to begin madly rehearsing. He perceived the recital as an obligatory step toward his degree and felt that he should somehow have been exempt from continually proving himself to his teachers via end-of-semester juries, convocations, and recitals.

As it turned out, both Carla's and Tom's recitals were well received. Carla's performance was musically expressive and skillfully executed; her major professor described it "very solid." Tom's, on the other hand, was more variable, including both innovative flashes and embarrassing memory lapses. Another trademark performance, it left everyone, including Tom, limp with exhaustion at the end.

What do these examples tell us about stress? Basically that the stresses of performing involve an interaction between the person, a challenging situation, and a characteristic style of coping. In their own ways, Carla and Tom evolved styles of performing that were both personal and, to some extent, adaptive. Carla placed a premium on note-perfect accuracy, a subtle interpretive style, and takes few chances during a performance. Tom left more to chance, practiced erratically, and relied heavily on his musical intuitions to carry him through a performance.

In the long run, Carla is more likely to develop a sustaining interest in and enjoyment of performing, even though Tom might be the more exciting performer. Her coping style, which integrates performing effectively into her daily life, is down-to-earth and practical. She is able to select music well suited to her capabilities and has learned to emphasize her strong points while not dwelling too much on her shortcomings. In contrast to Carla, Tom has never become comfortable with the experience of performing. What happened on stage would often surprise him as much as the audience, and although he has experienced some moments of exhilaration, he found the persistant unpredictability difficult to cope with. His attitude toward performing is a curious mixture of wanting to display his skills and feeling that doing so is a needless imposition. He seems unable to reconcile his rather grandiose image of himself as a virtuoso performer with the reality of his uneven accomplishments. In short, Tom is something of a stranger, an enigma, to himself.

We have observed that, in their drive to achieve top performance levels, many musicians pay too little attention to their psychological development. Moreover, the dedication required of a performer may deprive him or her of experiences considered desirable, if not essential, for the development of self-knowledge. The mythical standard of perfection is frequently the only goal deemed worth pursuing, beginning as it does with the simple dictum "practice makes perfect" to which every neophyte musician is exposed.

We believe that musicians who perform must come to terms with the same stresses that everyone else deals with, and they also must cope with additional sources of pressure. In the following chapters, we describe in detail a psychological approach to stress management designed to help performers become aware of and learn to cope effectively with the sources of stress in their lives. This approach is intended to be useful not only to performers, but to teachers, parents, and professionals as well. Although our attention is directed primarily toward the mature performer, we don't want to neglect the factors that may engender stress and anxiety during the early years of development.

Our approach to stress management is based on a model called "Stress Inoculation Training," or SIT, which owes much to the work of psychologist Donald Meichenbaum.[4] Basically, SIT refers to a set of procedures to help people under stress become aware of the source of the stress, develop effective coping skills, and put these skills into daily practice.

The first step, learning to identify sources of stress, is easy to overlook. Another term for this process is self-assessment, because it entails taking a relatively objective look at situations that affect how you feel and behave. Notice that the emphasis is on *self*-assessment, which we believe is the most relevant focus for effective stress management. It's natural to point to external factors as the cause of stress, such as teachers, conductors, difficult music, auditions, and the like. But, as we've suggested already, stress has more to do with how you evaluate and react to events than it does with the events themselves. Self-assessment is a process of getting to know yourself better, both as a person and as a performing musician.

One important facet of self-assessment concerns your reactions to the people for whom you perform. It's generally taken for granted that one of the occupational hazards of a career in the performing arts is exposing yourself to evaluation by other people, whether they are audience members, teachers, peers, or audition committees. How do you respond to being in the public eye? Do you tend to feel exhilarated, comfortable, anxious, or fearful? Do your reactions seem to depend on circumstances or on how you size up the performance situation? The following imagery exercise may help you see how self-assessment can increase your understanding of the factors that contribute to your feelings as a performer.

To begin, find a quiet place where you can relax and be by yourself without interruption. In this and subsequent imagery exercises, it's important to be relaxed and inwardly focused so that you can be as attentive as possible to your own responses. Letting go of excessive muscle tension, breathing deeply and freely, and closing your eyes are three aspects of this preparatory process and will help reinforce the effect of the imagery.

When you are comfortably relaxed, form the picture of an audience in your mind from your vantage point onstage. Personalize this audience by including among its members acquaintances whom you believe are musically sensitive and highly attentive to your performance. Once you have developed and can sustain the image of this audience, try to become aware of your reactions to it. How do you feel? What do you notice about yourself? Do you enjoy the experience of appearing before others? Or perhaps you feel nervous, despite the presence of audience members you regard as friends. Do you feel inhibited or anxious about making a mistake in front of others? If so, you're in good company. It's very difficult to escape the feeling that people in an audience—whoever they may be—are likely to be critical of you as a performer. We like to think of this as "the imaginary critic," who seems to inhibit the performance of many musicians, irrespective of whom they happen to be playing for. The imaginary critic is as much a product of one's way of thinking about performing as it is of the audience. Most performers seem to understand, at least on some level, that audiences want to support their efforts and see them succeed. But, on the other hand, it is difficult to escape the feeling that performing makes one extremely vulnerable to criticism.

As you continue to focus on your audience image, try to visualize the faces of each individual present. Initially, perhaps your reaction may have been rather global and impressionistic, but as you continue to look at the faces, you may begin to see differences in expression, levels of apparent interest, and other characteristics. Do you feel an affinity for any of these individuals? That is, is your attention drawn to any person in a positive way? If so, you are responding the way many performers do when they seek one individual in an audience and try to play for that person.

Some performers make every effort to block the audience from their awareness. Sometimes this is manifested by complete absence of eye contact, or by behavior on stage that conveys the sense that the performer feels no connection with those in attendance. We suggest that you learn to see members of your audiences as allies and friends who are almost always supportive of a performer's efforts. Even if you are playing for people you don't know, you may be able to develop a sense of kinship, or, at times, even empathy with somebody you feel is an especially sympathetic listener. In most cases, the greater your ability to relate to those in attendance, the more comfortable you are likely to feel as a performer.

Beginning in early childhood, performers learn to look to others for information about themselves. In part, they seek information about the quality of their performances, and the feedback obtained from a good teacher can be invaluable. But it is easy to carry this process too far and come to depend primarily on feedback from others as the only means of judging performance skills. A nod of approval, a passing grade on a jury examination, a successful audition, all convey evaluative feedback and give performers some indication of how their efforts are perceived by others. But there are at least two possible pitfalls in depending on such feedback, at least for the unwary. First, it can be difficult for performers to distinguish between evaluations of their musical skills on the one hand and their attributes as a person on the other. Statements like "good performance" or "you need work" can easily be interpreted as an evaluation of one's overall qualities as a person. Such a distinction normally is lost on young children, to whom phrases like "nice playing!" and "good girl!" are practically indistinguishable, particularly as they are likely to be accompanied by comparable gestures, body language, and affect. Thus, performance-oriented feedback from others may be tied with implicit messages about one's qualities as a person, and it is important to be able to tell one from the other.

A second common problem with feedback predominantly from outside sources is that you may get inconsistent, even contradictory, information. Those acting as critics may or may not possess sufficient information or background to make a fair assessment of your efforts. A teacher who is sensitive to musical nuances may react critically to your interpretation of a piece that greatly impressed someone else. What sounds exquisitely beautiful to one individual may seem like nothing but noise to another person. In almost any audience, there are inevitably going to be people who have something critical to say. If you depend exclusively on others to evaluate your musical skills, then at times you will feel that the feedback you get is inconclusive. Perhaps you will listen to a teacher, whom you believe to be highly credible, knowledgeable, and influential. Possibly you will listen to someone else whose opinion you respect and who you feel has your best interest at heart. Either way, you may be left with the nagging feeling that you don't know who is right and that you must pragmatically decide whom to believe, based on who exerts the greatest influence over you at that time.

A third potential problem with external feeback is that it prevents you from developing informed opinions about your musical skills, and more generally, about your qualities as a person. If, upon finishing the performance of piece of music, you habitually turn to anyone present—rather than yourself—and ask, "How did I do?" you are depriving yourself of a significant source of valid information about your performance. The cultivation of self-assessment skills—an integral part of SIT—is designed to counteract the tendency, especially common among performers, to seek evaluations from nearly everybody but themselves.

However, self-assessment does *not* exclude information from outside sources. Most musicians are familiar with performers whose overvaluation of their own capabilities leads them to ignore the comments of others and rely exclusively on their own appraisals. This one-sided perspective is a way of limiting, and therefore defending oneself against, information that may be helpful. Realistic self-assessment means taking stock of yourself both as a person and a performing musician by incorporating a wide range of information from a variety of sources, including both yourself and those whose evaluation you hold as important.

Self assessment can be applied fruitfully to a number of aspects of performance skills.[5] Some of the basic issues are:

1. Your personal motives for performing
2. Your inclinations toward one type of music or one particular composer more than others
3. Your capabilities and limitations as a performer
4. Your preferred mode of interacting with others who influence your development as a performer
5. The characteristics of your musical performances
6. Your inclinations concerning the circumstances under which you perform
7. Your plans and aspirations as a performer
8. Your preferred procedures for learning and preparing music for performance
9. The medium that best suits your capabilities and inclinations as a performer
10. The most appropriate means of assessing your personal development as a performer

Self-assessment may take a variety of forms, depending on what you wish to learn about yourself. As we discuss in more detail how to prepare for performances with an eye to effective stress management, we will suggest a number of techniques that you may wish to employ. Underlying all these techniques, however, is a capacity to attend to what you do and how you react in various situations. Often our experiences flow by in such a way that we are scarcely aware of what may be happening. In many situations, this heedlessness is desirable—for example, when a musician comes offstage in a euphoric state after a performance about which he or she remembers little but a sense of unity with the music. In our day-to-day affairs, as well, we tend to act first and think later.

One additional aspect of self-assessment should be clarified at this point: Self-assessment should not be confused with self-criticism. Musicians are very aware of how easy it is to be critical of a performance, even one that has apparently gone rather well. Self-criticism often includes an element of self-condemnation, a masochistic tendency that is sometimes almost self-indulgent. Self-criticism often arises from focusing on the most minute shortcomings of a performance, such as an erroneous note or even—as reported by one musician—a rest that was not fully observed. Self-criticism of this sort can serve several purposes. First of all, it's a way of anticipating the imagined criticisms of others, who are thereby "beaten to the punch." Second, self-criticism may be a way of attributing superiority to oneself by showing that you can detect subtle errors that no one else in attendance can perceive. More insidious, perhaps, is the capacity of self-criticism to induce habitually negative interpretations of one's performances. Many performers seem driven by an unrealistic desire to measure up to impossibly high standards set by themselves or someone else; and as a result, they never seem to take pleasure in what they do. Perfectionism frequently accompanies a self-critical attitude, and it is important to clearly distinguish such behavior from more balanced and rational self-assessment. Self-assessment may lead you to the useful discovery that you have perfectionist qualities; it does not, however, call for further self-criticism once you have made such a discovery. Self-assessment is simply a process of discovery, of learning to experience what you are doing in as honest and open a manner as possible.

The process of self-assessment is relevant to virtually all aspects of musical performance skill. Of particular importance, however, is the use of self-assessment techniques following a performance, because many performers seem incapable of appraising their own performances either objectively or helpfully.

On numerous occasions, we have listened appreciatively to performers not as sophisticated musical analysts, but as individuals who enjoy and love music. At the conclusion of many such performances, musicians nonetheless often turn expectantly to us, awaiting a detailed analysis of how they have done. The expectation of some sort of feedback, whether in the form of applause, compliments, or whatever, is deeply ingrained in virtually every performer. We have discovered that one of the factors that contributes to tension and anxiety during performance is difficulty in evaluating one's own performance skills. Performers who anxiously turn to listeners, irrespective of the latter's musical credentials, for reassuring or validating feedback are often very unsure of their own capabilities. It is important for performers to cultivate sensitivity to their own performance skills and to learn how to evaluate their own musical efforts. The self-rating form in table 2–1 provides one means of beginning to do this.

This rating form is entitled "SOAP," an acronym that stands for a four-phase assessment process encompassing: (a) a *s*ubjective rating, (b) an *o*bjective rating, (c) an overall *a*ssessment, and (d) a *p*lan. We suggest that performers make frequent use of this rating

**TABLE 2–1**

*SOAP (Subjective/Objective/Assessment/Plan) Self-Rating*

DATE: _____ TITLE: _____ SETTING: _____

AUDIENCE: _____

| Subjective Rating | Low | | Moderate | | | High |
|---|---|---|---|---|---|---|
| Tension level at beginning | 1 | 2 | 3 | 4 | 5 | 6 |
| Tension level at end | 1 | 2 | 3 | 4 | 5 | 6 |
| Distracting thoughts | 1 | 2 | 3 | 4 | 5 | 6 |
| Distracting sensations | 1 | 2 | 3 | 4 | 5 | 6 |
| Objective Rating | | | | | | |
| Technical proficiency | 1 | 2 | 3 | 4 | 5 | 6 |
| Interpretive sensitivity | 1 | 2 | 3 | 4 | 5 | 6 |
| Expressiveness (tempo, rhythm, phrasing, etc.) | 1 | 2 | 3 | 4 | 5 | 6 |
| Overall Assessment | | | | | | |
| Overall rating (self) | 1 | 2 | 3 | 4 | 5 | 6 |
| Overall rating (audience) | 1 | 2 | 3 | 4 | 5 | 6 |

Plan:

Based on: Problem-Oriented Medical Record (POMR)

form as a means of gaining more precise information about their assessment of a particular performance. Let's look at each of the four components of this self-rating in turn. The first part, or "subjective" assessment, concerns how the performer feels while performing. As you can see, there are a number of factors that bear on subjective experiences during a performance. We have found that different tension levels, distracting thoughts, and distracting sensations are all frequently reported by anxious performers and that these tend to vary during the course of a performance, depending on the circumstances. Some performers feel very tense at the beginning of a piece, but quite calm by the end. For others, technical problems or mistakes may cause tension levels to rise significantly from beginning to end. Distracting thoughts may come in the form of ideas, pictures, or reactions that have nothing to do with the task at hand. Sensations, including such things as awareness of one's heartbeat, changes in breathing, and so on may also serve as potent distractions. The "SOAP" form asks performers to rate each of these factors separately on a six-point scale that extends from low, (not much of a problem), to high, (there is a definite problem).

The "objective" assessment deals with factors that are more amenable to direct observations; and include technical proficiency, interpretive sensitivity, and musical expressiveness. (You may be able to devise other measures as well.) While it may be easy for a teacher to evaluate these aspects of a performance, it is equally important for performers themselves to rate these dimensions and then compare their own results with those of teachers or other listeners. A number of problems can be addressed by using such a rating form. Many performers make excessively subjective analyses of their performance—for example, by blowing a single mistake out of proportion and feeling that it "ruined" a performance. Being more objective and analytic makes it possible for a performer to obtain a more balanced and, ideally, realistic appraisal of his or her own skills. Because these factors can also be rated by other individuals in attendance, there is a basis of comparison that may help a performer develop a realistic sense of how his or her skills appear to other people.

The third component of this form, the "assessment", involves an overall rating of one's performance in terms of the global impression it makes on the performer and on the listeners. We suggest that performers first rate their performance at an overall level and then also try to make an overall rating of the audience's reactions as well. (As used here, the term "audience" refers to any listeners, not a formal audience *per se.*) The assessment phase attempts to capture the global impression of a given performance, and this rating can be evaluated over time to discern characteristic patterns in the evolution of musical performance skills.

The fourth aspect of the self-rating form is the formulation of a *plan,* which is based on responses to the three previous ratings. The plan is perhaps the most important feature of this evaluation process because it encourages the performer to use the feedback obtained in the first three areas to decide on an appropriate course of action. If one has performed poorly, the form should have provided enough specific feedback so that the plan can incorporate a detailed series of steps to help rectify the problems. If the performance has gone well, a plan can also help determine what to do next. For example, having performed well for one type of audience, a performer may decide to play for different listeners, perhaps potentially more critical or musically sophisticated. In any event, self-ratings are most beneficial when they result in useful plans to guide a performer's subsequent activities. This particular rating form represents one such technique to help performers develop a systematic approach to guiding themselves through the final stages of preparation and rehearsal for public performances.

The second phase of SIT involves learning stress management skills that you can employ in various performance situations. We like to use the term "skills" rather than "techniques" because it emphasizes a learning process rather than the idea of something you can just do without training. Common stress management skills include such procedures as relaxation training and mental imagery.[6] Relaxation training entails learning procedures to minimize tension in various muscles, either globally or with a high degree of selectivity. Mental imagery involves using internal visual images that you conjure up for a particular purpose. You might, for instance, imagine how you would like to appear onstage during a performance, picturing the scene in great detail.

On the surface, relaxation training and mental imagery seem simple; perhaps you feel you already are comfortable with them. Yet each of them involves practice and skill—not as much as is required to sing a Schubert *lied,* but definable skill nonetheless. Thus, the cultivation of stress management skills is likely to take time before you see any real benefits. Furthermore, like the skills employed to learn a new piece of music, stress management is best practiced when one is in a relaxed frame of mind. Music is best assimilated when we are in a receptive, open frame of mind, rather than when we feel pressured by deadlines or obligations that introduce a note of urgency into the preparation. Similarly, stress management skills such as relaxation training and mental imagery are best cultivated when you can consciously carve out a little free time for yourself, without demanding specific results within a specified time.

The best way to illustrate some of the problems in developing coping skills is to consider relaxation training. It has been said, "an effort to relax is a failure to relax," an idea that is worth considering, because it suggests that relaxation involves a frame of mind as well as a physical state. Learning to relax can be frustrating, particularly for anyone who has spent years accumulating psychological and physical tensions. The usual approach to relaxation is to conceive of it as a challenge, as something to be achieved or mastered, like a piece of music that will eventually yield to effortful practice. Yet most practitioners of relaxation skills find that they only begin achieve the desired results once they are able to surrender, to some degree, conscious control of the process.

There is an important difference between thinking of "relaxation training" as another activity in an already-hectic schedule and viewing it as an activity that really influences how and what you do. Approaching relaxation exercises as just another of your many daily activities is likely to encourage you to think in terms of such troublesome notions as mastery, perfection, success, and failure. And if you are driven by perfectionism as a performer, you may approach learning to relax in a similar manner. You may place yourself under the burden of having to succeed in relaxing perfectly to win the approval of your therapist, and you may feel increasingly frustrated as your conscious efforts prove counterproductive. Ultimately, you will probably feel less relaxed and more tense than when you began.[7]

Taken out of a broader context of attitudes that encourage a somewhat contemplative lifestyle, relaxation training is little more than a sterile exercise that may even make you feel a bit foolish. If you opt to explore this facet of stress management, you may have to make some adjustments in your fundamental ways of perceiving and acting. Ideally, this will have begun during the self-assessment phase that initiates the development of stress management skills.

Coping skills come in many forms, although relaxation and imagery are especially well-known techniques, derived from psychotherapeutic procedures that have been used for many years. Another, more recent development is what has been termed "cognitive restructuring" by its practitioners. Cognitive restructuring is a broad concept encompassing a variety of psychotherapeutic techniques that help people become aware of how thoughts affect feelings and actions. This awareness, in turn, is used to alter attitudes and beliefs that contribute to psychological distress. These techniques are based on a premise introduced earlier, that our perceptions of things greatly influence how we feel and act. Cognitive restructuring might be recommended, for instance, to an accomplished musician with a long standing fear of being unmasked as an "imposter," despite numerous successful performances and persistent critical acclaim. The well-known saying among actors, "you're only as good as your *next* performance," implies that one's past accomplishments are not accurate predictors of the future, and many performers seem to live by this dictum. Add to this concept the dread of being declared a fraud (a fairly common feeling among accomplished performers), and you have a situation in which stress and tension mount with each succeeding performance. Unlike the gambler who believes that success is just around the corner after losing several rolls of the dice, a performer may believe that each success brings *failure* that much closer. Without some exploration and alteration of the beliefs that underlie this apprehensive approach to performing, neither practice performances, relaxation training, nor imagery are likely to bring about any lasting change in such a musician's underlying beliefs about his or her capabilities as a performer.

The diversity of techniques for coping with stress can make it difficult for the performer to know which is most likely to be helpful. Not only do people differ in terms of the techniques they find useful, but any individual may find that different stress management techniques are called for at various times. For example, some people find it helpful to "psych themselves up" before a performance with statements that affirm their musical capabilites. Such positive "self-talk" may be reassuring and help minimize feelings of inadequacy or low self-esteem. But not everyone finds this technique helpful, as illustrated by a story about the great cellist, Piatagorsky. He admitted to being troubled by "nerves" before performing, and when asked what he did to overcome the problem, he said he constantly reminded himself, "You are the great Piatagorsky!" "And does it help?" came the question. He replied, "No, I don't believe myself!" (S. Beach, *Musicdotes*. Berkeley: Ten Speed Press, 1988)

Two basic rules apply when considering how to learn coping skills. First, don't try to learn complicated stress-management techniques when you are under pressure to prepare for a major performance. In the same way that you begin learning new music in comparatively relaxed circumstances weeks or even months before a performance, try to cultivate stress management skills under non-pressured conditions. However, while the time just before a performance may not be optimal for learning progressive relaxation techniques, it *is* a good time to arrange a series of practice performances before audiences of increasing size or critical knowledge. Second, coping techniques may need to be modified to fit the needs of a particular situation. Mental imagery can help develop and reinforce a positive representation of how you wish to appear on stage, but it is not likely to be helpful when you are just learning the music. If you want to use imagery at this early stage, try to develop an acoustic image of the music itself or, if you are an instrumentalist, a detailed picture of the hand and finger movements needed to produce the musical effects you are trying to achieve *at that time.*

Clearly, it's important to carefully choose techniques well suited to personal needs. Don't assume at the outset that you *must* learn deep relaxation, that imagery is the secret of a good performance, or that cognitive restructuring will rid you of stage fright. The procedures most helpful to you will become evident over a period of time, as you learn about yourself as a person, a musician, and a performer. Moreover, you will probably discover that some trial-and-error experimentation is needed to refine the techniques you employ to manage performance stress. Above all, allow yourself time to learn and put into practice these strategies, so that they eventually become a deeply-rooted part of your overall identity as a performer. The techniques we've mentioned thus far—relaxation, imagery, and cognitive restructuring—are but stages in a process of personal experimentation and fine tuning that occurs before tangible effects are likely to be experienced.

The third stage of SIT involves putting the skills you have learned into practice so that they begin to help counteract the stressors you have identified. As with the first two stages (self-assessment and skill learning) the implementation phase is not something that one should attempt to short-cut. Many performers, however, tend to rush into this phase in the same way that they may be inclined to perform a piece of music onstage before it is ready. We have already noted the value of learning and practicing stress management exercises when you do not have to use them immediately. For example, it's better to learn the deep-breathing phase of progressive relaxation when you're already moderately relaxed than when you're hyperventilating in the wings and waiting to go onstage! Or, as another example, three days before a major recital is *not* the time to experiment with cognitive structuring techniques to unearth the *real* reason for your addictive urge to perform.

Yet eventually, circumstances such as these will be the ones in which you count on the skills you have learned to help you cope with stress and anxiety. How can you achieve the effect when the circumstances under which you learn and practice coping skills are very different from those in which they need to be implemented? It's easy to become deeply relaxed when you're relatively relaxed to begin with, but what happens when you have a panic attack the night before a recital? How will the skills you've practiced hold up under this sort of pressure? These questions relate to the third stage of SIT—that of implementation.

The basic strategy for implementing skills for coping with stress is to try them out under circumstances that are milder variations of the actual stressor you are confronting. The concept of inoculation can be used as an analogy for this process.[8] In medical terminology, inoculation includes exposing someone to a weakened form of a virus to stimulate the natural antibodies of the immune system. Through attacking the virus in its weakened state, these antibodies strengthen the body's capacity to cope with more virulent strains of the virus. Stress management training can inoculate us in a similar way. Challenging, stressful events are analagous to viruses that may overwhelm our immune system unless we have developed the necessary antibodies. Coping skills are like antibodies used to fight stress, so the problem is how to expose oneself to stressful events that will stimulate, but not overwhelm, the coping skills that have been learned. The solution to this problem is through a process referred to by psychologists as "graded exposure," which involves putting oneself in situations that evoke mild or moderate levels of stress that challenge, but do not overwhelm, your coping skills.[9] The idea is that a series of such sessions, each progressively increasing the amount of stress, anxiety, or fear, provides us with a testing ground in which to practice coping skills that have been previously learned under minimally stressful conditions.

A good illustration of graded exposure is a technique in which performers engage in a series of "practice performances" prior to a major recital or audition. Practice performances should be deliberately arranged to include stressful qualities similar to, but less intense than, those of the actual performance. These events are not casual performances under informal circumstances, but rather should be carefully designed to bring out stress or anxiety in a controlled manner that allows the performer to practice effective coping behaviors. One might begin, for example, by playing a portion of a recital for a group of trusted friends, or by tape-recording your performance, (being recorded tends to put nearly everyone on guard). A simple, yet effective, strategy is to decide in advance to play a particular piece on a given day and time. Even if no one else is in attendance, you are likely to experience a heightened state of anticipation in the interim, which can give you some idea of how you may feel before the actual performance.

Graded exposure can be implemented in many other ways, as well. You can use mental imagery to visualize, in great detail, the circumstances you will face in an upcoming performance.[10] Depending on the vividness of your imagination, conjuring a detailed scenario of the performance can, to some degree, evoke feelings akin to those during a live performance. Irrespective of the techniques you employ, it's important to keep in mind two things you can accomplish through graded exposure. The first, of course, is gaining experience in a performance context. Generally speaking, the more you perform, the more comfortable you will be in what we will henceforth call the "performance state," which for many musicians can be an uncomfortable, alien experience. But exposure to performance situations alone is not enough to guarantee beneficial results, no matter how many times you force yourself onto the stage. Rather, the key is to use each performance as an opportunity to practice the psychological and musical skills you have learned to help you perform effectively. If, for example, you find yourself hyperventilating in even a mildly stressful situation (such as when playing for a few friends), practice counteracting the problem. Don't get sidetracked into thinking, as some musicians do, "If I'm this uncomfortable in front of my friends, imagine what a basket case I'll be when there's a real audience out there!" Instead, arrange even less stressful performances to practice any techniques you have learned for coping with hyperventilating (such as deep, regular breathing or calming mental images you have rehearsed). Remember that the purpose of practice performances is to deliberately make yourself a bit anxious so that you can implement stress management techniques you have learned without being overwhelmed by the circumstances.[11] This second idea—using practice performances to exercise stress management skills—adds an important psychological dimension to what might otherwise appear to be only a rehearsal focusing exclusively on musical issues.

Putting all of these components together—self-assessment, skills training, and implementation—may seem complicated, and certainly this approach to managing performance can be very demanding of your time and energy. It's important to emphasize the challenges at the onset, though, to help counteract common illusion that some quick and easy "magic formula" will take the stress out of performing. So far, no one has found it! Instead, musicians who become enthusiastic and competent performers generally do so through systematic analyses of their strengths and limitations, along with continuous experimentation with and exposure to performance opportunities.

One of the main premises of this book is that performers themselves are in the best position, in many ways, to understand how to conceptualize and solve their performance problems. But we also know musicians commonly feel that other people, particularly teachers and coaches, are the ultimate authorities to whom they must appeal for feedback on the quality of their performing skills. From the standpoint of psychotherapeutic intervention, however, it is very important for performers dealing with stress, tension, or anxiety to adopt a problem-solving approach to these issues. In other words, it is important for performers to attempt to couch performance problems so that they can be approached using solutions that they themselves can help develop.

Table 2–2 lists four common performance problems and potential responses which illustrate what we mean by a problem-oriented approach. The list developed out of our work with organists, whose instrument poses some special performance challenges, but the principle can be applied to any instrument. Notice that for each problem we suggest a series of "potential experiments" rather than "solutions." This wording emphasizes our belief that the most effective solutions to performance problems evolve in the course of

**TABLE 2–2**
*Problem-Oriented Experimentation*

| Problem | Potential Experiments |
| --- | --- |
| Troublesome learning | Competing tasks (e.g., pedal while moving a pencil) |
| | Vocalize polyphonic lines one by one |
| | Learn a new piece from *end* to *beginning* |
| | Transpose challenging passages |
| Lack of sensory awareness | Practice in the dark |
| | Practice silently (no stops drawn) |
| | Visualize hand and foot movements in detail |
| | Make a slow-motion analysis of movement patterns |
| Erratic memory | Use alternate measure (A/B) half scores |
| | *Imagine* playing a piece through in its entirety |
| | Practice with memory-enhancing sound cues |
| | Transcribe challenging passages into a notebook or log |
| Discomfort with performance-related sensations | Do a "cold" run-through with minimal warm-up |
| | Play immediately after physical exercise |
| | Play just after drinking caffeinated coffee |
| | Practice while playing a cassette tape of audience noises or other simulated background effects |
| | Make a video or audio cassette recording of preliminary performances |

thoughtful and active experimentation rather than through preset formulas. The proposed experiments all reflect a diverse range of ideas that are presented here to stimulate interest rather than to provide sure-fire answers.

The first problem, troublesome learning, is familiar to virtually all performers. This problem often emerges later in the need to exert considerable conscious control over one's playing, so that the slightest distraction is likely to cause the performer to falter or make mistakes. Thus a piece that feels comfortable in the practice room may seem unmanageable during a rehearsal or lesson. The central issue is that effective performing depends, at least partly, on becoming familiar enough with the music that it can be performed with minimal conscious control. Sigmund Freud once commented that the purpose of psychoanalysis is to "make the unconscious, conscious." In contrast, it could be said that the purpose of practice is to make the "conscious, unconscious."

To the degree that music is learned effectively, performing it is relatively resistant to distractions. For a musician, such distractions can come in many forms, including (a) irrelevant thoughts or sensations, (b) the presence of an audience and the significance accorded to its members, and (c) unfamiliar aspects of the physical environment. New music is almost always practiced and learned in distraction-free circumstances that are very different from those in which it is eventually performed.

Standing up to the rigors of the performance environment often requires a degree of "overlearning," a term that is difficult to define precisely. In practical terms, a piece is overlearned when it can be played coherently in the presence of competing stimulation, such as extraneous noise, an audience, or the unpleasant feeling of anxiety. How can one achieve this degree of solid and predictable security? Obviously, such time-honored techniques as slow practice, consistent fingering, and mastering the piece at a speeded-up tempo play an essential part in the solution. But many performers reach a plateau in their preparation at which they have derived maximum benefit from such techniques. Often they have become bored by the repetitiveness of this work and need some further challenge. In this case, some active experimentation may be useful. Each of the suggestions listed in table 2–2 adds a different challenge to the learning process. For example, an organist who can play a pedal passage effortlessly might try to do so while moving a pencil with one hand from one side of the music rack to the other. Probably the pedaling will become slow and halting, with many wrong notes, but continued practice in this manner will eventually lead to pedal work that is highly resistant to intrusions. (This preparatory technique was advocated by an American virtuoso organist, Lynwood Farnam.) Or, if you are concerned about having marginal control over a challenging passage, see how comfortable you feel playing it in another key. You may find that doing a series of transpositions helps you achieve a stable cognitive representation of the music that is independent of a particular pattern of notes or fingerings. Similarly, each of other proposed experiments may help deepen your learning of the music so that its performance becomes more resistant to distractions.

Certain performers who play with little awareness of the physical feedback from the muscles and joints used when playing may be surprised to experience excessive muscle tension while performing, when the tension has become too great to be ignored. For such individuals, practicing in ways that focus attention on subtle physical cues can be very beneficial. One pianist, for example, practiced by playing in a darkened room to help her become more aware of the sensations of muscular tension that usually intruded when she was performing. Without the distractions of visual cues, she became much more attentive to the subtle sensations of unnecessary tension in her hands, arms, and shoulders.

Memory slips—the most common source of anxiety for performers—can also be approached in imaginative ways. One violinst learned to play a short but difficult étude from memory by making two versions of the score, each containing only half of the measures. One score contained measures 1, 3, 5, and so on; the other, measures 2, 4, 6, etc. After learning the piece, he began to practice it using the half-scores, switching from one to the other each day, and in this way he quickly committed the entire piece to memory. Still another performer found that a particular background sound— ocean waves—during practice fostered a state of mind that aided his recollection of a piece he was memorizing.

Yet other techniques may help those who are uncomfortable with the common physical sensations of performing. The feeling of cold, stiff fingers at the beginning of many performances can be simulated by running through a piece with little warm-up. This technique tends to bring to light the problems that are likely to affect an actual performance. (Of course, playing without any warm-up is not advisable except for brief evaluations of this type.) Playing immediately after physical exertion helped one flautist become used to the way her heart pounded during performances, a symptom she had feared meant an imminent heart attack. Another performer, a cellist, used a cup or two of very strong black coffee, a stimulant, to evoke some of the physical effects of activation that he experienced on stage. When he could play a piece musically even after drinking so much coffee, he felt more confident that it was ready to perform. While we do not advocate the use of drugs to manipulate levels of activation, we were struck by this individual's imaginative way of dealing with a common problem.

When discussing performance problems with musicians, we try to encourage an active, problem-solving approach that effectively uses personal resources and ingenuity. Often an experimental and even playful attitude toward solving problems can be very beneficial. We suggest that you consider the problems and experimental solutions given in table 2–2 not so much as perscriptions that will work for you, but rather as guidelines for developing your own personal solutions.

This problem-solving approach can be illustrated through the example of Diane, an organist who, like many performers, was terrified of playing her music from memory. Doing so made her so anxious that she avoided it whenever possible. "I have a poor memory," is the way she first described the problem, but she immediately added, "I *have* to relax; I *know* I'm too tense." Is it reasonable to accept her initial assessment of the problem? Perhaps she was tense and needed to relax, but would it have made sense for her to immediately undergo relaxation training? A closer examination of the problem suggested several important points. First, the initial assessment of her memory seemed overly harsh, because she previously had performed successfully from memory. It was more accurate to say that, although capable of playing from memory, she found the experience extremely unpleasant and occasionally did have embarrassing memory lapses. Second, by jumping to an immediate solution to her problem ("I need to relax") she was not only limiting consideration of other options, but was on the verge of learning a new skill, relaxation, that would have required additional time and commitment. Third, the overall manner in which she talked about her problem seemed rather dogmatic and left little room for experimentation. Underlying all of these issues, of course, was the question of why she felt compelled to play from memory, since it was not really required of her.

In fact, learning to cope with these problems required more than relaxation training, and began with a broader consideration of why she wanted to play from memory. Diane's assertion that she viewed memorization as an intriguing, if sometimes frightening, challenge was accepted at face value, a realization which made it possible to remind her that playing from memory represented a conscious choice, not an obligation. This was really not a major insight, since she had known it all along, but by making the decision to perform from memory in a conscious way, she was able to take personal responsibility for her efforts, whatever the outcome. Her own self-assessment eventually identified a key factor in her anxiety: the abrupt transition from playing with the musical score to playing without it, with no intervening steps, caused her great discomfort. Although the problem had developed over the years and clearly had other aspects, this transitional point in preparing a performance caused her the greatest amount of distress.

When asked to consider how she might cope with this problem, she initially could only think of "more practice," the standard antidote, it seems, to almost any problem. Eventually, however, she began to see other facets of the problem. For example, most of the pieces she played from memory were technically difficult and demanded the utmost concentration and coordination. The obvious suggestion to play something less difficult was met with the objection doing so was not a true "test" of a performer's capability. It was interesting that even this particular suggestion evoked a great deal of anxiety. It was easier for Diane to accept memory lapses in a complicated piece than in a simpler one for two reasons. First, others would not be as likely to detect a memory lapse in a complex work as long as she somehow kept going, whereas forgetting something simpler, such as a hymn, would immediately be apparent to all those familiar with it. Her reaction was similar to that of a well-known folk singer, who claimed that having to sing the popular song "Blowin' in the Wind" almost drove him from the concert stage because he was constantly afraid that he would forget the words. Second, failure at a simple task would have constituted an even more powerful indictment of her suspect memory, because she would no longer have a ready alibi, such as "no one else I know can play it from memory, either."

To cope with this problem, Diane began a process of *experimentation,* which is essential to learning coping skills.[12] Rather than engaging in extensive cognitive restructuring, or learning imagery or relaxation techniques, she chose to focus primarily on the music. She did, however, learn to monitor her "stream of consciousness" for self-defeating thoughts that tended to discourage and distract her. She also employed a technique called "thought stopping," in which she consciously terminated such thoughts as soon as she became aware of them.[13] In a more direct approach to the problem, she developed several ways of gradually weaning herself from musical scores. After deciding to accept the risk of playing a simple hymn from memory, she selected one with an especially memorable melody, and then experimented with three different "cue cards." One consisted only of the hymn text, without any musical notation. The second was comprised of the melody line, while the third contained the necessary chord progressions.

By adopting such a focused problem-solving approach to her difficulty, Diane eventually came to terms with her "memory problem" in a practical, yet creative, manner. Gradually, she tried her system of using cue cards in circumstances in which she felt minimal pressure, such as during choir rehearsals and informal services. Finally, she settled on the melody line system because it provided her with the musical continuity of a full score, but still required her to supply most of the details.

In the end, she learned a great deal about strategies for coping with playing from memory, which had been so stressful for her. Her use of trial and error experimentation enabled her to develop a helpful approach to the problem that eventually allowed her to perform without cue cards whenever she chose. An interesting and beneficial side effect of her investigation into the problem came when she began to view playing hymns from memory less as a test of her musical skills and more as a bridge to the many creative possibilities of improvisation, for which she found she had real talent. No longer constrained by rigid adherence to the musical score, she began to experiment with variations on hymn tunes, much to her own satisfaction and to the delight of the congregation.

This performer derived a great deal of satisfaction from having successfully worked through what had previously seemed an insurmountable problem. In part, her difficulty had stemmed from her restrictive view of it, which severely limited her options. After all, what can someone do whose memory is "shot"? This obstacle illustrates the importance of the self-assessment phase of treatment. During this stage, Diane learned to focus on a specific, manageable issue—how to make a transition from playing with a score to playing without one—and then generated a range of possible solutions. She also learned to use the technique of thought stopping to shut out the myriad distracting and worrisome thoughts that tended to crowd into her mind during a performance. Such thoughts can interfere with memory or almost any other skill. It's important to note that the self-assessment phase extended for several weeks, during which she used a great deal of trial-and-error experimentation to try and refine various strategies for managing the stress of performing from memory. Eventually, the strategies that seemed best suited to her situation were put into effect in performances, which at first were deliberately arranged to minimize the amount of anxiety they evoked. By the time her efforts were completed nearly four months had elapsed, but her treatment had been a productive and rewarding experience.

# 3

## The Whole Performer

There is a tendency to treat performers like one-dimensional musical automatons. Because they spend years in single-minded training, it is often tempting to assume that they are psychologically one-sided and perhaps somehow stunted in comparison to other people. Some performers do seem almost machine-like in their approach to making music. Such individuals are practically inseparable from their instrument, have compulsive and driven practice habits, and seem to prefer the solitude of the practice room and the lights of center stage to the cultivation of social relationships. When problems develop with their performance skills, they are especially likely to take an overly narrow view of such difficulties and ignore broader issues that might give them a better perspective.

> Peter: *At age twenty-two, Peter sought the advice of a local physician for a problem with the extension of his left fifth finger when playing octave passages. He reported considerable physical pain in the finger following hours of sustained practice, and believed that this problem constituted a serious impediment to his aspirations of becoming a professional musician. An examination suggested that he had incurred some ligament damage as a result of excessive practice.*
>
> *A discussion with Peter about the basis of his problem revealed a number of factors that apparently contributed to his distress, only some of which were directly related to musical*

*skills. Among these, excessive muscular rigidity when main-
taining hand position, and arduous but counterproductive
practice habits stood out. But beyond these problems were
other difficulties that Peter tended to minimize or deny entirely.
He was an extremely tense and perfectionistic individual, and
was prone to setting excessively high performance standards
for himself. Socially isolated, he had made few friends in college, and he became extremely anxious in nonmusical social
situations where he could not use music as a vehicle for interactions with other people. Having virtually no outside interests
and being largely devoid of practical skills, Peter defined himself almost exclusively in terms of his musical skills, which by
objective analysis were at best only modest. His intense preoccupation with his little finger appeared, in a broader perspective, to reflect an overly narrow conception of the problems he
was experiencing as a* person.

*Fortunately, he consulted a physician who was familiar with
the problems of performing musicians and was thus aware of
the extent to which obsessive preoccupation with physical
complaints may cause one to lose sight of the effects of broader
psychological impairments. As a result, he not only successfully treated Peter's problem at a symptomatic level, but was
able to help him appreciate the need to explore the broader
factors that may have contributed to the problem.*

Peter's situation effectively illustrates how performers can become so focused on musical skills that they find it difficult to step
back and take stock of their general psychological status. There is
a sense, often conveyed to students by those with whom they study,
that the Arts transcend the concerns of the individual or are somehow "larger than life." In practical terms, this image is manifested
in a number of invidious attitudes about performers and other artists that either downplay or completely ignore their importance as
people. In this chapter, we develop a framework that gives an overview of seven dimensions of the psychological makeup of a performer that is based on the work of psychologist Arnold Lazarus.[1]
Our purpose is to encourage performers to assess their personal
situation in ways that transcend their functional capabilities as performers. Lazarus refers to the components of this model as the "BA-

SIC ID$^2$," an acronym that encompasses seven areas of our psychological makeup. Lazarus' BASIC ID provides a helpful way of gaining a broad perspective on one's psychological strengths and limitations, as well as promoting insight into how one may better cope with and solve problems relating to performance skills. Before considering Lazarus' BASIC ID in detail, however, let's look at some of the ways in which a performer's characteristics and needs as a person tend to be shunted into the background.

First of all, the attitude that performers and artists should subjugate their personal needs to pursuit of artistic excellence is very common. A cultural stereotype of performers or artists depicts them as impoverished, neurotic individuals living on the margin of society and driven by artistic impulses too strong to be ignored. That artists and performers will make many personal sacrifices is taken for granted and many people, the artistically gifted among them, also believe that the quality of an artist's craft is somehow enhanced by personal suffering. However, the general lack of jobs for highly skilled performers probably accounts as much as anything else for the impoverished conditions many endure.

Second, the personal, human qualities of performers are frequently minimized in their pursuit of high-level performance skills. Auditions place a premium on the ability to play at a standard of excellence that relatively few can hope to attain. The emphasis in such situations is on the quality of performance skills, rather than on personal characteristics. Audition committees traditionally go to great lengths to prevent anything but the music from entering into their decisions. The high premium placed on fidelity to the musical score may not leave much room for personal interpretation. Anxious to make a good impression, a performer will strive to attain technical and musical perfection, frequently at the expense of personal expression.

Third, encouragement of compulsive practice habits and, more generally, a highly structured lifestyle from early childhood on can combine to create behavioral rigidity that does not promote broader psychological growth. Children who come to believe early on that their musical skills distinguish them from their peers may develop excessive reliance on these capabilities to the exclusion of more adaptive social skills.

Manifestations of these tendencies are numerous at a clinical level. For example, when asked to describe the problem that led her to seek psychological treatment, one young pianist stated that it was her inability to play a particular chord in a specific sonata. Another focused on the fact that her legs trembled when she played in public; yet another was concerned about his inability to memorize an especially troublesome passage in a lengthy étude. Such self-reports display the tendency to view performance problems in a narrow, mechanistic context that, at least as stated, does not lend itself to an examination of broader psychological issues.

Part of the purpose of psychotherapeutic intervention is to help performers develop a broader perspective on their problems, to explore the ways in which a variety of factors may have bearing on what at first appears to be an isolated symptom of physical or psychological distress. A thorough evaluation of the performer's situation that takes into account a range of factors including psychological status, physical health, and musicianship should ideally be carried out before initiating a treatment program.[3]

As a first step, let us apply Lazarus' BASIC ID concept to performance skills. The phrase is an acronym that refers to seven basic functional areas of our psychological and physical makeup. By considering each of the seven components of the BASIC ID, we can begin to understand the range of factors that may have a bearing on performance skills. This analysis is important for two reasons. First, it can help with the process of identifying and assessing the specific manifestations of performance-related problems that need attention. Second, it provides a useful framework for tailoring treatment programs to the needs of each individual performer. By considering each of these seven functional areas, one can develop what Lazarus terms a "multimodal" approach to treating performance problems—that is, a plan that uses a wide range of therapeutic techniques appropriate to each area of concern. The following components make up the BASIC ID: *b*ehavior; *a*ffect; *s*ensation; *i*magery; *c*ognition; *i*nterpersonal factors; and *d*rugs/physiological components. Let's take a closer look at each of these factors in turn.

*Behavior.* "Behavior" refers to the observable aspects of performance skills, those that are most evident to members of an audience or anyone who is listening to and watching a performer. Some examples of behaviors related to common performance problems, including stage fright are:

Shaking or trembling
Idiosyncratic mannerisms or movements
Physical appearance
Patterns of movement
Grimacing after a mistake
Mechanical aspects of playing, such as hand movement

Behavior is the most directly observable dimension of performing, and consequently is a good starting place when attempting to reach common ground with a performer about the nature of a performance problem. At first, performers often describe their problems in rather vague terms—for example, "I just can't play the Brahms intermezzo!" (pianist); "I'm a "basket case" whenever I go out on stage!" (flautist); or "Everytime I perform, something goes wrong" (vocalist). A behavior-oriented analysis of these statements would focus on their observable manifestations in order to gain a clearer, more concrete picture of the problem. The inability to play Brahms, for example, might have any of several behavioral manifestations, including (1) becoming visibly tense while playing; (2) making an inordinate number of errors, or (3) being physically unable to span the required range of keys in certain passages. The performer who is a "basket case" onstage might (1) avoid eye contact with the audience; (2) shake uncontrollably; (3) walk on- and offstage timidly and self-consciously; or (4) manifest postural constrictions that contribute to poor breath control.

Focusing on such behavioral concomitants of performance problems makes it easier to describe the difficulties in terms that both the performer and the clinician can understand. This is especially important because the many *musical* aspects of performing involve subjective evaluations that can be difficult to translate into meaningful, practical terms. Furthermore, encouraging performers to specify their problems in concrete terms makes it easier, in the long run, to devise useful solutions.

There are several effective ways of assessing behavioral aspects of performing that performers, teachers, and clinicians may find helpful. Videotaping, in particular, is a very useful, but underused, assessment tool that provides feedback concerning both auditory and visual dimensions. Frequent videotaping of a piece of music while preparing it for public performance provides a useful record of progress and contains information that the performer can incorporate into subsequent practice sessions. Videotaping can be especially helpful when performers are given an opportunity to share their own evaluations of a recorded performance, rather than simply asking a teacher or coach to analyze it. Watching video tapes without listening to the sound track is a useful way to help draw attention to issues of appearance, posture, or playing technique that are otherwise easy to overlook.

Videotaping a performer playing "trouble spots" in a piece provides an especially useful form of behavioral feedback. The focused concentration required to play a difficult passage is sometimes converted into excessive muscular tension, which can be evident in facial grimaces, hunched shoulders, and postural rigidity.[4] Performers who think they are concentrating effectively may only be making themselves physically tense, and they can become aware of this by seeing how they look while playing. Videotaping segments of the music preceding and following the troublesome passage is also recommended as a means of detecting manifestations of the anticipatory and residual tension that frequently accompanies difficult passage work. The ebb and flow of muscle tension is often quite subtle and can be difficult for the performer to detect, particularly in the early stages of preparatory learning. Because one's attention at this time is focused fully on the music, it's often quite difficult to simultaneously perceive developing patterns of tension. Often such unnecessary tension is completely imperceptible until it becomes excessive and difficult to counteract. Reviewing videotapes is a helpful procedure for detecting the early manifestations of excess tension that otherwise may remain unnoticed.

Other behavioral manifestations of performance problems can be assessed by videotape as well. For example, the correspondence between the mood of a piece of music and the degree to which the performer's behavior projects that mood can be fruitfully evaluated in a video feedback. Discord between the moods of the music and the performer can be illustrated by one example of an organist, seated at the console in full view of a congregation, who played the Buxtehude "jig" fugue while remaining practically motionless, with no facial expression. What came across was a dissociation between musician, instrument, and music; the performer did nothing to convey the mood of the music. Another performer, a skillful classically trained violinist, was preparing to audition for a summer theme park orchestra to augment her income. She had been asked to play a rousing "fiddle tune" as part of the audition. However, while practicing the piece, she had adopted the most serious, grim facial expression imaginable. Fortunately, she decided to tape one of her last rehearsals, and burst out laughing when she saw how incongruous her expression was in the context of the music. Visual feedback was invaluable in helping her become more aware that she needed to accurately project the spirit of the music, rather than playing it through in so studious a manner.

Such spiritless performances can occur for several reasons. Some performers are overextended by their music and can do little more than manage to play a score accurately. Because they are overtaxed, they—somewhat paradoxically—feel tense while attempting to communicate an entirely different musical mood. Other performers are not aware of the degree to which listeners interpret the meaning of live music from what they see as well as from what they hear. "You looked as though you were really enjoying yourself up there" is the sort of compliment that communicates the importance of the visual element of performing. For other performers, a dissociation between behavior and musical mood reflects a basic constriction of emotional expressiveness. These individuals may have a diminished capacity to respond emotionally to music—a fact that is not lost on the listener.

The behavioral dimension of performance skills can be evaluated in other effective ways as well. Rating scales, for example, can focus on the behavioral aspects of performing. Table 3–1 shows a three-point rating scale designed to assess some basic behavioral aspects of performance; in this scale, values of 1 = absent, 2 = occasionally present, and 3 = consistently present.

A simple rating scale like the one in table 3–1 can be used effectively by student and teacher (or other listener) to provide a quantifiable way to assess the behavioral components of a performance. Behavior rating scales offer a number of advantages over less formal feedback. First, they focus attention on specific behaviors. In table 3–1, posture, facial expression, and movement are the key elements. A means of focusing on specific areas needing improvements can help make what needs to be accomplished more evident to the performer. Second, rating scales provide a standard to compare rat-

**TABLE 3–1**

*Three-Point Rating Scale for Performance Behaviors*

| Behavior | Rating (circle one) | | |
|---|---|---|---|
| | Minimal or Absent | Somewhat Evident | Clearly Evident |
| Posture | | | |
| Flexible, supple | 1 | 2 | 3 |
| Self-assured | 1 | 2 | 3 |
| Well suited to instrument | 1 | 2 | 3 |
| Facial expression | | | |
| Relaxed | 1 | 2 | 3 |
| Expressive | 1 | 2 | 3 |
| Matches mood of music | 1 | 2 | 3 |
| Movement | | | |
| Well integrated | 1 | 2 | 3 |
| Fluid | 1 | 2 | 3 |
| Economical | 1 | 2 | 3 |
| Total score _____ (maximum 27) | | | |

ings of two or more individuals. It's helpful, for example, to have both performer and listener(s) fill out rating scales and then compare notes. Disagreements are almost inevitable and can be the basis for fruitful discussions about what accounts for the discrepancies and how they can be resolved, if necessary. Third, rating scales provide a way to assess changes over time. Making weekly ratings is a good way to gauge whether or not the behavioral aspects of a performance are improving. Finally, systematic behavior rating scales can reduce some of the ambiguity that can occur when performers and listeners attempt to discuss musical ideas. Instead of telling a performer that he or she isn't communicating with the audience effectively, this analysis can be couched in terms of specific behaviors that could help achieve a desired effect. Breaking the concept of communicating down into elements such as making eye contact with the listener, becoming more physically relaxed, and varying facial expression appropriately can help define the needed changes more effectively.

The behavioral aspects of performance skills encompass the act of playing, as well as one's appearance while playing. How accurately one performs a piece of music is also an important measure of skill, provided there is agreement on what it means to play "accurately." At the most basic level, accuracy can be defined as fidelity to the musical score, or performing just what is printed. Beyond this level, the issue of interpretation comes into play, because no two performers will perform the same piece of music identically. In fact, no two successive performances of a piece of music by the *same* performer will ever be precisely the same. Since note accuracy is on the most obvious, observable aspects of performing, we'll confine our attention to a behavioral analysis of musical errors.

Mistakes are the bane of every performer, yet it's hard to imagine a live performance without errors.[5] The sheer number of notes in a typical piano sonata, for instance, makes it very difficult to navigate the entire piece without error. Recorded performances create the erroneous impression that note-perfect renditions are the norm, but the amount of editing and splicing needed to get a perfect "take" makes it clear that such musical "perfection" is highly artificial.

As a behavioral manifestation of performance skills, mistakes are interesting in their own right. Unfortunately, most performers tend to believe that mistakes must be eradicated as quickly as possible, and seldom pause to evaluate their meaning. But it's important to try to understand their significance, because there are so many possible contributory factors. Here are some factors that can contribute to making mistakes; some are obvious, others are not:

1. Performing at a tempo beyond one's control.
2. Misreading a score.
3. Exerting too much conscious control while performing.
4. Performing music beyond one's capabilities.
5. Being excessively tense while performing.
6. Being unable to focus one's attention effectively.

Technical mistakes frequently trigger self-depreciating thoughts, such as "I'll never be able to play this piece well" or "If I make a mistake like this while practicing, just imagine how badly I'll play when it really counts!" Such thoughts are troublesome not only because they are negative, but also because they divert the performer's attention from the music. For now, it is sufficient to say that analyzing musical mistakes is an important means of gaining insight into one dimension of performance skills. Because of their significance, we will consider the topic of mistakes in a later chapter. For the present, we will simply assert that mistakes are a key item in the behavioral assessment of performance skills.[6]

*Affect.* This term refers to how we express our emotions.[7] It is one of two terms used to characterize patterns of emotional expression. Affect relates to moment-to-moment variations in a person's emotional state, and includes expressions such as crying, laughing, fearfulness, and anger. The other term, *mood,* refers to a person's prevailing emotional tone, which does not normally fluctuate as rapidly as effect.

Affect and mood are important concepts to consider in our discussion of performance skills for two reasons. First, affect and mood are essential elements of musical expression. Without emotional expressiveness, music loses much of its power and appeal. Second, affect and mood comprise a performer's emotional bedrock and can both influence and be influenced by the emotional connotations of music.

Performers differ markedly in their affect and mood. Some experience extremes of emotion, ranging from elation and euphoria to anxiety and depression. Others seem to be on a more even keel and rarely, if ever, show much variation in their emotional state. Emotional expressiveness is partly related to a performer's *temperament,* which is the overall pattern of responsiveness we were born with. If you have ever observed infants in a hospital nursery, you may have noticed how their behavior differs from one to another. Some are placid, others are agitated no matter what efforts are made to comfort them, while still others are very alert, responding to minute changes in their environment.[8]

Most people's characteristic patterns of emotional expressiveness develop at least partly from their in-born temperament. If you are nervous, high-strung, and edgy most of the time, as an infant you may have been highly reactive to the things around you; as a child easily stimulated, but not readily reassured. As a performer, such tendencies might express themselves in extreme physical and psychological tension, but might also imbue your performances with "electricity" that listeners find very exciting. Or, you may be more placid, with little variation in the way you express your emotions.

If so, as a performer you may maintain your poise regardless of what happens on stage, and others are likely to turn to you for reassurance at moments of crisis. Because you are less emotionally reactive, however, it may be more difficult for you to invest your performances with the emotional colorations that capture listeners' attention.

Performance problems related to affect and mood may take several forms. Perhaps the most common of all, however, is stage fright, a significant component of which is the affective state of fear, or anxiety. Although we discuss stage fright elsewhere, we will briefly consider the relationship between stage fright and affect here, because affect is one of the most noticeable and troublesome aspects of the problem.

Affective states like fear and anxiety involve such high levels of emotional intensity that we are likely to feel extremely uncomfortable or even physically threatened. These states develop when we perceive ourselves to be in danger, and they mobilize our physical resources to deal with the threat. Unfortunately, the intense emotional arousal can be so distressing that it becomes the focus of our attention, rather that the perceived threat itself.

Consider anxiety, which virtually everyone has experienced at one time or another. Anxiety is a warning signal that alerts us to danger.[9] A performer's anxiety before going onstage is often a response to fears of failure, criticism, or memory slips. The physical signs of anxiety are familiar to most of us, and may include a dry mouth, profuse sweating, rapid heartbeat, shallow breathing, trembling, and an urge to urinate. All of these symptoms arise from a response system controlled by the automatic nervous system (a part of the central nervous system) that prepares us to take immediate action, particularly in response to *physical* threats. It's important to know that these reactions also occur when we're not in physical danger, although the feelings are still very unsettling. The degree to which performers interpret such sensations as signs of danger or as dangerous in their own right is related to how anxious they feel. In other words, the anxiety of stage fright results from a combination of our physiological response and our tendency to be distressed by that response. Both veteran and novice performers frequently report being emotionally "worked up" before and during their performances, despite the common assumption that only those without much stage experience feel nervous. The difference between how veterans and novices react—at least to some degree—arises from how they interpret their feelings. Seasoned performers tend to be less threatened by their physiological responses and have learned to accept it as a given of performing.

Another common affect reported by performers is depression. The term actually refers to a pervasive mood characterized by sadness, loss of pleasure, and apathy. Severe depression can interfere with one's ability to function and may require professional treatment. But performers are prone to feelings of depression that are not necessarily clinically significant. For instance, many musicians report feeling depressed following a major performance. Within a matter of hours, the excitement of performing gives way to an equally intense, but opposing, feeling of depression and apathy. This swing may be partly a natural response to the tremendous amount of mental and physical energy required to perform, and it's common for a musician to feel "wrung out" and exhausted after a performance, sometimes for days afterwards.

Musical affect is not, of course, limited to anxiety or depression in the context of performing. It's equally important to consider how music makes us feel. Much has been written about music's capacity to arouse the feelings of listeners, but the impact of music on performers themselves is often overlooked. There are many reasons why one is attracted to a particular piece of music, but an important aspect of the selection ought to be the feeling evoked by the music. Music's power to evoke emotional, or affective, responses, stems from several sources. The various scales and keys have long been associated with certain affective states, as have different systems for tuning instruments. Musical moods are conveyed by components of the sound as well: its dynamic level (loudness), *tessitura* (average pitch level), and timbre (sound quality) all contribute to our emotional responses. Vocal music in addition uses text to create affective responses. Finally, a piece of music may trigger nonmusical memories of past experiences that we associate with particular emotional states.

Our affective responses to music partly determine our preference for one piece over another.[10] In selecting music to perform, consider how it affects you emotionally as a naive listener. Your reactions to the music may change while learning and preparing it for a performance, but if your emotional response to it is positive on first hearing, you will probably find that it both sustains your interest and allows you to perform more meaningfully.

As we have seen, depression and anxiety are the affective factors most commonly related to performance problems. Most performers have had to deal with these affective states, and for many performers, they are constant companions. Assessing the impact of these feelings on performance skills is important because intense affect—particularly anxiety—can markedly inhibit the musical expressiveness of a highly skilled performer.

*Sensation.* The third component of Lazarus' BASIC ID, sensation, refers to sensory perceptual experiences. The perception of music, of course, relies primarily on the sense of hearing, and musicians are acutely responsive within this sensory system. The sensations associated with performing, however, go beyond simply what the performer hears, although this factor is obviously very important.

To some extent, the sensations that are experiences while performing are affected by the degree of autonomic nervous system (ANS) activity.[11] Activation of the ANS results in a preparatory state of alertness in which sensory acuity is enhanced. Performers in high states of ANS activation frequently report hearing previously unnoticed nuances in the music. They may also see things for the first time, such as notes in the score which suddenly stand out in bold relief. In other words, they experience a state that psychologists call *hypervigilance,* a heightened stated of alertness and perception.

It is interesting to consider hypervigilance in terms of its impact on our subjective feelings. Hypervigilance arises when the autonomic nervous system becomes activated; as a result, our perceptual acuity is enhanced compared to a nonaroused state. We are more sensitive to sensations that might otherwise escape notice. But the ANS activation that occurs during performing is not only marked by hypervigilance but by an increased intensity of sensations to which we are more acutely sensitive. Arousal brings about both an increase in sensitivity as well as more intense sensory experiences. The combined effect of heightened sensitivity and more pronounced sensations are responsible for much of the psychological distress reported by performers.

Figure 3-1 graphically illustrates our explanation of hypervigilance. When we are hypervigilant, we are more acutely aware of things going on both around and inside us; the more highly aroused we are, the sharper our senses and the greater our ability to detect events that might otherwise escape notice. Moreover, when you undergo ANS activation, not only do you experience more symptoms of anxiety, but you are more acutely aware of them. Thus, even a minor change in heart rate, for example, may seem to have major significance. Many performers report that, when nervous, they feel as though their heart is visibly pounding in their chests. In an activated state, not only may you experience distressing symptoms, but you feel them with a clarity that cannot be matched when your arousal level is lower.

This figure helps explain why, when you are ready to perform, you may be much more acutely aware of internal events than at other times and may notice things you never observed before. One performer, for example, at the time of a recital discovered several

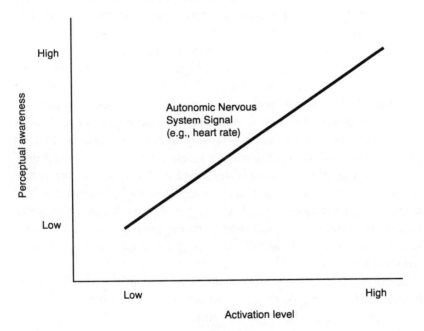

**FIGURE 3-1**
*Perceptual Salience and Arousal*

notes that he hadn't remembered seeing previously in the score. Such hypervigilance frequently causes performers to experience high levels of anxiety about their symptoms even though, by objective standards, they do not appear to be nearly as distressed as they report feeling.

Performers troubled by anxiety frequently report alien and uncomfortable sensations, many of which are related to anxiety. As we have already noted, this state can be intensified due to misinterpretations of sensations arising from ANS activation. Such sensations are difficult to ignore because of their intensity. Consider, for instance, heart rate. Normally it's inaudible and we pay little attention to it, but in a state of activation, our perceptions of it change. When, as a result of ANS activation, heart rate increases markedly, the change is often experienced not only as an increase in rate, but intensity as well. We become much more aware of our heart beat. Many performers describe the sensation as one in which their heart seemingly threatens to burst through their rib cage. This feeling is so distracting that it, instead of the music, can become the focus of the performer's attention. The combination of heightened vigilance (or sensitivity) and an increased heart rate contribute to this unpleasant, distracting sensation.

Other sensations associated with activation can be troublesome to performers. Some report difficulty breathing, as if they are suffocating, or in catching their breath. Nausea and dizziness are also common. Others report feeling disembodied or somehow separated from their physical selves. This condition, popularly described as an "out-of-body" experience, involves feeling like one is floating or hovering, and looking down on oneself almost like a spectator. Clinically, this phenomenon is described as *dissociation,* and it can occur when one is subjected to intense psychological pressures. Extreme cases of dissociation may result in "going blank" and being unable to remember what has just happened. This condition, known as amnesia, is almost always a response to an extremely stressful situation.

Performers frequently note that their perception of time is affected during a performance.[12] Sometimes, time seems to crawl, making the interval between one note or chord and the next seem endless. When experiencing this effect, a performer may speed up the tempo of a piece so much that the likelihood of making mistakes is much greater. In other instances, time appears to speed up, so that events seems to take but a brief percentage of their true duration.

Such sensations although associated with performing, embody many of the characteristics of an "altered state of consciousness" caused by mind-altering drugs. Most of the sensations we have described so far are unpleasant; however, many performers experience pleasant altered states of consciousness that may constitute a significant motivation for performing. Or, perhaps more correctly, such pleasant responses may stem from the performer's capacity to enjoy some of the altered sensations and perception already described. Some performers, for instance, enjoy the experience of time distortion, especially when time apparently slows down and they have the luxury of savoring their music practically on a note-by-note basis. Out-of-body experiences, including feeling that one is floating away from the stage, may be frightening to some individuals but pleasant to others.

Many performers routinely talk about getting a "high" from being onstage, and this experience at least partly stems from changes in physical state that lead to altered states of perception and sensation. There is often a thin line between exhilaration and fright. You may feel buoyed up at one point in a performance, highly sensitive to what's happening, and on top of the music, and yet the next moment, you may become intensely apprehensive. This experience is especially prevalent among novice performers, for whom going onstage and expecting to survive may require an act of blind faith. One music student, a pianist, compared the experience of performing to surfing. His experience of performing had fluctuated in terms of how comfortable he felt onstage. He likened the thrill of a good performance to being on the edge of a wave that seemed to carry him effortlessly. On the other hand, he had also "wiped out" several times, but in the process he had learned that he could survive such mishaps and even learn from them.

You may experience other types of sensations as a performer. Hallucinations, often a symptom of certain severe mental disorders, involve sensations that, though perceived as real by the individual, are not detectable by anyone else. Common hallucinations include hearing voices talking to you or seeing things that do not exist. Some of the most common hallucinations result from drug use, especially hallucinogenic drugs like LSD and mescaline. Artists have sometimes taken such drugs because they alter basic perceptual capabilities and thus change the way they see the world. Chronic alcoholics who abruptly withdraw from alcohol go through a period of physical and psychological distress during which they commonly report hallucinations.

Sometimes it can be difficult to distinguish between hallucinations in the clinical sense and the sensory experiences linked to artistic creativity. Some composers, for instance, report hearing musical themes running through their minds, often in vivid detail, before they capture the themes on paper. These experiences are not hallucinatory in the ordinary sense of the word, but are more like the intense images discussed in the next section.

Another type of sensory experience is fairly common among musicians and performers—*synesthesia*. This occurs when one sensation triggers another in a different sensory modality. Some musicians, for instance, associate notes of particular pitches with certain colors. This form of synesthesia results from the association between two different sensory modalities—vision and hearing. The significance of synesthesia is cause for some debate, and it is not clear whether the phenomenon is necessarily associated with musical talents.

*Imagery.* The fourth component of the BASIC ID is imagery, which refers to the mental pictures we habitually create.[13] People vary considerably in their ability to experience imagery, but musicians and other artists are known to be especially open to this aspect of consciousness. If you were asked to imagine being onstage during a performance, you would probably be able to describe clearly the feelings, sounds, and sights. You might, for instance, imagine how you would look, with complete details of your physical appearance, your clothing, and the expression on your face. The image may be kinetic—that is, almost like a videotape of yourself in action being played in your mind. Your description might include what the music would sound like, particularly if you have a good musical memory and are able to recreate a score in your mind. You might also be aware of your feelings in this hypothetical situation and describe some of the sensations and feelings discussed earlier.

Mental imagery can be a powerful tool for the performer when used to reinforce performance goals. We will say more about the use of imagery in a later chapter. For now, however, we will focus on the assessment of imagery, so that you can analyze your current use of imagery and its relationship to problems you may have with stress or anxiety.

Many performers find themselves afflicted by unwanted imagery. In particular, anxious performers tend to generate unpleasant images of catastrophic failure during performances. They may often feel that these unpleasant, uninvited images are a preview of what will inevitably happen onstage. "I have this recurring image of myself being onstage, forgetting my music, and having to run off in a panic!" is an example of vivid and powerful imagery that is distressing both because of its theme (embarrassment, humiliation) and because of the difficulty of controlling it. The distress may be intensified by the fact that the performer feels powerless to control the image, which seems like a premonition. Sometimes we dwell on such images because they have a morbid fascination. Though distressing, such images can be intriguing in a voyeuristic way, as strongly attractive or repellant imagery often is.

Persistent distressing imagery can strongly affect our feelings. Harboring detailed images of onstage catastrophes may increase anxiety, and there is a direct relationship between the amount of elaborated mental imagery you engage in and the intensity of your feelings. A detailed image of what you anticipate will happen onstage can, under certain circumstances, cause perceptible changes in feelings and lead to the accompanying physical changes. By imagining a stressful recital in detail, for example, you may experience a sudden rush of adrenalin or a perceptible increase in your heart rate. It is almost as if we can deceive our bodies into acting like the experience is real, when nothing but active visualization is occuring. In a subsequent chapter, you will discuss using this effect to advantage, because it is possible to employ imagery as an anticipatory *rehearsal* in which the images of performance conditions are used to foster adaptive emotional states.

To assess whether the anxiety or stress you experience may be related to imagery, consider the following questions. First, to what degree does imagery play a part in your everyday stream of consciousness? Do you frequently find yourself daydreaming or becoming lost in vivid fantasies? Daydreams and fantasies are both forms of mental imagery characterized by a state of consciousness in which day-to-day reality is temporarily suspended. Reflect on what you recall about your dreams—the frequency with which you remember your dreams, the content of your dreams, and the degree to which they seem to mirror your waking life. Dreams also involve a suspension of reality, even more than daydreams or fantasies. In dreams, our experiences—both pleasant and unpleasant—often seem indistinguishable from reality. The "reality" of dreams, however, suspends both logic and plausability, a fact that only becomes evident when we awaken and recollect our dreams. A singer, for instance, who had a recurring dream about beginning to fly while onstage recalled feeling anxious during the dream about falling and being injured; while dreaming, she lacked the sense of realism that would otherwise have caused her to realize the absurdity of the situation. Upon awakening, with a proper sense of reality restored, she could appreciate the irritational quality of the dream.

Do you pay attention to dreams, and perhaps attribute significance to them? How aware you are of your nocturnal dreams, daydreams, and fantasies gives some indication of how important they may be to you. People differ substantially in the degree to which they report such experiences, but most of us have them whether or not we pay much attention to them.

For the performer, images can take a variety of forms. When people talk about imagery, they usually mean visual imagery, and this form is the most widely described. The term "visualization," of course, brings to mind images of visual mental pictures. And when most performers talk about visualization exercises, they are referring to generating pictorial images. But musicians also have access to other types of imagery, including those based on hearing and even touch. Auditory imagery may commonly take the form of hearing a piece of music without performing it; an experience quite different from actually playing a piece of music from memory. The use of auditory imagery involves the capacity to construct, in the course of learning, an internal representation of a piece of music as it might actually be performed. This can be done in a number of ways, including imagining how a piece would sound while reading the score, or reconstructing an entire piece of music from memory, much like playing a tape recording. Many performers have this capacity, but probably only a few cultivate it systematically.

Imagery involving the sense of touch, called *tactile* imagery, can also take several forms. A common one can sometimes be seen when performers, just before going onstage, move their fingers in patterns corresponding to the music, but without playing the instrument. By doing so, they can imagine playing the piece, or at least what it would feel like if their hands were on the keys. Even without finger movement, it is possible to imagine how it might *feel* to play if one is sensitive to this sensory modality.

The musician's capacity for imagery, then, is a rich and varied source of stimulation that can contribute to both distressful anxiety and positive performance skills. Imagery can play a role in anxiety, for example, when performers visualize various catastrophes that might befall them onstage. But imagery also can be a powerful tool for enhancing skills, particularly when the performer cultivates sensitivities in auditory and tactile as well as visual modalities.

To illustrate how good use can be made of mental imagery, consider the example of one performer who we previously mentioned (p. 61). He complained of intense and chronic anxiety every time he was required to play in public. His initial complaints were followed by two years of therapeutic work. During this time, this individual struggled with the problem of performing and his constant anxiety. Eventually, through dedicated work and persistence, he learned to play in public in a musically expressive way that was not as constricted by anxiety. Many systematic therapeutic steps led to this breakthrough, but one particular step stands out, having to do with mental imagery. During a performance when he was playing a technically difficult piece, it occurred to him that the experience must be like riding a surfboard on the crest of a large wave. At such a time, the chances of making it to shore and "wiping out" appear equally great. During this performance, he felt it was equally probable that he would get through the piece without embarrassing errors. The more he thought about this analogy, the more apt it appeared to be. We talked about this image at length, and several points of comparison became obvious. First, performing, like surfing, involves skills. Second, both the performer and the surfer subject themselves to risks. The risks to the performer are primarily social, whereas the surfer faces more physical dangers; however, both are very real and need to be taken into account. Third, performing and surfing involve moments of exhilaration as well as episodes of sheer panic. Both feelings appear to be inevitable, and if you want to experience one, you will probably have to put up with the other. The emotional highs and lows that go with performing and surfing are well-known to their respective practitioners, and it is a mark of skill in both pursuits to learn to take the good with the bad. Finally, in comparing the risks, this pianist commented that wiping out is not necessarily life-threatening and, similarly, making a mistake during a performance should not threaten a performer's very identity, unless it is interpreted as a catastrophe. The common element is that, even though one makes mistakes, few mistakes are fatal.

The image of surfing on the waves of anxiety proved very helpful to this performer as he continued to learn new ways of coping with anxiety. His idea was important not only because it comforted him, but also because it was he who developed it. Throughout this book, we emphasize that the performer is ultimately the best authority on the detailed experience of a particular performance problem. Notice that we say experience here—not necessarily understanding. From that vantage point, the performer is often better equipped to develop ideas and solutions to problems than a therapist, teacher, or coach. Whether or not the surfing image is helpful to you in thinking about anxiety, it illustrates that every performer is potentially able to develop ways of coping with anxiety and other performance problems that might seem insoluble.

*Cognitions.* A psychological profile would not be complete without a consideration of how performers think about themselves and their music. The term cognition encompasses a range of capabilities, but psychologists usually use it in two general ways. The first concerns "cognitive skills," which are the basic building blocks of performance skills. Memory, our capacity to retain images of events after their termination, is one such cognitive skill. Memory, for example, enables us to make sense of a musical composition because musical expression occurs over time and thus very little of an entire piece is expressed at a given moment. Our experience of music, however, contains both continuity and structure, even though we cannot hear an entire piece at any one time. Memory also comes into play in terms of performing music without a score. In this context, the musician not only appreciates the music's continuity, but has a highly detailed "blueprint" of its structure. Not all performers are equally adept at memorizing music, but for most soloists this skill is a prerequisite to playing that is frequently taken for granted.[14]

In the first sense, then, the term cognition is often used to describe certain basic performance capabilities, of which memory is an excellent example. The second way the term is used involves how we think about what we are doing. Most people hold an inner dialogue with themselves that parallels their daily activities, but most of us are not aware of how these thoughts interact with our behavior. It has been found that people who suffer from anxiety disorders, depression, and other psychological problems have characteristic ways of thinking that affect their feelings.[15]

Many of our thoughts are surface signs of deeply seated beliefs that we have acquired since childhood and of which we're usually only minimally aware. Such thoughts are like instructions we issue to ourselves, and are referred to as "self-statements," or simply "self-talk."[16]

You are probably aware that you spend a lot of time talking to yourself. We don't mean the type of self-talk that may signify a mental disorder but, rather, the commentary that regularly runs through everyone's minds. If you make an effort to notice the flow of these thoughts, you will probably find that they contain themes or ideas that tell you something about both yourself as a person and a performer. Such thoughts, which may be very positive or more negative, originate in experiences that few of us can remember in detail. The following list provides examples of a number of ideas—frequently translated into potentially restrictive thoughts—that many of us grew up with. For example, most of us try to work so that we always get "the right answer." As performers, we are told to "follow the rules." And, course, no self-respecting musician would ever want to make a mistake because we have all been taught that "to err is wrong."

1. Practice makes perfect.
2. Pay attention.
3. I should play better.
4. Play exactly what's written—don't improvise.
5. I can't play Ives.
6. Why try?
7. Don't take chances.

8. Memorizing is too hard.
9. One mistake and the piece is ruined.
10. Playing by ear is a waste of time.

By becoming aware of these thoughts, you can attend to a part of your makeup that significantly affects your feelings and your confidence as a performer. We recommend, as a basic exercise, that you take some time to monitor your thoughts and look for themes or ideas that may contain clues about your view of your skills as a performer and yourself as a person. You may find, for example, that much of your self-talk involves rules or warnings about making mistakes or doing anything original. If this is the case, as a performer you probably feel excessively anxious when you attempt a novel interpretation of a piece of music or cultivate a style of playing that breaks new interpretative ground.[17]

Almost everyone engages in self-talk, whether a performer or not. Self-talk can be positive, negative, or neutral, but it almost always has some influence on our behavior. To the extent that a person pays attention to it, self-talk sometimes can be very distracting. But if it remains just outside our conscious awareness, it can influence our behavior in ways of which we are, at most, only dimly aware. Consider, for instance, a violinist who reported feeling mildly anxious every time she began practicing a particular piece of music. Even before she played a note, she was aware of a moment of apprehension that seemed quite foreign to her. Her feeling did not stem from the emotional quality of the music, which was a lively, tuneful, fast-moving piece. Upon reflection, she noticed that, when preparing to play, she thought, "I'll never make it all the way through" regardless of how well she had previously played the piece. The basis of this thought was unclear, but it appeared to be related to an excessively cautious attitude she had acquired while studying with a highly demanding and critical teacher.

The self-talk of performing musicians can take many forms, but much of it appears to stem from beliefs acquired during early training. "Practice makes perfect" is a good example of such a belief that is drummed into the head of every beginning student. For the beginner, the rule is clear, because "practice" simply means playing a piece a certain number of times, while "perfect" means being able to play all the notes correctly. Surprisingly, however, the self-talk of many older and technically advanced musicians still reflects this same belief. They tell themselves things like "ten more repetitions and I'll have learned this" or "I won't quit until I can play this piece *perfectly,*" despite the fact that nothing guarantees the truth of such statements. Such self-talk is simply a byproduct of an outmoded belief that may have been useful years before but now needs to be reevaluated in light of their subsequent development as musicians.

Self-talk can make a significant contribution to feelings of anxiety. The self-talk of anxious musicians is marked not only by themes of risk and danger but by statements that increase the psychological pressures. "I'm *certain* that I'll have a memory slip," "I just *know* that it won't go well," "I've *never* been able to play this piece right yet—there's no way I'll ever be able to perform it!" are forms of self-talk guaranteed to increase anxiety. Statements such as "I *must* play this perfectly or else I'll be totally humiliated," and "X can play this piece, so I *should* be able to play it too" emphasize words like "must" and "should," which can generate unrealistic expectations and cause performers to become excessively self-critical.

The cognitive dimension of performance anxiety is a very important facet of the problem, as it is of anxiety in other circumstances as well. Anxious cognitions (self-talk) not only divert attention from the tasks at hand, but can also intensify a performer's anxiety. Anxious cognitions arise when we appraise how much danger situations pose. Generally speaking, if the demands of the situation seem to exceed our coping skills, we are likely to either avoid the situation or approach it reluctantly and fearfully. Often, the musician's assessment of performance situations, rather than the actual circumstances, determines whether or not he or she feels anxious. A music student, an organist, expressed considerable anxiety about his forthcoming senior recital, and his way of thinking about the event significantly contributed to his apprehension. He asserted, for instance, that his performance had to be flawless in order for him to pass his performance course and graduate. He believed that portions of one of the pieces he was to play, a sonata by the French composer Louis Vierne, were beyond his technical skills, and as a result, he was convinced that he could not get through the whole piece. He worried on one hand that no one would come to hear him play—an indication that he had few friends—but at the same time he was terrified that the recital would be well attended and that the audience would include expert organists, from whom he anticipated devastating criticism. All these thoughts occurred to him in advance of the performance and created so much distress that more than once he nearly cancelled it. He did not do so partly because he realized that such thoughts were not necessarily realistic—, even though he was inclined to believe they were. The performance went quite well, despite all his apprehension. The musical quality of his playing was impressive, despite occasional wayward fingering and pedaling, and he passed the course without difficulty. His performance of the Vierne was fine in the areas where he had anticipated problems, but was slightly ragged in an opening passage that he had taken for granted and practiced comparatively little. The audience, of moderate size, was enthusiastic and supportive, and a group of his friends staged a surprise reception for him afterward. So much for his dire predictions and anxious self-talk!

Self-talk in advance of a performance can add measurably to musicians' apprehension, particularly when they feel powerless to counteract its effects. Moreover, one can engage in self-talk and play instrumental music at the same time, because the two involve different expressive modes. This means that while you are performing a piece of music, your mind can wander to thoughts that have nothing to do with the music. This effect is perhaps heightened because most musicians learn—or overlearn—their music so thoroughly that they can perform it without much conscious attention. When the playing becomes automated one's attention is free to wander elsewhere, frequently into irrelevant thoughts. You are, in effect, consciously doing two things at once—performing and thinking—but not directing your full attention to either one. Since these two activities are coincident, not strictly related to each other, you may find yourself attending first to one, then the other, and feeling that you're not focused on the music. Instead, you are self-consciously aware of both thinking and playing, without being fully involved in either.

Some performers, to avoid troublesome thoughts, try to distract themselves with thoughts of their own choosing. They repeat to themselves thoughts like "I can do it!" and hope that doing so will keep more troublesome thoughts at bay and at the same time help them perform well. Athletes employ a similar strategy before big games, when they "psych themselves up" with self-talk to feel more confident than they otherwise might.

In reality, self-talk, whether deliberate or involuntary, is not very likely to affect a performance that has been systematically prepared. Many seasoned performers find that just before and during a performance their minds enter an open, yet passive, state in which they are maximally receptive to their music and relatively undistracted by positive or negative thoughts. Self-talk is usually considered a sign of self-consciousness, because it reflects a tendency to think *about* what one is doing rather than simply being caught up in the activity.

Keeping track of your self-talk is an important part of learning what may be making you feel anxious. To the extent that you think about performing, either in advance of or during it, you will probably be self-conscious about it. To the degree that your thoughts are positive or negative, your emotional state will probably vary accordingly when you perform. By keeping track of your thoughts and looking for common themes, you may be able to uncover underlying attitudes that affect how you feel while performing.

*Interpersonal.* Are you by nature a loner who prefers to make music in the solitary world of the soloist? Or are you drawn to collaborative musical activites in which you play an integral role as part of a group?[18] Performing by its nature sets you apart from other people, even in ensemble playing, in which the audience is likely to know more about you than you know about them. Soloists, however, are the most vulnerable performers of all; they must succeed or fail on their own merits and seldom have an alibi to cover a poor performance.

Performing can be at once a very solitary act and yet very intimate. To the audience, a performer often seems physically and psychologically distant, yet great performers somehow make their music touch those in attendance in a very personal way. It's easy to spot performers who are disconnected from the audience. They initiate little eye contact, seem guarded in their movements, and generally play in a careful, defensive manner. Their self-consciousness is readily perceptible to the audience and can make everyone feel slightly ill at ease.

When considering interpersonal factors in performing, it's useful to assess how you relate to people in general. Do you, like some musicians, welcome the solitude of the practice room because it gives you a good alibi for avoiding others? Some performers develop compulsive practice habits mainly to minimize contact with other people and set rigid time schedules in order to minimize their personal interactions. What about performing? Are you drawn to the experience because of a desire to share yourself with others or because you feel that you can communicate something special through your music? Or do you see audiences as adversaries, as critics to be impressed or skeptics who doubt your musical abilities?

Learning to feel comfortable in the social settings of performances can take a great deal of time. In their youth, many musicians were singled out because of their special talents and made to perform for others. This experience can be unsettling for children, who may be prone to anxiety and highly distressed about having attention called to themselves. Many otherwise capable musicians have had second thoughts about performing in public because of unpleasant early experiences in which they were coerced into playing or singing despite their discomfort. Almost every musician can remember performing in recitals that—however well intentioned— often served more to help teachers justify their efforts to parents than to benefit the students. Such situations can make performing something done to impress other people, not to communicate anything to them.

Some mature performers admit to ambivalence about relationships in general. This attitude can be expressed in a great many ways, such as never seeming to have time to do things with others, practicing constantly, and finding other direct or indirect ways to isolate themselves. There are many reasons why performers may feel this way, and its worth examining some of these in detail. One reason might be that performers, who are used to being the center of attention, may have difficulty establishing personal relationships in which they have to share attention with another. Interpersonal factors are one of the primary sources of performance anxiety, because many performers feel that their self-esteem depends on how others regard them. Many performers feel anxious partly because they believe others are excessively critical of them. Such performers may become defensive at the slightest perceived criticism, whether intended or not. As a performer, therefore, you may want to explore your personal relationships to determine whether you are excessively sensitive to criticism. Relationships entail a great deal of give and take, and if you are used to being the center of everyone's attention, you may feel disappointed when other people seem to "ignore" you.

A second problematic aspect of relationships for performers concerns the conflicts that frequently arise over time commitments. Working to become a top-flight musician often seems to require so much commitment that no time is left for personal relationships. Outsiders often perceive musicians as single-minded people who have little time for anything except the pursuit of their careers. It can be difficult to balance the time required to maintain a relationship with the time needed for one's music, and musicians frequently have trouble achieving this balance.

Relationships with teachers, coaches, and others with whom one works daily are another important personal factor for the performer. If you have been troubled by anxiety in performance situations, you may need to evaluate how you get along with those on whom you depend for feedback and training. Interpersonal factors can play a significant role in a performer's motivation. Think back to a piece of music you learned for a performance and reflect on the factors that led you to select it. Perhaps you had no choice, but had to prepare the piece for a competition or an audition. On the other hand, you may have been motivated, at least partly, by knowledge of the effect that the music would have on someone else. The most obvious example is choosing music because you know that it will bring pleasure to other people. But there are other social motives for selecting music. Young musicians, for example, often select music to please their parents, impress their friends, or to live up to their teachers' expectations. In the competitive world of the conservatory, where one-upsmanship is a given, some performers select music to show off to their peers and belittle other performers. Another example might be an anxious performer who cautiously selects music that will be inoffensive to others and that presents little risk of making mistakes. In each of these examples, decisions about music are clearly affected by social considerations.

For ensemble players, the social aspects of performing are obviously significant. Relationships between members of a group— whether a string quarter, choir, or other ensemble—are often important in determining the quality of their music. Of course, there are stories about musicians who, though unable to get along with one another offstage, put their differences aside because of their common love of their music. But many ensemble players gravitate toward this medium because it offers several psychologically beneficial interactions with others. First, there is the simple pleasure of sharing music with other skilled musicians who enjoy playing together. Many performers who initially pursued the solitary career of soloist eventually gravitate toward ensemble playing because of the enjoyment of collaborating with others. Second, many performers prefer playing in groups because they feel less anxious as a result of sharing the responsibilities with other musicians. As part of an ensemble, a performer is less likely to be singled out as the center of attention, and this anonymity can help an otherwise anxious musician feel less self-conscious. Many ensemble performers feel as though they have allies to help them confront the psychological threats posed by an audience.

One final social aspect of music is the relationship between performers and those in a position of authority, such as teachers or conductors. The interpersonal dynamics of these relationships significantly affect a performer's skill and level of confidence. Traditionally, such relationships have been based on a highly authoritarian social structure in which those in power are accorded the utmost respect and deference. Many teachers and conductors are known for their strong personalities as much as for their musical capabilities, and these personal qualities may have the most significant effect on the performers who work with them. While many such relationships are personally and musically productive, in many instances interpersonal problems get in the way of effective musical collaboration.

Consider, for example, an accomplished vocalist whose professional career seemed to lose momentum just when she was receiving some important concert bookings. She complained that although she was singing well, she was increasingly apprehensive about performing and was having difficulty in getting along with the conductors who had engaged her. The more successful she became by external standards, the more her anxieties increased. In her eyes, each performance was more important than the last because it meant that she had more to prove. As a result, each glowing review of her performances increased her apprehension about her ability to live up to the claims about her musical sensitivities. She became overly deferential toward conductors, feeling that her slightest misstep would result in an unflattering reputation as a prima donna. Unfortunately, she also believed that her success was somehow a matter of luck and that sooner or later she would be unmasked as an imposter. As a result of these beliefs, she was cool and distant in her relations with her colleagues. Although this defensive behavior was intended to mask her feelings of vulnerability, it was interpreted as standoffishness—the image she had hoped to avoid in the first place. For this performer, the treatment focused on assessing her relationships with professional colleagues and helping her develop more effective social skills. Her musical skills were never in question, despite her doubts, but it took a great deal of time and many concert engagements to convince her that she possessed the abilities routinely attributed to her by others.

*Drugs (biological/physiological factors).* The final component of the BASIC ID is the biological and physiological underpinning of musical performance skills. The term "drugs" is used because it fits the acronym BASIC ID, but it represents a much broader range of factors that contribute to the performer's basic makeup. Of course, drugs are of interest in their own right, and many performers have experimented with pharmacological agents ranging from tranquilizers and alcohol to the more contemporary beta-blockers to calm their nerves while performing. Our discussion, however, will focus on the effects of physiological factors on anxiety, the way in which biological responses contribute to anxiety. In part, our responses to the stress of performing are grounded in our temperament, a biologically based pattern of response that each of us was born with. Temperament is a component of one's personality, but it is also a specific biological pattern of responses. This use of the term differs from what is meant by "artistic temperament," which is used broadly to describe general personality patterns of performers. Temperament is reflected in a variety of ways, such as how we respond to stimuli, how quickly our physiological systems react and change, and how much we are troubled by distractions. A performer who by temperament has low reactivity to external stimuli may be less affected by an audience than one who is highly responsive. Performers whose physiological systems react strongly to the slightest stimulus may find it more difficult to maintain psychological equilibrium during a performance than those who are characteristically more placid.

We mention here, but do not discuss in detail, one important issue concerning musical performance—anti-anxiety drugs and their effects on performance skills. There is currently a great deal of interest in the use of a particular type of medication called "beta-blockers." Beta-blockers were originally used to treat certain heart problems, but were also found to alleviate some of the symptoms of acute anxiety reported by performers. These symptoms are primarily caused by autonomic nervous system arousal and are commonly a pounding heart, shallow breathing, excessive sweating, and so forth.

The use of beta-blockers by performers has generated considerable controversy. We suggest that, if you are contemplating the use of beta-blockers, you do so only under the careful supervision of the prescribing physician.

A decision to use medication such as beta-blockers should not be undertaken lightly. A number of potential risks, as well as benefits, are associated with this approach to managing performance anxiety.[19] We also suggest that any performer considering the use of these drugs treat them as part of a broader solution that incorporates the psychological techniques discussed in this book.

Based on our discussions with many musicians, stage performers, and physicians, we believe that use of drugs, such as beta-blockers, may be appropriate under certain conditions. First, when other measures have failed, performers with chronic, disabling anxiety in performance situations may benefit from the use of medications that help control the disturbing symptoms. Performers with histories of chronic anxiety may find that the abrupt cessation of some of the physiological symptoms of anxiety brings a tremendous sense of relief. In other words, these drugs may be useful in breaking entrenched anxiety that does not yield to other techniques. The advantage of the medications is that they provide an immediate and often dramatic reduction in the symptoms of anxiety and thus may give the performer a glimpse of what it is like to perform in without disabling anxiety symptoms. This experience may be an incentive to engage in future performances with the goal of eliminating the symptoms through other, more permanent techniques.

The second situation in which one might consider using beta-blockers would be a performance that is absolutely critical to a performer's development or career. Under such circumstances, it might be argued that a performer should use any therapeutic agent that will result in or contribute to optimal performance. Some performers have reported that using beta-block medication before an important recital or audition has made the difference between performing with confidence and being highly anxious. However, this approach to the use of medication raises several issues. First, of all, one might wonder whether a performer with this advantage is comparable to an athlete who takes steroids or other drugs to improve physical conditioning or athletic capabilities. Beta-blockers do not offer performers the across-the-board advantages that steroids may for athletes; moreover, these drugs may permit performers to play musically and expressively when they otherwise might not attempt a performance. Nonetheless, the use of chemotherapeutic agents to give a performer an edge over others creates an ethical dilemma. Second, a one-time use of beta-blockers, or other medications, requires advance preparation, because no one can predict how a performer is likely to react to these drugs. Even trial doses taken under circumstances that simulate the actual performance may give misleading information about the effects to expect. Certainly, trial doses of any medication should be taken well ahead of a particular performance, and the drugs' main effects and side-effects should be carefully monitored. It is important for performers to understand that a chemical agent that provides some relief from anxiety may have side effects that interfere with practice and preparation. For example, sleep disturbances and fatigue are common side effects of beta-blockers.

We recommend that any performer considering medications to help treat anxiety carefully discuss the matter with both teachers and physicians. No drug is a magic panacea that delivers complete and lasting relief from anxiety. Moreover, musicians who become dependent on medications to quell anxiety may never have the experience of reducing symptoms through their own direct efforts.

Let's now consider some of the basic physiological processes that affect the level of anxiety, at least as experienced by performers.[20] (For a more detailed description of anxiety, see chapter 5.)

*Physical signs of anxiety.* The subjective impact of anxiety is its most compelling feature and may be so acute that it seems intolerable. A person's outward appearance is not a reliable indicator of the amount of his or her subjective distress, but performers tend to assume that what is so obvious to them cannot be overlooked by others. This supposition is frequently erroneous because the impact of the subjective sensations is magnified by the heightened perceptual acuity that accompanies anxiety. That is, the anxious individual not only experiences certain somatic symptoms (such as racing heart, altered breathing, and sweating), but is more finely attuned to these symptoms than would be the case if they were not anxious. Anxiety not only triggers physical changes, but also increases awareness of the sensations, thus exaggerating their severity in the performer's mind.

An instrumentalist interviewed shortly after a recital commented on the intensity of his heart beat and muscle tremors. "My heart was pounding *so hard* at one point that I thought it was going to burst through my chest." He also added that he had trembled *violently*. Yet those in attendance, who had no reason to mislead him, said he appeared calm and relaxed throughout his performance. His experience exemplifies the alteration in perceptual acuity that can accompany altered physical status. This combination results in a tendency to overestimate the intensity of the symptoms.

The effect is something like reverse biofeedback. Many internal signals are practically undetectable and require external amplification before a client can be taught to work with them effectively. But when an individual is anxious, such sensations become all too evident, because they are amplified by the heightened perceptual acuity that results from hypervigilance. Conversely, relaxation training, which should lower ANS activation, not only diminishes physical symptoms, but reduces awareness of them by reducing the effects of hypervigilance. When more relaxed, the person is less highly aroused and less aware of the signs of activation.

The hypervigilance associated with performing can create other problems. Greater perceptual acuity may suddenly make one aware of things that previously were only dimly sensed. For example, a performer may notice problematic fingering in a passage that was glossed over with ease during rehearsal. Minor variations in tempo suddenly may be perceived as significant disruptions in the rhythmic fabric of the piece.

It is important for performers to learn through direct experience about the alterations in perceptual acuity arising from hypervigilance. Music is learned under relatively relaxed conditions, when arousal is low and, as such, is perceived in one way; in the state of arousal caused by its public performance the performer may percieve the music very differently. This heightened acuity can be adaptive in many ways, as observed by many performers, who speak of being more alert and more aware of what they're doing during a live performance. But only through repeated performances can one begin to sort out the adaptive from the maladaptive aspects of hypervigilance. Awareness that one's perception of internal sensations is likely to be exaggerated can help reduce the distress caused by believing that everyone can see the symptoms of one's anxiety. Channeling this heightened acuity to enhance the musical aspects of a performance is the next and most critical step, because this orientation can bring out sharpness and excitement in a live performance.

*Breathing.* Breathing problems are commonly reported by anxious performers. Wind players and vocalists are more likely to report breathing problems than string or keyboard players, but their dependence on an adequate wind supply makes them more aware of it. Many nonwind instrumentalists have breathing problems as well.[21]

Breathing, which can be both a voluntary and an involuntary function, is a unique phenomenon. A performer has more control over breathing rate and depth than heart rate or sweating. Being somewhat more voluntary than other correlates of arousal, breathing requires less conscious attention to be effectively modulated. By the same token, it is among the most easily modified physiological responses to performance.

It has long been known that breathing patterns are significantly affected by anxiety and other emotional states. Two of the most common breathing problems of anxious performers are breath-holding and hyperventilation. Breath-holding and spasmodic breathing are especially common among nonwind instrumentalists, for whom regular, full breathing is not essential, and can result in high levels of muscular tension, dizziness, and physical discomfort.

There are two basic modes of breathing: "upper chest" (thoracic) and "diaphragmatic". Breath-holding involves constriction and rigidity of both chest and diaphragmatic structures, whereas hyperventilation tends to involve more chest than diaphragmatic breathing. In general, upper chest breathing is more commonly associated with anxiety and other negative emotional states than the diaphragmatic form.

Hyperventilation, or rapid and shallow breathing, is a common correlate of anxiety and frequently accompanies panic attacks or performance fear. Common symptoms of hyperventilation include dizziness, light-headedness, nausea, confusion, and tremors. These symptoms may directly exacerbate anxiety in performance situations and, moreover, may heighten anxiety if the performer finds them distracting or even disabling.

Because of the voluntary-involuntary nature of breathing, treatment of breathing problems requires concerted awareness. In general, it's best to practice—perhaps rehearse—the desired breathing patterns in conjunction with the music being prepared for performance. First, however, the performer must know the difference between upper chest and diaphragmatic breathing and be able to recognize the characteristics of each.[22]

Breath-holding and related spastic breathing problems can be treated using several strategies, which will be most effective if practiced while the music is being learned. Breathing times can be marked in the score, ideally in a way that corresponds with the phrasing of the music. Singing musical lines (initially without playing) engages breathing quite naturally. Listening to a recording or mentally visualizing the music while relaxed and periodically focusing on the desired pattern of breathing is an effective way to make the response more automatic during a performance.

Hyperventilation has been successfully treated through training in both diaphragmatic breathing and slow breathing. One study reported success in diminishing panic by teaching anxious subjects to breathe diaphragmatically, and lower signs of autonomic nervous system activation were reported in subjects instructed to breathe at half the normal rate (eight versus sixteen breaths per minute). In another study, researchers found that subjects taking only eight breaths per minute were less anxious while watching a stressful film than those breathing at a normal pace.

The main conclusion reached by these and other studies of breathing patterns is that people have greater capacity to control their respiratory systems than most other physical systems activated by anxiety. Moreover, the relationship between breathing and other correlates of anxiety is substantial enough to achieve an overall decrease in arousal level through effective breathing techniques. Other types of performers—not just wind instrumentalists—need to be aware of the importance of breathing in overall levels of tension and apprehension, even though breathing is not essential for sound production.

There are, of course, other factors to consider in terms of a performer's make-up. Those that we have considered—behavior, affect, sensations, imagery cognition, interpersonal, and drug/physiology factors—are especially useful in clinical work with performing musicians.

By now you should know that our perspective on performance stress and anxiety takes into account a range of factors far wider than the performance itself. The notion of the BASIC ID was introduced to emphasize the importance of a broad perspective on performance stress and anxiety. To summarize and clarify the use of the BASIC ID, we will present a case study showing its application to problems posed by one performer. This performer was a twenty-one-year-old organist whose history of performance anxiety dated back two years. George was preparing for his senior recital at the university music conservatory, and four months before the recital he reported bouts of alternating anxiety and depression. Table 3–2 gives a detailed assessment of his problems.

Notice that the seven aspects of the BASIC ID are considered in table 3–2—*b*ehavior, *a*ffect, *s*ensation, *i*magery, *c*ognition, *i*nterpersonal, and *d*rugs-*p*hysical. We can see from analyzing this performer's problems according to the BASIC ID that he had difficulty in a number of functional areas. He had three behavioral problems. First, he tended to avoid practicing whenever he thought of the recital because even the thought of the recital made him very anxious. Second, when he did practice, he found that he made many errors, and, during difficult passages, he trembled noticeably. Third, he had to contend with the fact that more than one manual of the organ would be coupled together during certain passages of the music. On the instrument that he was playing, this factor added to the physical strength required to depress the keys because as additional ranks of pipes were engaged, the necessary amount of force to acti-

**TABLE 3–2**

## Multimodal Assessment

*Presenting problem:* A twenty-one-year-old organist with a history of performance anxiety for two years. Preparing for senior recital in four months; experiencing alternating bouts of anxiety and depression.

| Factor | BASIC ID Assessment—Complaints | Treatment Plan Action | Priority |
|---|---|---|---|
| Behavior | Avoids practice at thought of recital | Learn to use anxiety as a cue to practice | 1 |
| | Frequent note errors and motor tremors | Modify compulsive repetitive practice style | 2 |
| | Loss of key control with manuals coupled | Finger strengthening exercises | |
| | | Practice performing with moderate stressors | |
| Affect | Anxiety, fearfulness, depression | Normalize anxiety; AWARE | 1 |
| Sensation | Pounding heart, sweating, time distortion, spectatoring/dissociation, faintness | Biofeedback training to improve discrimination between activation and nonactivation states | 3 |
| | | Adjust/compensate to arousal as needed | |
| Imagery | Physical incapacitation | Log preparation/performance experiences | 1 |
| | Ridicule by younger students, teachers | Practice mastery and coping imagery | |
| | Losing balance, hitting the tutti piston | | |
| Cognition | Various "musts" and "shoulds" | Elicit, monitor automatic thoughts | 3 |
| | "Practice makes perfect" | Explore, modify anxiogenic assumptions | |
| | "Only as good as your next performance" | Formulate adaptive concept of performance | |
| Interpersonal | Isolated, self-conscious, unassertive | Practice performances for supportive group | 1 |
| | | Explore isolating effect of practice style | 2 |
| | | Promote collaborative relationship with therapist/teacher | |
| Drugs, Physiological | Episodic drinking to alleviate anxiety | R/O endogenous depression, other medical problems | 1 |
| | Previously used Valium for excess tension | Evaluate for substance dependence (?) | |
| | | Evaluate for beta blocker trial as needed | |
| | | Biofeedback training to monitor tension levels | |

*Note:* Priority 1 = immediate; 2 = short-term; 3 = longer term.
[1] From Lazarus, A (1989), *The practice of multi-modal therapy.*

vate them increased. These three factors embodied the behavioral aspect of his performance problem.

In the affective (or, emotional) domain, George, like many performers, reported alternating bouts of anxiety and depression. When depressed, his thoughts tended to be negative, characterized by hopelessness and helplessness. When anxious, he felt that he was incapable of coping with the risks presented by the performance. These emotional states alternated cyclically, so that he was on an emotional rollercoaster.

The third dimension of Lazarus' BASIC ID, sensation, refers to sensory-perceptual experiences. George, in previous engagements, had experienced a number of very unpleasant, even frightening, sensations, including pounding heart, profuse sweating, and time distortion. The latter is reported by many performers, some of whom feel that time speeds up, and others of whom feel that time is stretched out almost endlessly. Either way, the experience can be disorienting. He also reported the sensation of "spectatoring," in which people feel as though they are watching themselves from a distance. In some instances, performers feel as though they have floated away from their bodies and are watching the performance from another part of the room. Finally, he felt faint at times, a sensation he feared might be a sign of an impending heart attack or equally dangerous physical problem.

Imagery is the fourth component of the BASIC ID, and here George reported several trouble spots. First, he imagined becoming physically incapacitated, and had, on numerous occasions, imagined fainting, having a heart attack, and even dying while on stage. Second, he pictured being ridiculed by younger students and his teachers because he felt that his performance skills were not "up to par." Finally, he was terrified of losing his balance while seated on the organ bench and accidentally pressing the "tutti" piston, which turns on the full organ. In this catastrophic image, he imagined falling off the bench, striking the "tutti" piston, falling across the entire organ, and lying prostrate on the pedal keys. George was well aware that his images were not realistic; however, he worried that his fear itself might cause the events he imagined to actually happen. Moreover, the images were so intensely vivid and fraught with such danger that they evoked physiological responses of the same type, though not to the same degree of intensity, that he had experienced on stage.

Like many performers, George found that his cognitions reflected many directives, which he had absorbed from teachers, books, parents, and other performers. He lived by many "shoulds" and "oughts," which had been part of his early upbringing and training. Examples of some of these rules were "I *must* do well," "practice makes perfect," and—a phrase that many performers believe—"you're only as good as your *next* performance."

These thoughts made George particularly anxious because he realized that he was unable to live up to most of them. For example, though he believed that "practice makes perfect," at the same time he realized that the hours he had spent learning music and trying to live up to this dictum did not necessarily pay off with flawless performances.

Interpersonal factors also contributed to his anxiety. He had become very isolated, cutting himself off from people who might have provided him with social and emotional support. He was not particularly assertive, and therefore he tended to doubt his ability to play with conviction and credibility. Instead, he isolated himself in the practice room for hours to go over and over pieces of music that he was too frightened to play for other people. In other words, compulsive practice habits were to some degree a defense against social contact.

Finally, a number of physiological factors contributed to his problems. First of all, George had begun to drink episodically to alleviate the anxiety that alternated with depression. Although his problem with drinking had not reached clinically significant proportions, he clearly had a tendency toward this problem and was at risk for drug abuse. He previously had been prescribed Valium for "nerves," by a family physician to whom he had described his chronic anxiety.

Collectively, these many symptoms distributed across the seven basic areas painted a broad picture of this performer's difficulties with anxiety. His own description of the problem was more limited because he did not realize that it had so many facets.

The BASIC ID analysis for George provided a framework within which a treatment program could be designed; this program is also outlined in table 3–2. Notice that each of the seven areas has been addressed with a variety of therapeutic recommendations. Also notice that many of these recommendations were assigned priority ratings, which indicate their relative importance. For example, George's tendency to avoid practicing because the thought of the recital made him anxious was considered a very debilitating and maladaptive reaction. Therefore, efforts were made to address this problem at the outset of therapy. He had to learn to use the thought of the recital as a cue to practice, rather than to avoid preparation. When questioned about this, he decided that he could tolerate the mild apprehension triggered by the thought of the rehearsal. When he became aware of his feeling, he learned to approach practice gradually by beginning with some preparatory activity, whether it was something as simple as looking at a score or as direct as going into the practice room to get to work. Also assigned a high priority was helping him relabel his anxiety from something catastrophic to a more adaptive response to the demands of a performance. He was taught the therapeutic acronym AWARE, which stands for learning to *a*ccept anxiety, *w*atching it, *a*cting with it, *r*epeating these three steps as needed, and finally *e*xpecting anxiety in performance situations.[23] By learning these techniques, Geroge came to accept that, although anxiety might be an inevitable part of performing, it was not particularly dangerous and did not signify that he was an inadequate performer.

As you can see from table 3–2, therapy for George involved a multimodal approach and contained a number of interventions for each of the seven components of the BASIC ID. A variety of other techniques were also implemented, some of which had lower priorities than the ones described. George had been fortunate in seeking help some time before his performance, although four months before a major performance is none too early to begin work on chronic anxiety. Although at first somewhat sceptical that he could manage this longstanding problem, he found that by breaking down his anxiety into manageable components he was able to learn new techniques and practice procedures that led to greater comfort when performing. He eventually performed his recital as scheduled, and although he reported feeling anxious, it did not markedly interfere with his performance and he completed this phase of his educational program successfully.

# 4

# Stress and Performing

*Music is a wonderful thing, a fine profession. Write it, arrange it, conduct it, record performances of it; but for God's sake, if you ever want to get anywhere don't play it!*

—*Philip Green*

**P**erformers tend to view the time immediately surrounding (and including) their performances as the time of maximal stress and tension. In terms of the obvious manifestations of excitement, tension, and perhaps anxiety, this is probably true, and many performers, professional and amateur, have described such experiences as "frightening," "overwhelming," and even "terrifying." Such subjective reactions are mainly a response to the dramatic physical and psychological changes that accompany the immediate anticipation and experience of performing onstage. Related to a protective reaction to perceived danger often termed the "fight or flight" response, these physical changes mobilize one to take action.[1] Unfortunately, this response may easily alarm the performer and be interpreted to mean that something ominous is about to happen, even though it's usually a false alarm. It's interesting that even seasoned veterans of the concert stage routinely feel this way before performing, despite never having experiencing the catastrophic outcomes that they may anticipate. What does appear to change is their interpretation and subsequent response to such feelings. Effective and experienced performers are more accepting of their physiological changes before a performance and experience less anxiety.

If we focus all of our attention on the performance, we can easily lose sight of some of the more subtle preparatory aspects of performing and how these may be related to stress and tension. Despite all the emphasis on practicing, for instance, there have been few systematic investigations into how preparation techniques relate to performing skills onstage.[2] Yet every performing musician knows that practice and preparation are often filled with both physical and psychological tensions. It seems likely that one's frame of mind while practicing will have a substantial influence on one's thoughts, emotions, and sensations onstage. Practicing is more than simply rehearsing music to commit it to memory or to achieve a particular level of refinement; in a more subtle way, practice also causes beliefs, attitudes, feelings, and physical patterns, or muscular tensions to become associated with the music. You don't only memorize a Beethoven sonata, you build a complex internal representation of the piece that includes thoughts, feelings, and sensations. Our consideration of stress, therefore, needs to focus on the conditions under which practicing takes place, as well as the manner in which it is carried out. We suggest what is perhaps obvious: the how you practice, as much as what you practice, is likely to affect how you feel when you perform. If your practice and preparation strategies cause you physical or psychological strain, your performance of music learned under such conditions is likely to reflect the strain as well as the tensions arising from the performance situation itself.

There is another stage in the process of performing that is important to consider. Selecting the music to perform raises a host of issues that can lead to stress and tension. Commitments to perform are often made unreflectively long before the performance and without a clear rationale for the musical selections. Such poor planning may predispose the performer to select and learn music that is not well suited to the anticipated performance.

In order to comprehensively and realistically appraise the stresses of performing, it is necessary to consider the preparation process as a whole, beginning with selecting the music and one's motivations for playing. A stage of active learning and preparation comes next, when certain conditions that can subsequently cause problems may develop. The time just a few days before the performance is a third, uniquely stressful, stage. The performance warrants consideration in its own right, as does the time from a few hours to several days after the performance. From a psychological standpoint, each of these time periods constitutes a distinctive interval during which conditions that can lead to tension, stress, or anxiety may arise. Let us consider each of these phases in more detail.

*Phase One: Choosing to Perform.* Dealing effectively with performance-related stress must begin much earlier than the performance. The music you select and your reasons for selecting it are both important factors to consider. How do you choose music for a performance? You may be required to play certain pieces by a teacher or to play a particular repertoire for a course or audition, but in many other circumstances performers have some choice in what they play. Some exercise this option, whereas others leave the decision to teachers, parents, friends, or a chance encounter with music they impulsively decide is a "must" for impressing their audience.

It is an obvious but often overlooked fact that the impact of music differs substantially from one person to the next. Moreover, this impact may differ from one hearing to the next, as most of us have experienced. In learning to cope with the stresses and anxiety of performing, we feel that it is very important to have some sense of one's own musical likes and dislikes. In many cases performers have to play certain pieces of music for an audition or jury, but often performers have more leeway in selecting their music than they may imagine. Too often, performers feel that they must play a particular piece of music to impress a teacher or coach but entirely leave aside their own feelings about the music. The following two quotations illustrate how the reactions of individual people to a particular type of music can radically differ. Admittedly, the contrast is a bit extreme, but it does help illustrate the contrasting views that muscians often have of one another.

1. Extract from the diary of Franz Schubert: "Immortal Mozart! How many, yea, innumerable impressions of a brighter and better world have you imprinted on our souls."
2. Overheard in a pub, where two members of an orchestra were conversing before a concert: "What's on the program tonight?" The baleful reply was, "Bloody Mozart."[3]

The first example, eloquently praises the spiritual and transcendental qualities of Mozart and his music. The second passage, a remark by a professional musician, shows how one's attitude towards music can become utilitarian and jaded, particularly after one has become overly accustomed to performing. Many factors influence personal preferences about music, and we strongly recommend that performers take their own preferences into account and allow these preferences to evolve as they become more musically knowledgeable and sophisticated.

There can be many reasons for selecting a piece of music to perform in public: a desire to impress other people; enjoyment of the challenges posed by new and difficult music; interest in the works of a particular composer; simply because you like the way the piece sounds. Frequently, music is selected because of its expected effect on other people, rather than because the musician has particular interest in the piece. It's advisable to examine your motives when selecting music, because you may find it difficult to sustain the expenditure of your time, attention, and energy when the primary motivation is to please others. One major problem with this approach is that it can divert you from your real task by raising questions such as "Will X like hearing this piece?," "Will I disappoint Y if I play this piece poorly?," or "Will Z belittle my efforts and make me feel humiliated, no matter how well I play?"

Although it's certainly important to consider the characteristics of your audience, it's easy to become overly concerned about others' reactions. Psychologists term this tendency "external locus of control," a characteristic of people who primarily rely on others for approval and direction.[4] If you have an external locus of control, you are more likely to rely on other people's evaluations of you than your own judgment. As a result, your feelings of self-worth are largely determined by how you perceive other people responding to you. If feedback from others is favorable, then you think well of yourself; if not, you are likely to feel that you and your accomplishments are inadequate.

It may not be easy to resist the temptation of playing music that is beyond your technical capabilities or that doesn't fit your own musical tastes when you receive comments like "We'll be so disappointed in you if you don't play the Chopin ballade," or "You really need the experience of performing this piece soon if you expect to make any sort of progress." As children, one of the first things we learn is the importance of pleasing other people, and this tendency is carried over to the realm of performing. Performers seldom think about this attitude, particularly because they work in a discipline that places a premium on adherence to the authority of teachers. Nevertheless, most performers reach a point at which their personal sense of what is musically appropriate or feasible conflicts with that of a teacher, parent, or peer. This type of conflict can develop when you identify the music for which you feel a particular affinity.

You can develop your personal sensitivities to music quite simply. Collect several unfamiliar pieces of music of varying difficulty. Spend some time playing each piece, and focusing on your personal reactions to them. You may find that you have a "sense" of how to play certain technically demanding pieces with little difficulty. Others may be accessible, but dull and uninteresting. Have another musician (colleague, peer, friend) do the same thing, and then compare notes. Learn to pay attention to your initial reaction to each piece in terms of (a) your emotional reaction, (b) what it makes you think about, and (c) how readily it "falls to hand." Use this information to learn about your musical inclination and take it into account when you next select music for a performance.

We wish to emphasize the importance of considering your own needs and interests as a musician when selecting music for public performance. If you present a piece of music that has captured your own interest—rather than one you've been told you should play—you are more likely to be interested in sharing the music with your audience.

This is not to say that the suggestions of others are unimportant. For a performer, an external locus of control has some advantages. First, it makes you sensitive to the reactions of people who can influence the course of your development as a performer. The realities of being a performer require you to please and impress others—parents, teachers, juries, audition committees, and so on. But you do not have to make others the sole focus of your performing. Far too many performers are driven by "shoulds" and "oughts" ("I *should* play the more difficult of the two pieces," "I *ought* to play this piece to avoid risking failure," and so on) when selecting music to perform. Doing what you believe others think you should has several pitfalls. First, public opinion is very fickle, and it's difficult to predict what others will or will not like. Second, the judgment of listeners is likely to be based on a very different perceptual experience of the music than your own. Listeners don't invest the same amount of time and energy preparing to hear you perform as you do in preparing to play. And while playing for a teacher or a knowledgeable performer may reduce this gap, your physical and psychological state at the time of the performance will be different from that of those in attendance. Consequently, your experience of the music will be different from anyone else's, even someone who knows the piece well. A third potential problem of selecting music with other people in mind is that we may believe we must play music beyond our current capabilities. There are three simple reasons for this belief. First, such music sounds impressive to us at first hearing, and this attraction constitutes a significant part of its appeal. Second, performers usually seek challenges and select pieces because they pose new technical or musical problems. Third, many performers feel that playing excessively difficult music is one way of eclipsing their peers and impressing teachers.

As a result of these tendencies, the performer can easily create a number of potential stressors at the beginning that may become significant stumbling blocks at the time of the performance. Paramount among these stressors is choosing excessively difficult music that leaves little margin for error, which the performer may have under tenuous control, at best, during non-performance conditions. Tackling such music represents a failure to consider how one experiences the performance state, with all its attendant heightened activation and accompanying psychological correlates, which may range from euphoria to utter panic. This radical alteration can markedly change one's experience of a piece of music, so that it becomes almost unrecognizable compared to what one is used to hearing in the practice room.

What does this imply about self-assessment? First, spend some time at the outset evaluating your motives for performing the music you have selected. Who or what are you doing it for? Do you get any intrinsic pleasure from it? Is it sufficiently challenging without posing insurmountable hurdles? Like a deep personal relationship, will it wear well once the novelty of hearing it has worn off? Is there something about the music you would like to communicate to or share with other people? Aside from being a vehicle for displaying your talents and perhaps virtuosity to teachers, peers, and colleagues, what more does the music offer? Does the music evoke feelings, or moods, that strike you as intriguing or perhaps seductive? In sum, what personal meaning can you bring to and cultivate in this music?

Second, it's important to gauge the discrepancy between your musical skills and those required to play the music to performance standards. Go through the entire piece to isolate the passages that are most challenging. Are you sufficiently skilled to master them? Would this piece be better studied as an étude to help you develop your skills rather than as one suitable for performing? Resist the temptation to select a piece for performing that you can learn in all but a few passages you think you will eventually master. Such seemingly minor segments can later undermine your confidence in the piece as a whole.

Third, consider the music as a form of self-expression that allows you to communicate with your audience. Perhaps as a naive listener you are taken by certain qualities of a piece. If so, you may want to try to express the music in a way that will evoke comparable feelings in your audience. Perhaps a particular composer's works greatly appeal to you, maybe someone relatively unknown who you feel should receive more attention. If you select music with a purpose in mind, you may have a rationale for its performance other than feeling obligated to play it. If you can bring an element of active choice into the situation, you are likely to feel less psychologically trapped and more involved in performing.

In general, the more active you are in selecting the music, the greater will be your personal investment in bringing the performance to fruition. The element of choice in this process is very important, as it is in more general stress management techniques. People feel pressured to the extent that they believe they have no or limited options, whether the issue is planning a performance or taking a new job. As a performer, you may feel pulled in different directions by the whims and wishes of those with a significant impact on your development—parents, teachers, peers, members of audiences, audition committees, and the like. Under these circumstances, you can easily feel trapped by forces you can't control and feel victimized or exploited. "Where," you may ask, "do my own needs and inclinations come into play?" When related to performing, such feelings may evoke negative motivations, such as a sense of martyrdom, a compelling need to please (or avoid disappointing) others, or anger accompanied by determination to show up an "unfeeling" teacher or "cruel" parent. Since musical taste is subjective, there are an infinite number of preferences and rationales for programming a performance. We suggest that you take an active role in this process from the beginning so that, as the performance nears, you feel assured that you have relied, at least in part, on your own preferences and judgment in assessing the suitability of the music.

Exercising decision-making power, however, does not entitle you to behave like an ill-informed tyrant! Rather, engage in a process of self-assessment while planning a performance so that you can learn more about yourself as a person *and* as a performer. Actively consider suggestions made by others as well as developing a rationale for your choice of music to perform. You may have to play selections chosen by an auditions committee, but if so, you can still exercise the choice of whether or not to perform the audition. Approaching the decision-making process actively means weighing the potential costs and benefits of auditioning, or not. Could the audition benefit your development as a performer? Are you prepared to be judged by others? Do you have any underlying feelings—one way or the other—about the feasibility of the audition? Call them gut reactions, hunches, inner voices, or whatever you like, but pay attention to what you may be trying to tell yourself. However you feel at the time of a performance, it is helpful to look back on the entire process, beginning with your choice of music, and perceive an element of active choice. Ultimately, only you can *choose* to perform. Parents can plead, teachers can encourage, and peers can challenge, but your presence onstage is your own personal responsibility, a result of a choice you have made.

It is an obvious but often overlooked fact that performers spend comparatively little of their time onstage. Most of their time is taken by planning, practicing, preparing, rehearsing, fine tuning, and related activities. Even if you perform frequently, you are likely to spend most of your time preparing. Comfortable and enjoyable performing is not divorced from daily activities but, rather, is the natural result of systematic planning and preparation. Perhaps because one often feels very different when performing, it tends to be separated from daily life, but there is actually a strong underlying continuity that begins when you actively choose to perform.

Phase Two: Getting to Work. Musicians differ markedly in how they prepare music for performing, and what works well for one individual may be entirely inappropriate for another. Moreover, one individual may need to take different approaches to practicing and preparation depending on the nature of the performance. It is also noteworthy that musicians practice a great deal of music that they have no plans to perform simply to develop particular musical skills, for personal enjoyment, or for other reasons.[5]

Our analysis of the performance process focuses on the psychological factors involved in learning music for performance. The distinction between learning a piece of music and learning to *perform* that music is important, but is easily overlooked. Very different skills are involved in these two activities, and the common tendency to lump them together almost always reduces the effectiveness of each task. One way of looking at the distinction is to think of learning a piece of music as forming an internal, mental representation of the score and the information in it. As it becomes internalized, this representation becomes a "cognitive map" that we use to guide ourselves through the music. In much the same way that we refer to a map for directions to a place, we use a cognitive map to direct us through a piece of music.[6] The more detail contained in this cognitive map, the less one will be dependent on the musical score. Presumably with practice, one develops a gradually more complete map and relies increasingly on the internal representation for playing a piece of music.

One of the most anxiety-provoking experiences for performers is having to play music from memory. Over the years, performers and teachers have developed many techniques and devices to help overcome the problems of playing from memory. There are many helpful discussions of such techniques, but few (as far as we know) have addressed an important component of effective learning: many people learn best by gradually decreasing their dependence on the printed or written material. For musicians, playing from memory usually involves moving directly from playing with the score to playing without. For some musicians, this transition may be too abrupt to make in one step.

One way of circumventing this problem is through the use of partial scores that contain only a portion of the actual notes and markings of a composition. With this technique, you can gradually wean yourself from the complete score. We recommend that you try this primarily with pieces or passages that are especially difficult to memorize, because preparing the score can be somewhat tedious. One way to produce half the original score is to block out alternating measures of your score (1, 3, 5, and so on) using blank "post-on" labels. Practicing from such a score can help with memorization because you are intermittently given musical cues that help maintain your sense of the overall structure of the music. These cues are like guideposts to keep your memory on track as you play. Once you have mastered this version, then switch the blank labels to cover the previously exposed measures, and continue practicing until you can play this second version accurately. Over time, you will find that you can blank out more and more of the score until it is fully memorized.

This operation can be more time consuming and tedious than most performers would tolerate. Nevertheless, we recommend this type of exercise occasionally, if only to help the performer think in terms of musical cues based on partial information. Once several scores have been broken down and analyzed in this way, it is easier to adopt the same approach to an entire score by looking away from the score at regular intervals or temporarily deleting alternating measures.

Forming an internal representation of a piece of music occurs in several ways. Obviously, reading a musical score provides us with the basis for a visual representation of the music. A particularly well-formed visual image may enable a musician to give a note-by-note account of the score. However, a purely visual representation of a musical score may not convey sufficient information to provide a sense of what the piece sounds like. Often musicians who can visualize a score have no clear idea of what it sounds like musically. The reverse situation, in which someone can hear a piece but cannot clearly imagine the visual correlates of the sounds, is more common.

The capacity to hear a piece of music that is not being played raises some interesting questions. Frequently, when musicians claim to be able to do this, they mean that they have a global sense of the music in terms of—for example—its melodic and rhythmic structure. But how detailed is the internal representation that allows you to "hear" a piece of music? Can you, for instance, attend to the individual voices in a polyphonic fugue, highlighting some and ignoring others, and still keep the piece "going"? Can you "hear" a piece of music played in one key, and then "replay" it in another? Like a tape recorder, can you start and stop a piece in specific places, or perhaps carry out the mental equivalent of fast forwarding and rewinding? When you listen to music internally, do you ever hear mistakes? Can you alter various interpretive factors in your internal performance?

Considering questions such as these may help you assess the degree to which you can formulate a structurally and musically complete internal representation of a piece of music. Saying that you can internally "hear" a piece can mean several things and does not necessarily imply that you have a fully formed, detailed representation. We discuss mental imagery in more detail elsewhere; here it is sufficient to note, the very clear connection between how you learn a piece of music (that is, acquire a cognitive map of it) and the degree to which you will be able to hear it in your mind later.

A third element of the cognitive map that provides the basis for our internal representations of music concerns how it feels to play a piece of music. The terms "tactile" and "kinesthetic" are used for this aspect of music and refer to the sensations of touch and movement, respectively. Tactile and kinesthetic cues tell us how to position the physical structures required to achieve musical effects by playing or singing. Ordinarily, our awareness of tactile and kinesthetic cues is limited because we are more attentive to visual or auditory information. A pianist, for example, will probably find it difficult to attend to the sensations of his or her fingers and joints while listening to the effects of these hand movements. Some pianists use "silent keyboards" for practice, but usually just to avoid disturbing other people. However, such a device allows you to separate the sound from the *feel* of music; keyboard players can easily practice this awareness on electronic keyboards, which are widely available.

Trying to imagine how it feels to play a piece of music by recalling the sensations of the muscles and joints is quite challenging and normally not included in imagery training. However, this type of internal representation constitutes a source of musical information that is very different from the visual and aural aspects of playing a piece of music. To see how this type of information can be important in forming a mental representation, visualize a series of movements (such as fingering patterns for a keyboard player) that you consistently employ. Imagining the successive activation of each finger (or muscle set) will give you an idea of what it means to "feel" that you are playing a piece of music in your mind.

In speaking about learning a piece of music, we focus on how one forms a mental representation of it, a cognitive "map". Such representations are usually derived from a combination of the different sensory sources, among which the most obvious are the visual, auditory, and tactile senses.[7]

Phase Three: The Final Stage. The stresses that performers deal with change significantly as a performance approaches. We have already seen how the music one selects and the way in which it is learned can have affect a performer's susceptibility to anxiety either before or during a performance. In the third stage of performance preparation, our focus shifts to the psychological processes that arise when one is confronting a potentially stressful performance in the near future.

Effective performance preparation does not end with learning a piece of music, though musicians often confuse the two. In learning phase, you acquire such a detailed internal representation of the music that you can play the piece fluently, often without the score. However, learning music, in addition, entails absorbing so that your own characteristics and capabilities are reflected in the result. Musicians both affect and are affected by music as a result of learning it. No matter how religiously you attempt to adhere to the composer's intentions about how a piece should sound, you will learn it in a way that is uniquely your own.

Learning music, therefore, is the process of encoding a score so that it becomes highly familiar to you. One of the main criteria for assessing how well someone has learned a piece of music, of course, is their ability to perform it. But performing music and being able to play it are two fundamentally different things.

No matter how well a piece of music may be learned, its readiness for a *performance* shouldn't be presumed. There are several reasons from a psychological perspective. First, the physical and emotional state under which pieces are usually learned is markedly different from that under which performing takes place. The former is generally without tension and the related manifestations of physiological activation; the latter feels unusual, often quite alien, to a performer. The difference between these two states is enough to make the experience of the latter quite distracting—to the point of taking one's mind entirely off the music. Second, performing music requires a different set of skills than does learning. Although there are widespread differences in how people learn music, in most instances they begin by using their analytic skills to "take the music apart."

A straightforward way to help with this process is to keep a musical notebook. Figure 4–1, a page from one such notebook containing musical passages, recreates a section of a Bach organ chorale. Keeping such a notebook can be helpful for a number of reasons. First, it lets you isolate specific passages that may benefit from added attention. It is too easy, when reading from a full musical score, to pass a difficult point and continue to other portions that are easy to play and may already have been learned. Second, the act of writing down the notes in a passage is valuable in itself. One

**FIGURE 4–1**

*A Page from a Musical Notebook*

interesting exercise is to begin writing a passage from a score and then try to figure out, without looking at the score, what notes come next. In other words, try to adopt the composer's perspective and try to imagine how the composition was actually created. Often, notes on a page appear arbitrary, without logic, but if you attempt to discern a composer's intention by trying to predict the direction of a score, you may gain insights that will aid your mastery and interpretation of the music. Keeping a notebook makes it easy to record not just the musical score, but your thoughts about the music as they evolve. You may observe, for example, that your thoughts about the piece when beginning to learn it were very different than they became weeks or even months later. It can be instructive to make notes of these thoughts because they may eventually help you develop your interpretation of the piece or other perspectives that contribute to the overall musicality of your performance.

Although it's not evident from this example, you can also use a notebook to try out different ideas, from different fingering patterns to interpretative strategies. The piece in this example was worked up several different ways, and the final version is shown here. Isolating sections of a piece of music, though not always helpful, is certainly recommended when a performer is challenged by the music's technical demands. By removing the troublesome section from its context—as a mechanic might take a carburator out of a car, disassemble it, clean it, and then replace it—this analytic activity can contribute to making the performance of the piece technically secure and musically valid.

Analytic skills are applied in such tasks as studying the harmonic structure of a piece, isolating and working through its challenging passages, and playing or singing the music at gradually increasing tempos. Thus, the development of an internal image of a piece of music is almost invariably preceded by an analytic process that fosters the image. Performing, on the other hand, involves taking what one has learned and giving it expression. But what does this really entail? Musicians often talk about "letting go" or "releasing" the music when performing. The idea underlying such expressions is that, when performing, a musician gives up the conscious, effortful control that characterizes the learning process. Too often, a performer's style of playing reflects an effort to control every note.

Such performing has a strained, constricted quality and seldom reveals any spontaneity.

We believe that this overly controlled style arises from four factors. First, it is a natural response to the risks that many musicians associate with public performances. Becoming cautious and trying to avoid mistakes are rational responses to a perceived threat. Playing before a large or authoritative audience, a performance jury, or at an audition can make a performer especially prone to such tendencies. The second factor is the tendency of many musicians to perform with the same analytical, cautious approach they take to learning music. Because far more time is spent learning music than performing it, it is easy to adopt styles during practice that are unconsciously carried over to performing. Obsessive concern for note accuracy is appropriate when learning a new piece, but too often this obsession is retained during performances because it has become internalized in the individual's style of playing.

What you learn during practice is more than just the music; your style of practicing also becomes integrated with the music. The phrase "style of practicing" encompasses a great many things, some of which are more obvious than others. For example, the habit of practicing slowly and systematically is part of one's style. So is the amount of time you devote to practice. But other, less obvious elements may carry over into your performance. For example, do you think a great deal when you practice music? If so, what do you think about? Do certain ideas or themes accompany your practice? If so, they may offer clues to attitudes and beliefs about yourself as a person or performer that accompany you onstage. Do you habitually practice with too much muscular tension? Are you aware of how tense you are when you practice? Tension may also stay with you outside the practice room. Just as the muscles needed to produce music develop characteristic response patterns, other muscles not directly related to the production of music can become conditioned. We consider this problem in more detail later; for now it is enough to emphasize that there can be a great deal of carry-over from practice sessions to performance that affects not just the music, but how you produce it, what you think about, and how you feel.

A third factor that contributes to overcontrol is lack of self-trust. Leaving aside whether you feel comfortable letting go on stage, consider the broader question of how relaxed and open you are in other circumstances. Do you approach relationships with others cautiously? Do you engage in any other activities in which you "cut loose" your control over things? Sometimes, musicians who complain of being unable to "loosen up" onstage discover upon reflection that they feel equally constrained in their every day lives. In other words, the aspect of performing that calls for letting go of the music may be very foreign to you.[8]

Finally, in a related vein, it's important to consider what the "performance state" feels like. If you are unaccustomed to freely expressing your feelings and keep a tight rein on your emotions, you may be unprepared for the strong physical and emotional sensations that performers may experience onstage. Recall one of your early performances, preferably when you were relatively young, and how you felt at the time. If you are like many performers, you may have been distracted by sudden feelings during, and perhaps before, the event. It is interesting to ask how you learned to deal with such feelings. If you found them distracting or frightening, what happened the next time you performed? Did you feel better or worse? If you experience significant distress as a performer now, you probably encountered some situations early in your performing history that made you somewhat fearful of how your body and mind unexpectedly responded onstage. You are therefore likely to have developed a tendency to control things because of the unpleasant and unexpected sensations you had at the beginning.

In summary we suggest that you consider at least four factors if you attempt to consciously control your performing:

1. Fear of risky situations, such as playing to an audience that is perceived as unsupportive, performing excessively difficult music, and so on.
2. Carry-over from your practice and preparation style that gives you a cautious, controlled approach to performing.
3. The broader question of how spontaneous you are in nonperformance, everyday situations.
4. Your manner of interpreting and responding to the intense emotions that frequently accompany formal performances and that catch many musicians by surprise.

If any of these factors, either singly or in combination, have affected your development as a performer, then you will probably benefit from developing a system for preparing for a performance once you have learned the music. Obviously, any performer can benefit from systematic preparation, and it's worth noting that seasoned, veteran performers tend to invest enormous amounts of time and energy in refining their music for public performance. Such preparation strategies are designed to promote self-assurance and confidence as the performance draws near. It goes without saying that this period of preparation is preceded by a much longer phase of learning, which we have already discussed in some detail.

The point at which you enter the final stage of preparation obviously differs from one situation to another. However, some performers allow far too little time between learning the music and performing it. As a result, they have very little time to become familiar with the music in anything other than a technical sense. Not having lived with the music for very long, they may find that it seems alien at a formal performance. Although capable of performing it capably in the practice room or during a lesson, they find themselves feeling very differently about the music—and themselves—at the performance. Even a flawless dress rehearsal does not guarantee that the performance will go smoothly.

There are, of course, many ways of getting experience of playing in public. Often teachers will schedule regular playing classes for students to try out a new piece of music before their peers and see how they will perform under the resultant pressure. Other performers find opportunities to play their music to relatively uncritical listeners. One pianist, for example, periodically played the music he had learned in piano showrooms, under the pretext that he was contemplating buying a new instrument. He also sought out shopping malls and other public places that have instruments for public use. He reasoned that his potential audience in such circumstances was not likely to be critical of his performance, but would at least be aware that he was playing.

Our approach to this phase of performance preparation helps performers develop a systematic plan to ensure adequate exposure to performance situations and derive maximum benefits from them. We suggest the following steps in this process.

First, establish a deadline for having your music ready to perform that is well in advance of the formal event. The amount of time between your deadline and your performance can vary, depending on the circumstances, but it's a good idea to set a target date (which can be changed if necessary) for learning the music. Bear in mind that it's easy to underestimate the amount of time required to learn and refine music for public presentation. The successive refinements needed to bring a piece of music to performance standards can easily require as much time and effort as learning the music in the first place. The audible results of this additional effort, however, tend to become less obvious with each succeeding degree of refinement.[9] Thus you are likely to invest significant amounts of time for what may seem like diminishing gain. Many performers feel that once they have learned the notes, they have mastered the music, but this is seldom the case. One can spend an unlimited amount of time on refinements, experimentation, and fine tuning. Try to set aside a period of time that will allow you to progressively refine your music without becoming disaffected with it.

The next step is to develop a system for gauging how much progress you're making as you develop your performance plan. A "performance log" is a simple way of keeping track of your performances and the circumstances surrounding them. You might begin with a separate entry for each piece of music you're preparing. Previously, we suggested that, when you begin a new piece of music, you jot down some notes about it, including a brief list of some realistic goals you hope to achieve as you learn and perform the music.

If you want to be even more systematic, consider using the performance assessment log shown in figure 4–2. This log consists of four basic components. First is the title of the piece; second is the composer. In the third part, the performer enumerates the goals that he or she has set for the performance of the piece. These goals are subdivided into technical, interpretive, and personal aims.

Technical goals are specific musical skills that the performer may wish to cultivate while learning a new piece of music. For example, a piece of music may be studied because it requires skill at octave passages, or rapid thirds, or trills, that would be useful for a pianist to add to his or her repertoire.

Musical/interpretive goals are what the performer wishes to communicate with the music. One goal might be as direct as conveying the composer's original intentions as faithfully as possible; an alternative might be to develop a unique or innovative interpre-

Name:_____

### Performance Assessment Record

I. Title: _____

2. Composer:_____

3. Performance Goals:

A. Technical:_____

_____

_____

B. Musical/Interpretive:_____

_____

_____

C. Personal: _____

_____

_____

4. Performance Log:

| Date | Time | Setting | Occasion | Audience |
|------|------|---------|----------|----------|
| | | | | |
| | | | | |
| | | | | |
| | | | | |
| | | | | |
| | | | | |
| | | | | |
| | | | | |
| | | | | |
| | | | | |
| | | | | |
| | | | | |
| | | | | |

**FIGURE 4–2**

*Performance Assessment Log*

tation of the music. Whatever the goal, the interpretation of music requires thought and planning, and we recommend that performers begin thinking about their interpretation when they contemplate learning a new piece.

The third performance goal concerns one's personal aspirations. In effect, you should ask yourself, "What's in it for me?" Perhaps you are attracted to the melodic aspects of the music or to sounds created by juxtapositions of various notes. Perhaps you are interested in learning the piece because it will help advance your career or prepare you for an important audition. As with musical and interpretive goals, personal goals can vary considerably. When learning new music, it is important for you to have a personal stake in the learning. If you invest personal meaning in the music you are attempting to learn, you will probably find the music more meaningful, so that you can perform it with greater confidence and conviction than music about which you feel, at best, lukewarm.

The fourth component of the performance assessment record is a performance log, which can be used to make brief notes about successive performances of the piece. The log has spaces for the date, time, setting, occasion, and type of audience. You may find that you want to note other aspects of the performance as well. This process is, at best, very sketchy and may be amplified with additional notes or personal reactions to a particular performance. At least, however, the performance log provides a means of documenting successive performances and the conditions under which they were given.

Keeping a record of your performances, particularly as a major event nears, is helpful for two reasons. First, such a record provides you with an organizational structure that can greatly aid systematic preparation. Second, it can offer reassurance as the performance becomes imminent. Reviewing and thinking about your previous performances (provided they have gone reasonably well) can significantly reinforce feelings of preparedness and bolster self-esteem.

Give some consideration to the number and nature of your practice performances. On one hand, it's important to perform often enough to feel very comfortable with the music; on the other hand, it's easy to go to the other extreme by performing too often or in a manner that will be of little benefit. The following suggestions may help you settle on a happy medium. First, try to schedule your practice performances at a specific date and time, rather than arranging them on the spur of the moment. Scheduling these events will enable you to experience the anticipation, and perhaps tension that may precede the performance. It's not a bad idea, by the way, to schedule these sessions for the same time of day that you will eventually be performing.

It's also very important to give yourself sufficient time after each practice performance to evaluate the feedback you've received and further refine the piece. Consider as well the type of audience for your practice performances. Playing a piece ten times for a friend or colleague may be less valuable than two or three well-planned performances for larger or more critical groups of listeners. The size of your practice audience is probably less important than the degree to which you perceive them as authoritative or potentially critical.

As much as possible, try to simulate in each practice performance the conditions of the actual performance. Of course, a dress rehearsal is intended to provide this type of simulation, but consider arranging other practice performances with the same care and planning.

As far as actual performances are concerned, it's important to learn as much as possible from each experience. To make this task easier, we recommend using the brief self-assessment rating form, which can be filled out quickly after any performance. (See page 30) The "SOAP" form allows you to efficiently describe your performance subjectively, form a more objective opinion of it, assess the status of your overall goals for the piece, and plan what needs to be done next.

The most important part of this process is planning what to do based on the feedback you've derived about your performances. At this stage, try to be as specific as possible. "Planning to practice more," for instance, is too vague to be of very much help. "Planning to make fewer mistakes" is praiseworthy but lacks a clear-cut means for achieving the desired effect. Moreover, planning to *avoid* doing something is usually not effective. Generally, it's more helpful to decide specifically what you want to achieve; in doing so, you are likely to find that the problems you wish to avoid take care of themselves.

What about a statement like, "I need to concentrate more when

I perform"? Although this might seem a worthwhile goal, it can be difficult because there are so many ways to define concentration. Some performers describe concentration as an effort, using terms like "bearing down" or "focusing as hard as you can" on the music. Others describe concentrating as being "caught up" or "lost" in the music and aware of little else. The issue, then becomes deciding what you mean by concentrating (or paying attention or practicing).

These examples should clearly show that a plan for subsequent performances will benefit from thoughtful consideration of your goals. The most effective way to do this is to review your self-ratings and investigate the troublesome areas. For instance, suppose that during the performance you were troubled by distracting thoughts that reflected fears of failure or embarrassment.[10] An obvious immediate response to this problem would be to plan to avoid such thoughts in the future. But this type of plan is less of a solution than it is a wish to avoid the difficulty in the future. Instead, you need insight into the problem and a thoughtful analysis of how the problem can be addressed systematically. Let us, therefore, look at this issue in more detail.

Troublesome thoughts may occur at almost any time. In the sense used here, troublesome means that the thoughts are unwanted, distracting, and difficult to control. Troublesome thoughts often seem alien, as if springing from outside our conscious awareness, and they are usually unpleasant because they focus on risk, danger, failure, or other threatening themes. Because these thoughts are unwanted, they tend to be distracting and may make us feel as though we are in imminent danger. Such distraction involves two factors. First, the thoughts compete in our consciousness with whatever else we are focusing on at the time. Second, if sufficiently disturbing, such thoughts may redirect our attention toward an in-depth consideration of their meaning and significance. It's possible to become entangled in a spiraling pattern of increasingly abstract thinking, in which you become aware of intrusive thoughts, focus on their content, and then start thinking about why you're having such thoughts—all of which, of course, leads you further from the point where you began.

The difficulty of controlling such thoughts is their third, and perhaps most troublesome, quality. Most of us conceive of thoughts as a kind of physical reality that enables them to be manipulated at will. A strong sense of physical control is implied in this idea. For instance, a performer might say "I don't allow anxious thoughts to cross my mind" in much the same way that a guard might forcibly prevent a car from passing an international border. But distracting thoughts are maddeningly free-spirited; they float in and out of our consciousness, diverting our attention as they go. Generally speaking, trying to force them out of mind or prevent them from occuring can be extremely frustrating, particularly if we attempt to do so abruptly or forcefully.

Let's return to our overriding concern here, that of developing a plan for preparation and subsequent performances. Thus far, we have determined that our specific problem is not so much musical but, rather, cognitive (including, perhaps, troublesome mental images). On further reflection, we have noticed that unwanted thoughts are distracting and difficult to control, at least when we effortfully try to drive them from our consciousness. A plan for coping with such unwanted distractions needs to take these factors into account. A simple plan at this stage might be to develop increasingly task-oriented behavior, finding ways of becoming more focused on performing and less on distracting thoughts and images. Deciding on specific ways to do this may require some detailed thought. You will probably discover that no single, sure-fire method can accomplish this task, but that certain techniques are more likely to work for you than for other individuals. You might find, for example, that saying "stop!" to yourself whenever you become aware of unsettling thoughts may gradually cause them to diminish. On the other hand, you may discover that you're more prone to the problem when you play a difficult piece rapidly. In this case, one obvious solution would be to slow down until you've achieved the required mastery. A plan that contains these sorts of specific strategies is more likely to be helpful than the general directives we spoke of earlier.

When conducted with care and with an eye for detail, practice performances can be extremely beneficial when preparing a performance. By no means casual events, they should be realistic simulations of the actual performance itself. Although self-rating forms may not be necessary for everyone, they can be very useful if you find it difficult to evaluate your performances concretely and specifically. There are several clear advantages to such a system. First, it provides you with a cumulative record of your performances and thus makes it relatively easy for you to gauge your progress. Second, it can help you isolate problem areas and analyze approaches to them. Third, it can help you distinguish between the musical and psychological factors that affect your performing. Although the two are related, it's important to distinguish the contributions of each factor to a problem, because your efforts to correct the problem should vary according to its source.

The advantages of practice performances vary considerably depending on the nature of your practice audience, although many performers overlook this fact when planning a performance. Formal dress rehearsals, which are usually held without deliberately inviting an audience, differ substantially from practice performances as we use the term. Several studies have shown that the size and nature of an audience affect a performer's responses, and thus you should carefully consider who you ask to attend practice performances.[11]

We recommend that you gradually increase the size and sophistication of the audiences to whom you give practice performances. Begin with one or two people whom you trust and feel comfortable with. Explain your intentions and make every effort to communicate your music to them without considering them as "only" friends. Even at this early stage, schedule your practice performance for a specific time and place, rather than just asking someone to listen to a piece as soon as you feel you've mastered it. Scheduling practicing performances ahead of time allows you to experiment with how you perform at different times of the day, and your practice performance schedule should include times corresponding to that of the actual performance. Second, advance scheduling allows you to experience a period of anticipation during which you can test and enhance your coping skills. You may find, for instance, that shortly before a practice performance, you experience a certain amount of the queasiness that precedes a major performance. Don't be shaken by this reaction, because it's perfectly normal. Instead, try to "make friends" with the feelings, allow them full expression, and attempt to regard them as natural physical changes that are a normal part of performing. Rather than being seen a danger signal that makes you anxious, they should signify heightened readiness to undertake a skillful, creative venture.

Practice performances are especially helpful if you get useful feedback after each performance. There's a tendency, particularly among musicians who are good friends, to offer support by avoiding criticism. Indeed, we generally have an almost reflexive desire to applaud or praise performances, no matter how critical we really feel. Peer-oriented practice performances, although intended primarily to simulate performance conditions, are also undertaken to obtain accurate feedback. Soliciting criticism can be touchy, because at times we want to deny critical comments to maintain our psychological equilibrium. Furthermore, feedback—whether positive or negative—is often too vague to be of much use. Finally, feedback from another person, however well-intentioned, may or may not contain the type of information you're seeking. If, for instance, you are especially concerned about your melodic phrasing, a comment that you looked relaxed misses the point. Performers often invite such comments, however, because of the way they solicit feedback. "I'd like you to listen to me play this piece," is a common request, "to see how it's coming along." Issued with such vague guidelines, even someone highly motivated to help will be unable to understand what you're really looking for. Do you need support? Reassurance? A truly critical appraisal?

For these reasons, you should give your listeners, in advance, some idea of what to look and listen for. If you wish to be formal, ask your audience to complete the relevant items on the SOAP performance rating form. Also complete one of these forms yourself, and then compare your assessment, point by point, with others' to see how closely you agree. Even if you choose a less structured approach, it's still a good idea to give your listener(s) an idea of what to look for in the music and your performance. It is impossible to attend carefully to eveything that occurs during a musical performance. Because music unfolds over time, our principal means of deriving meaning from it are remembering and reconstructing images of what we have heard. Focusing on one aspect of the music necessarily means ignoring others, and so it is important to remember that listeners are highly selective in what they pay conscious attention to.[12]

In summary, even your initial practice performances, held for listeners you trust, can provide you with useful feedback, but to ensure this result, you should provide your audience with a helpful frame of reference for their opinions. Using rating forms, providing an overview what you're trying to communicate musically, and making it clear whether or not you want explicit feedback are all ways of enhancing the value of these sessions.

An interesting parallel can be drawn between a performer and listener and two people involved in a personal relationship. In both instances, problems frequently develop because of a lack of clear communciation between them. Musicians sometimes assume that other people can listen with the same critical acuity that they themselves possess, but this is seldom the case. Because of this tendency, performers often make erroneous assumptions about what others hear or do not hear. Similarly, people in relationships often assume that the other person sees the world in the same way, despite evidence to the contrary. In either situation, failure to be explicit about one's wants or needs is likely to create too much ambiguity for effective communication.

Once you have worked through some of the challenges of performing for one or a few individuals, you can expand your audience so that you progressively increase the stress you experience. The key, of course, is to voluntarily expose yourself to stress that does not exceed your coping abilities, but that allows you to practice what you have learned in previous encounters and further refine your performance skills. Performance classes frequently are conducted by teachers of specific instruments to give their students experience of playing in public. The manner in which such classes are conducted, however, can significantly affect how much benefit the performer derives from the experience. At this stage in developing public performance skills, research has shown that four factors can have beneficial therapeutic results:[13]

1. A nonthreatening, friendly audience.
2. Accurate feedback and nonpunitive, helpfully critical reactions following performances.
3. Gradual exposure to anxiety-producing performance situations.
4. Assured success during early rehearsal performances.

A graduated exposure to performance situations helps the performer tolerate gradually increasing levels of performance stress.

Too often, student performers make the transition from their practice rooms or teachers' studios to the stage before live audiences without any intermediate steps. Either singly or in combination, the following techniques can be used to generate a gradient of increasingly demanding situations:

1. Gradually increasing the audience size, perhaps beginning with only the teacher and one or two other students.
2. Gradually increasing the status of the audience. The presence of even a single teacher—especially one considered very important and critical—can outweigh even a large but untutored audience.
3. Audio- or videotaping the performance.
4. Requiring the piece be played from memory rather than with a score.
5. Performing in the setting where the actual performance will eventually take place.

The last component of this model, assured success, means arranging performance challenges that are well within the performer's grasp. Many students (and some teachers) facing an important performance select a repertoire that overly taxes their technical and artistic skills—even before anxiety-provoking cues are added to the equation. Choosing very demanding music leaves little margin for the extra demands on attention, concentration, and motor coordination usually imposed by performance situations. Selecting a repertoire that has already been learned and that is comfortably within your present technical and interpretive level is a sensible way to approach performance.

Acting against this recommendation is the perception of many performers that the familiarity and even boredom that result from knowing a piece well will be communicated to the audience as a lackluster, uninspired performance. However, the state of mind associated with by performing will probably make an overly familiar repertoire very welcome. Many performers who become acclimated to performing try to cope simultaneously with the performance situation and a relatively new piece of music; the resulting demands on their attention, concentration, and dexterity make them likely candidates for an overwhelming panic attack.

You can take advantage of other factors that increase the likelihood of successful performances. Most of these center on your advance preparation, and some have already been mentioned, but four of them bear repeating.

1. Using mental imagery to rehearse away from one's instrument offers an effective means of reinforcing and consolidating the effects of live practice.

2. Performers can also benefit from simulating performance conditions through systematic advance planning. Important rehearsals, for instance, can be preceded by the same preparatory activities that will precede the actual event. For many performers, these activities become like a ritual that helps get them into the flow of a performance.

3. Prior exposure to the setting of the performance can also combat anxiety. Getting used to the room, its acoustics, and other aspects of its ambiance leaves less to adjust to at the time of the performance.

4. Conceptualizing the performance as "risk free" can be beneficial. Even a practice performance can easily evoke enough anxiety to interfere with effective performance. Your perceptions of the performance can greatly influence your response to it. For instance, if you regard mistakes as catastrophies you may be able to reframe them less dramatically in a supportive group setting. The clarinetist Anton Weinberg suggested using the intriguing term "musical misunderstandings" in place of "mistakes." Try to conceive of the performance as an experiment or a learning situation, in which the goal is to learn about yourself and your skills, rather than as a situation in which you must either succeed or fail. A performance has so many potential outcomes that it seems unnecessarily limiting to categorize one's efforts so strictly.

These strategies are intended to help you develop confidence through a series of positive experiences that do not make excessive demands upon your coping abilities. Frequently performing an overlearned repertoire may sound very boring, or even unmusical, but this approach enables the performer to explore and come to terms with the surprising and sometimes disconcerting alterations in consciousness that accompany performing. From this vantage point, the music is a means to an end, which is the exploration of subjective experiences that all experienced performers must become accustomed to.

To further broaden your performance opportunities, you may want to explore some additional performance environments to gain more experience:

1. Churches, where soloists may be invited to perform preludes, postludes, or other service music
2. Schools, where combined performances and talks about music are often welcomed
3. Special interest clubs (auxiliaries, support groups, boards), which offer programs on a wide range of topics
4. Music companies, which may sponsor musical instruments in shopping malls, retail stores, or other outlets
5. Social service agencies, hospitals, and convalescent homes, which provide extended care
6. Colleges and universities, where performance facilities are sometimes made available as needed to members of the larger community

Widespread interest in the arts, and specifically in music, makes it relatively easy to find opportunties to refine your performance skills in public settings. Of course, simply performing in public does not guarantee an attentive audience, because in many of the settings mentioned previously, people have assembled for other purposes or have little formal knowledge of music. Regardless of how your efforts are perceived, however, such experiences invaluable sources of the self-generated feedback you will inevitably obtain before, during, and after performing. If you feel that a particular performance is not sufficently challenging, look for ways of increasing its demands on you—for example, by relying more on your memory than a printed score or by playing a piece that is more demanding then normal. In general, try to develop a systematic plan for engaging in public performances based on the principle of graded stress inoculation (see chapter 2). Essentially, this process means performing for others in situations that require you to master progressively increasing levels of stress until you can tolerate the stresses inherent in a major performance. Scheduling such events ahead of time, preparing systematically in the interim, and engaging in an honest process of self-appraisal after each can help ensure that you derive the maximum benefit from the experiences. It is in this way that one really acquires and refines performance skills—not in the practice room.

*Phase Four*: The Performance State. As a major performance becomes imminent, many musicians notice a significant shift in their feelings, thoughts, and actions. Often, a few days before the performance, performers begin to feel "keyed up," and this feeling often increases until the time of the performance. For the uninitiated, this experience can be trying, because it introduces feelings that are either alien or associated with risk or danger. This change in physical and psychological status gradually progresses in intensity and many musicians carry the feelings into the performance, where, depending on the circumstances, they may either further intensify or else diminish as time progresses.[14]

After a performance, musicians frequently say they feel "wrung out" and attribute this fatigue to the amount of energy they have just expended. However, how one feels immediately after performing is a product not only of the energy expended during the performance but of the hours and days beforehand when one was in a state of pre-performance tension.

Having become aware of the unique feelings that arise in the period before a performance, many musicians have developed characteristic, even ritualistic, behaviors that support them during this last phase of preparation. In general, these pre-performance activities may have any of three effects: reducing excessive stimulation, enhancing concentration, and draining excess physical energy. All of these activities are related to a central fact about the time surrounding a performance: it entails heightened physical activation, which tends to increase until and sometimes into the performance and then diminish markedly, both during and following the performance.

Musicians often want to isolate themselves for a period of time before a performance. One pianist, for example, disconnects his phone three days in advance of a concert and talks with as few people as possible during this time. The amount of isolation differs from person to person, but the common element in this behavior is the desire to reduce the stimulation one must deal with. As one singer described it, "I go into a phase where I think that having one more thing to deal with will drive me crazy!" She feels incapable of dealing with much besides the performance when it is two or three days away. During that time, she becomes a comparative recluse, seldom venturing from her apartment and avoiding the television, radio, and other common activities that she otherwise enjoys. This isolation is not particularly pleasant, she says, because she is cut off from the people who ordinarily give her a great deal of support. But during this phase she finds talking to other people irritating and gets quite impatient with "small talk".

Reducing stimulation can be handled in other ways as well. You may, for instance, develop familiar, comfortable rituals, such as re-arranging your music or reading passages from a book you habitually turn to. Sometimes such rituals are directly related to the preparatory activities, such as the habits of one woodwind player who carefully trims three extra reeds the day before each performance, or the pianist who methodically reviews the score of each piece she'll be performing four times the day before. Why three reeds or four reviews? There's no obvious logic. But rituals clearly serve several important functions apart from their adaptive purpose. First, they reduce stimulation, leaving you fewer unexpected experiences to deal with. Second, they provide the comfort that comes with repetition. It somehow feels right to repeat things over and over and perhaps learn something new about ourselves or the activity in the process. Third, very simply, rituals are a means of passing time, which to many performers seems to drag in the days or hours before a performance. Almost everyone faced with stressful situations— stage performers, soldiers preparing for battle, athletes before matches, and so on—finds the time immediately before the event to be the most psychologically taxing. During this time, one's fears often become most intense, but little can be done to determine how realistic they are.[15] Under such circumstances, it's very sensible to engage in activities over which you have some control, whether it's trimming reeds, studying scores, or other repetitive tasks that have no direct bearing on the performance.

It should be clear from the preceding discussion that we are talking as much about minimizing internal as external stimulation. External distractors—phone calls, interruptions, television, and so on—are easy to identify. Such events can be clearly labeled as distractors when we are in a state of pre-performance activation, but otherwise we passively attend to them daily without being fully aware of their impact. More subtlely stimulating aspects of the environment may also require regulation, however, including such things as ambient lighting, noise levels, and temperature. It's worthwhile trying to notice the types of stimulation you are sensitive to and learning as much as you can about how your surroundings affect you when you are in different moods, including your characteristic mood just before a performance.

Many musicians extend their efforts to reduce stimulation before performances to internal sensations as well, such as the thoughts, feelings, and physical sensations that compete for our attention. The pre-performance activation experienced by many musicians generates many such sensations. In this condition, best described as a "preparatory state," physiological activation is accompanied by a variety of sensations (which might be called symptoms) that frequently draw attention to themselves. Consider your heartbeat, for example. Normally, it's difficult to detect unless you happen to focus intensely on it. But as you move into the preparatory state, you may experience episodes of tachycardia, or rapid heartbeat, that occur unexpectedly and are distracting or even frightening. Similarly, you may become preoccupied with extremely worrisome thoughts or images about your upcoming performance. Fears of collapsing onstage, forgetting the music, losing the place in the score, and similar concerns are all commonly reported by performers of many different levels of training and accomplishment. This point cannot be emphasized enough, because many relatively unseasoned performers erroneously imagine that seasoned veterans seldom, if ever, have to contend with such distracting thoughts. However, such occurrences are common among experts and novices alike: it's just that the professionals have learned that such fears are seldom truly predictive of what will happen during the performance. In other words, they treat such thoughts as a normal part of performing and are not unduly distracted or frightened by them.

Having troublesome thoughts and being bothered by them are two different things; thoughts, after all, are not "reality," but reflections of our *interpretation* of some actual or potential event.[16] Unfortunately, some performers become frightened or anxious in response to such thoughts, saying things like, "I'm *certain* that my worries about having a memory slip mean that I'll forget such-and-such a passage" or "Having thoughts like these must mean that I'm just not cut out to be a performer", when nothing could be further from the truth. However, these types of thoughts often reach a crescendo shortly before a performance, no matter how well prepared the musician may be. Preoccupation with such thoughts can take time away from beneficial preparatory activities and *can* result in self-fulfilling prophecies if taken seriously enough.

Clearly, reducing stimulation associated with both internal dialogues or external factors is highly desirable because there are limits to the number of things we can attend to at any one time. It is important that a performer's focus of attention be as task-relevant as possible. Sometimes, our attention is very focused, a condition that we associate with intense concentration. At other times, our attention is drawn to different ongoing events, so that we feel distracted.

Attention is an important component of the mental fabric that underlies a musical performance. Figure 4–3 illustrates the concept of attention and the potential impact of anxiety on attention. Attention could be perceived as a circle; Stanislavski used the term "circle of attention."[19] You might think of this circle as analogous to a spotlight shining on a stage. In the center of the beam, the light is most intense, and it gradually fades and then blends into darkness at the edges. In the top drawing, the circle of attention encompasses a number of components of a musical performance. This illustration shows that certain events capture our attention while performing, while others fall outside the sphere of our immediate awareness. Notice, for example, how motor and technical skills are both in and outside the circle; this indicates that, after a performer has prepared for the performance, the motor skills needed to play the piece should be so well-learned that they do not require much conscious attention. If a performer needed to attend to motor skills, less attention would be left for other tasks, such as the focal task of interpretation, which occupies the center of this circle. However, other factors occupy our attention during a performance. Feelings and emotions, for example, are experienced by all performers, and may become the center of their attention. In addition, performing has cognitive aspects—for example, when a performer formulates a plan for playing a section of a piece. This largely conscious activity may occupy a performer's attention during the performance. In a well-prepared performance, most musicians can focus on interpreting the music, because their technical command of the music

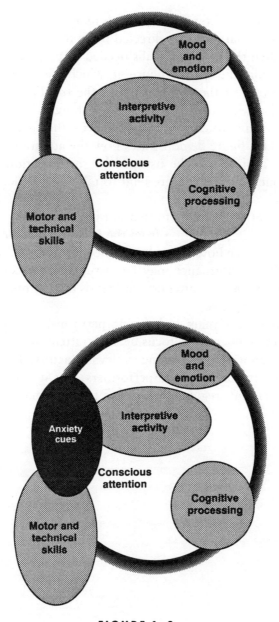

**FIGURE 4–3**
*The Circle of Attention*

Adapted from C. Stanislavski, *An actor prepares*. New York: Theater Arts.

allows them to play literally without thinking. Thus, in the top figure, the circle of attention is directed more to the interpretation of the music than the technical skills needed to play it.

Now consider the bottom figure, in which the circle of attention encompasses all of the components in the top figure, but is also occupied by anxiety cues. These cues are shown as darker than the other components to convey their salience—they are very difficult to ignore. This figure demonstrates how the attention we focus on performing a piece may be usurped by the sensations caused by anxiety, which by their nature tend to take precedence over other information.

The concept of a circle of attention illustrates how anxiety can distract our limited attention from the task at hand. In the bottom figure, you can see how your ability to concentrate on the essential elements of a performance may be disrupted by anxiety that not only competes for your attention but tends to take precedence over almost everything else.

In summary, the main task facing performers at the time of a performance is effectively focusing their attention on the critical tasks while ignoring or screening irrelevant factors. This task is not easy, especially for neophyte performers, but it can be achieved through persistent, regulated exposure to performance situations.

# The Nature of Anxiety

*Early in life, I was visited by the bluebird of anxiety.*
— *Woody Allen*

**D**uring most of human history, daily life was filled with physical risks and dangers. In contrast, modern times are filled with anxiety, manifested by apprehension, physical stress, and physiological activation. Anxiety has provided the inspiration for works of art ranging from W. H. Auden's poem "The Age of Anxiety" to the second symphony of Leonard Bernstein. It has been the object of countless treatises and psychological studies. Because anxiety has become a household word, it may have ceased to have a clear definition—if it ever had one to begin with.

This chapter reviews the complex concept of anxiety because we need a useful working definition for performers, teachers, and clinicians alike. Following a brief account of modern scientific findings, we present a historical overview of anxiety and the terms used to describe it. We then proceed to a detailed consideration of a contemporary model that integrates a large body of clinical and research data. Next, we develop our working model of anxiety and consider some assessment procedures that are useful in clinical contexts. Finally, using some case histories, we consider some of the most salient symptoms of anxiety likely to be encountered by performers.

## Some Modern Views of Anxiety

A very wide range of terms and concepts have been used to describe the anxiety. "Fear," "phobia," "nervousness," and "panic" are among the words used often interchangeably with "anxiety." In the clinical realm, "neurotic anxiety" was used by Sigmund Freud nearly 100 years ago to describe a pattern of distress that he believed afflicts almost everyone. At present, the use of the term anxiety appears to have two aspects. The first aspect concerns its effect on how we think and feel. Considerable evidence suggests that anxiety is accompanied by habitual patterns of thought. The second aspect focuses on how anxiety apparently limits basic cognitive capabilities such as memory and attention. For the performing musician, both of these aspects can have important implications.[1]

Among psychological disorders, clinical anxiety ranks first in six-month and second in lifetime prevalence according to recent data from a large-scale study.[2] This survey estimates that anxiety disorders and a related group of psychological impairments called somatoform disorders affect more than eight percent of the current U.S. population, or approximately 18 million people. So if you have been troubled by anxiety (whether related to performing or not), it may comfort you to know that you share this problem with many other people. Of course, the prevalence of this condition does not minimize its impact on an individual, nor do we wish to suggest that it does.

The prevalence of anxiety compared to other forms of psychological distress has been explained in a number of ways. First, many psychologists have argued that anxiety is a part of the "human condition," a fact of life. A brief reflection on the many uncertainties we must face will convince most of us that life offers no lasting peace of mind. So, the apprehension many of us feel may partly come from awareness of our human frailty and vulnerability. From this vantage point, anxiety appears to be a normal part of our psychological make-up.

A second explanation for anxiety's widespread prevalence is its link to a very primitive self-protection mechanism termed the "fight or flight" response, which virtually all mammals possess.[3] Central to this response is physical activation that has much in common with our feeling when we are anxious. The fight or flight response triggers profuse sweating, clammy hands and feet, rapid breathing, a perceptible increase in heart rate, and so on. Although the experience of these sensations is often unpleasant, they actually serve the useful purpose of mobilizing us to take some sort of immediate action. This response may have evolved as a means of responding to direct physical threats, such as an attack by a wild animal in prehistoric times. Now that we are seldom confronted by such physical dangers, this response is usually elicited by situations that pose psychological threats. Facing a large audience as a soloist is a perfect example of a psychological threat, at least to the degree that the performer finds this experience challenging and frightening. Although the risk of physical harm is quite low, such circumstances can trigger the reactions that accompany the fight or flight response, which we experience as extreme tension. So the next time you find yourself sweating, shaking, and feeling threatened before a performance, remember that your response is partly a normal reaction to a situation perceived as dangerous.

Another way of explaining the prevalence of anxiety lies in the fact that it often is found in conjunction with certain physical conditions. Symptoms of anxiety, for example are routinely reported by individuals suffering from drug and alcohol abuse, metabolic and neurological conditions, and cardiovascular problems. Of these, the association with cardiovascular conditions is especially strong. The next time you feel anxious, notice that your heart is literally pounding—probably the most clearly evident symptom of anxiety you're likely to experience. The term "soldier's heart" was first used many years ago to describe the cardiac distress of soldiers in battle. It can sometimes be difficult to tell if such symptoms signify an underlying physical problem or are manifestations of anxiety. Evidence suggests that a high percentage of patients with atypical chest pain symptoms clearly meet the diagnostic criteria for a form of anxiety known as "panic disorder." There appears to be an overlap between the symptoms of cardiac problems and those of anxiety. Thus, although anxiety is not usually symptomatic of a medical problem, it is a possibility to consider when attempting to understand the origins of a person's anxiety, especially when severe and chronic.

## Historical Perspective

The philosopher Soren Kierkegaard described the subjective quality of anxiety in great detail in his essay *The Concept of Dread:*

> And no Grand Inquisitor has in readiness such terrible tortures as
> has anxiety, and no spy knows how to attack more artfully the man
> he suspects, choosing the instant when he is weakest, nor knows how
> . . . (quoted in D. W. Goodwin, *Anxiety,* Oxford Univ. Press, 1986)

These words, written in 1844, vividly capture the relentless, pervasive impact of anxiety as it is experienced by many people in contemporary society. Kierkegaard's description of anxiety is one of the earliest phenomenological descriptions of this unpleasant subjective state, which is characterized by vague, unremitting uneasiness and dread of nonexistent danger.

Another common use of the term anxiety pertains to discomfort more clearly focused on a specific situation or object. The intense anxiety associated with speaking in public or taking an examination or with fear of heights, nightfall, or animals is what is meant by the second definition of the term. This condition is different from fear, which entails an appraisal of and reponse to a realistic, objective threat. Instead, the intense discomfort of situation-specific anxiety is not only disproportionate to the threat, but functionally disabling. These reactions are examples of phobias, a word derived from the Greek *phobos* (flight) after the deity of that name who was able to induce fear and panic in his enemies.

Historical examples of phobias abound. Hippocrates described two cases, the first involving an exaggerated fear of cats (*ailurophobia*), the second disproportionate fear of nightfall (*nictophobia*). Julius Caesar was morbidly afraid of the dark (*achluophobia*), while the philosopher Blaise Pascal feared crowds and open spaces (*agoraphobia*).

Despite the relatively clear-cut distinction between the two different anxiety reactions, the underlying concept is elusive. Anxiety is diverse and varies significantly from person to person and from situation to situation. Although conceptually heterogenous, it encompasses behavior patterns ranging from discomfort while playing a musical instrument to intense trepidation at the prospect of going to a shopping mall. It may occur as a circumscribed clinical syndrome or in the company of other psychiatric conditions, including depression and some personality disorders. Moreover, it can accompany many medical disorders as a primary (diagnostic) and secondary (psychologically reactive) condition. Thus it is not surprising that the nature of anxiety has been so difficult to pin down.

The evolution of the concept of anxiety is interesting. An early precursor, termed "irritable heart" or "cardiac neurosis," described the association between psychological distress and physical symptoms, particularly those involving the cardiac system. It was also know as Da Costa's syndrome (after the nineteenth-century surgeon who first described it), neurocirculatory aesthesia, nervous exhaustion, and even war neurosis. The focus on the heart and psychological distress is easily understood because a rapid heartbeat is one of the most apparent sensations of anxious individuals.

Freud's characterization of *anxiety neurosis* was a clear landmark in the evolving concept of anxiety. Freud distinguished two distinct forms of anxiety, the first of which, free-floating anxiety, had much in common with Kierkegaard's description of a generalized, pervasive apprehension. Freud also described a more sharply focused form of anxiety, which he characterized as the sudden eruption into consciousness of acute discomfort. He formulated two explanations of anxiety at different times in his career. The first viewed anxiety as a consequence of the failure to drive (or "repress") painful memories, impulses, and thoughts from conscious awareness. Later, he formulated the "signal" theory of anxiety, which viewed anxiety as a response to impending danger either from within or outside the individual. The importance of the signal theory is that it characterized anxiety as an adaptive response to a potential, realistic threat. This viewpoint is echoed in many current explanations of anxiety, which stress its functional utility as a rather primitive, but effective, warning system.

Despite the widespread contemporary acceptance of anxiety as a signal or warning system, anxiety loses much of its adaptive value when it becomes a maladaptive response that interferes with effective coping. For example, consider a pianist who feels overcome by stage fright. Initially, he or she may experience an appropriate degree of anxiety evoked by the prospect of being watched by others. This reponse may cause the performer to become more alert and careful while playing. But if the intensity of the anxiety spirals out of control—well beyond the level where it had been helpful—it may cause the very problems, such as technical errors or loss of motor control, that the performer feared to begin with. As the philosopher Hoch stated, "why should the alarm burn down the house?"[4]

Not only does the intensity of anxiety vary considerably, but the circumstances that evoke it are comparably variable. Freud, for example, distinguished several subtypes of anxiety, which he termed realistic, moral, and neurotic. Realistic anxiety (*realangst*) corresponds to what is commonly termed fear, the response to a genuine external threat; *moral anxiety* is apprehension stemming from overly restrictive superego development; and *neurotic anxiety* is an exaggerated response to inner feelings and sensations misconstrued as threatening.

As influential as Freud's theories of anxiety were, many other explanations have also been advanced. The American psychologist William James, for example, discussed anxiety and fear at length in his analyses of emotional states. In the James/Lange theory of emotionality, James and Carl Lange contended that emotions arise from our muscular and visceral responses to threatening situations. This idea became embodied in the phrase, "you are afraid because you run," which is another way of saying that physical responses to threats provoke the emotional reactions. It seems more accurate to say that such reactions have two parts that work in concert to produce an emotional response. The first part comprises the physical sensations of an emotionally arousing situation. Following this response, and equally important, is mental appraisal, in which the physical sensations are interpreted in some fashion. We refer to this two-part process as "cognitive appraisal" because it involves attributing meaning to our experiences.

Evidence of a relationship between cognitive appraisals and the internal sensations evoked by anxiety comes from several different sources. However, all of this evidence rests on the idea that anxiety is the product of internal physiological arousal plus a tendency to react to this state with thoughts of risk and danger.

## A Three-Factor Model of Anxiety

The psychologist Peter Lang and his associates developed an important contemporary model of anxiety that connects the earlier Freudian perspective to one that incorporates a broader range of contributory factors.[5]

According to Lang, emotional states such as anxiety arise from an interaction between three psychological components: cognitive (or verbal), behavioral, and physiological. The cognitive component is represented by thoughts and related mental images of risk or danger. The behavioral manifestation of anxiety is a tendency to avoid or escape from anything perceived as dangerous. The physiological component of anxiety involves the somatic reactions that accompany heightened arousal. Any of these three components may be activated by anxiety-provoking stimuli, and often one component can stimulate either or both of the others. An interesting illustration of this effect was found in a research study in which the subjects were asked to imagine a weight lifter. When doing so, they experienced a measurable increase in the tension of muscles that weight lifting would require.

Even though these three psychological components all appear to be involved in anxiety, they are not necessarily present to the same degree or at the same time. Our own observations of individual performers supports the contention that there are significant individual differences in how the three components of anxiety manifest themselves. This effect is *response system desynchrony.* Desynchrony can be illustrated by imagining three ensemble players who play "out of synch" with each other. The degree of response system desynchrony varies according to the intensity of a person's anxiety, so that desynchrony is greatest at low levels of anxiety and least at higher levels.[6]

The ways in which these three components of anxiety interact present diagnostically useful information. For example, the presence of all three components suggests extreme anxiety and substantial response synchrony. A situation in which behavioral and cognitive components are evident without a physiological response may reflect the effects of medications like beta blockers, which selectively reduce arousal without substantially altering behavioral or cognitive capabilities. Mild anxiety could be represented by troublesome thoughts without significant physiological arousal or avoidance.

The three-factor theory of anxiety offers a number of clear advantages over previous formulations. First, it ascribes a significant role in anxiety to both overt (behavioral) and covert (physiological and cognitive) components. Second, it accounts for the observation that the different components of anxiety may be only moderately correlated except under conditions of intense anxiety. Third, it acknowledges that the activation of any one of these three anxiety systems can in turn stimulate the others.

Lang's three-factor model has received widespread support and has markedly influenced contemporary clinical treatments. The key to this model lies in evidence that our thoughts contribute to anxiety when we appraise situations and conclude that there is danger. Over time, anxious people tend to develop an automatic response to situations that, although potentially stressful, do not pose much objective threat. The perception of risk may center on a specific event, such as performing in public, giving a speech, or taking an examination; on the other hand, it may be less focused, entailing a vague apprehension that "something terrible is about to happen." We can summarize this by referring to the work of Beck and Emery, who argue that disabling anxiety reflects cognitive activity in which a person (a) believes him- or herself to be in imminent danger; and (b) feels inadequately prepared to deal with the threat. These two features apply to situations of both focused and diffuse anxiety. The complex response pattern comprising anxiety can be oriented either toward specific stimuli, as with a phobia, or more generally toward the outside environment or diffuse internal sensations.

## Adaptive Aspects of Anxiety

Clinicians and theoreticians alike accept that anxiety is both an inevitable part of life and a highly adaptive response to certain circumstances. This point is worth remembering the next time you feel nervous onstage and wish that you could banish anxiety forever. Such an attempt is neither feasible nor desirable, because anxiety is part of primitive instinctual patterns that have played a role in survival since the beginning of human evolution. Recalling the distinction made by Freud (and others) between realistic and neurotic anxiety, an anxious client must learn to interpret anxiety as a warning signal, not as something dangerous in itself. Although anxiety may be unpleasant and aversive, it helps if an anxious person can perceive the sensation as at least potentially helpful rather than as an inevitable source of risk and danger. This adaption often requires us to recast our experiences with anxiety in new ways.

Psychologists use the word "reframing" to refer to reinterpreting an experience in ways that we previously may not have considered.

One good example is the way we tend to think about anxiety. For many people, anxiety is negative, a sign of psychological vulnerability or even pathology. For some, it causes shame or embarrassment, and for others it shows that they are not cut out to be performers. The case of André Watts, a well-known performer, illustrates how anxiety can be reframed in quite a different light than that in which most of us think about it.

A seasoned veteran of the concert stage, Watts reports feeling anxious every time he plays, but he has come to accept such feelings as simply a "fact of life." Even when his nervousness occasionally triggers a memory lapse, Watts remains philosophical and doesn't take the incident too seriously.

His viewpoint is illuminating for two reasons. First, because of his open admission of nervousness, which he accepts as "just a fact of life." Many of us have the mistaken impression that anxiety affects only novices and that highly accomplished performers are immune. But anxiety has been a fact of life for many accomplished performers, including the late Sir Lawrence Olivier, Luciano Pavarotti, Arthur Rubenstein, Jean Stapleton (from "All in the Family"), and many others.

Watts' remarks reveal another important clue about anxiety and its management: he accepts it as something inevitable and normal—no more, no less. This attitude stands in marked contrast to the fearful and self-deprecatory responses that anxiety evokes in many people. His comments echo the attitude of humanist psychologists such as Rollo May, who view anxiety as part of the human condition.

Watts' response to anxiety reveals an important psychological mechanism that can help reduce the impact of anxiety. He has adjusted, or "reframed," his perception of anxiety from something ominous to something more benign, which he no longer feels is the end of the world. Tolerating the distressful anxiety provoked by an upcoming performance without making catastrophic predictions is one mark of a performer who has come to terms with anxiety.

Psychologists such as Rollo May have long maintained that anxiety is an essential part of the human condition and, as such, cannot be eradicated. In effect, it "comes with the territory."[7] May believes that anxiety is linked to the realization, which most of us eventually grasp, that our existence is tenuous. Dealing with anxiety thus entails exploring the vulnerabilities that underlie it, rather than attempting to eliminate or minimize it.

As a survival mechanism, anxiety (incorporating cognitive, behavioral, and physiological components) is surprisingly adaptive. The psychiatrist Aron Beck and the psychologist Stephen Emery have discussed some of the adaptive aspects of ANS activation, which is closely linked to anxiety. First, physiological arousal checks careless or indifferent behavior in critical situations. Second, it facilitates rapid coping responses by short-circuiting more deliberate but time consuming reactions. Third, like pain, anxiety is a powerful motivator for overcoming lethargy and replacing it with intense alertness. Fourth, by being part of the fight or flight response, anxiety contributes to self-preservation.

Unfortunately, as Beck and Emery have pointed out, these adaptive aspects of anxiety and arousal are frequently obscured by the intensity of the response. Rather than simply alerting a lethargic organism to a potential threat, arousal may become so intense that it inhibits adaptive behavior—perhaps to the point of freezing or blanking out. If arousal and anxiety are to exert beneficial regulatory effect on behavior, their intensity must be moderate and appropriate to the requirements of the situation.

Psychologists have described a relationship between task efficiency and level of activation. This is called the "Yerkes-Dodson Relationship," named after the investigators who first noted the effect. If you look at the figure 5–1, you will see that the relationship between these two factors is represented by a curved line. The Yerkes-Dodson relationship suggests that task efficiency changes as a function of activation. The term activation in this sense refers to the state that most of us associate with anxiety; however it is important to distinguish between activation and anxiety. Anxiety involves activation, but is also characterized by thoughts, feelings, and symptoms that go beyond the activation itself. According to the Yerkes-Dodson relationship, very low levels of activation tend to be reflected by relatively low efficiency. As a performer, you can probably recall times when you have performed lifelessly or distantly. Such performances probably involved a relatively low activation level. On the other hand, if activation becomes too high, then efficiency again suffers. Many performers can relate to the experience of feeling so anxious that they are literally unable to play.

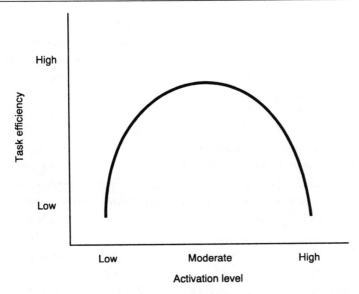

**FIGURE 5–1**
*The Yerkes-Dodson Relationship*

Somewhere in between these two extremes is an optimal state of activation. Most performers understand this intuitively, and with experience have learned to recognize the particular activation level that makes them feel most comfortable.

One important implication of this illustration is that activation is nothing to be afraid of. It is a natural physical state that can help you perform as long as it is neither too low or too high. We recommend that you try to monitor your feelings during performances to help you become more sensitive to variations in the sensations associated with activation states. You then may be able to discern which feelings tend to reflect an optimal "performance state".

## The Self-Perpetuating Quality of Anxiety

One of the most troublesome features of anxiety is the way it can spiral out of control in the absence of corrective, regulatory feedback. This effect, which has been noted by many investigators, arises from the fact that different components of anxiety—thoughts, physical responses, and behavior patterns—can be both stimuli and responses to one another. An example of this effect can be found in panic disorders, a condition similar to performance anxiety. According to one current theory, panic attacks are generated by unwarranted, catastrophic interpretations of physical sensations accompanying activation. For example, a weekend skier who experiences tachycardia upon emerging from the chairlift at the top of a steep slope might imagine that a heart attack was imminent. This erroneous interpretation of a sensation more plausibly associated with fear of heights may then trigger added activation, which further intensifies the unpleasant affect. Thus a trigger stimulus (internal or external), when perceived as threatening, leads to apprehension and vigilance. The arousal levels reflected in heightened vigilance manifest as characteristic physical sensations. When catastrophic implications are attributed to these sensations, the level of perceived threat increases, so that activation and activation is also heightened. Without corrective feedback, this spiral effect can continue indefinitely.[8]

This explanation of the cyclical pattern of panic attacks is supplemented by an important observation about the development of anxiety. Contemporary cognitive/behavioral formulations of anxiety stress the idea that anxiety can begin anywhere within the cycle just described. Catastrophic thoughts, for example, may evoke heightened activation, which in turn can generate intense apprehension and led to avoidant behavior. Conversely, arousal states may give rise to catastrophic thoughts, which then motivate avoidance. The genesis of anxiety, therefore cannot be attributed to any specific stimulus, because all of the components in the cycle can be either stimuli or responses. Thus, a cognitive/learning explanation of anxiety stresses the interrelationship between the components without designating any particular one as the cause.

## Critical Features of Anxiety

A helpful working model of anxiety that embodies many of the concepts discussed thus far has recently been proposed by Rick Ingram and David Kendall, who suggest that anxiety reflects the interaction of (a) certain critical features, (b) broader characteristics associated wtih psychological distress, and (c) a component reflecting individual differences in reaction.[9]

Among the principal critical features of anxiety is the perception of danger. In addition, anxiety is self-perpetuating and often includes a tendency to worry about the future. Most people who feel anxious are troubled by what *might* happen rather than by current or past events. Coupled with this concern about the future is the corresponding belief that they will not be able to cope with the anticipated danger.

The functional impairments frequently associated with anxiety are intensified, according to Ingram and Kendall, by aspects of the condition common to most other forms of psychological distress. These include (a) heightened self-absorption, (b) the activation of automated thought patterns (schemas), and (c) limitations on the effectiveness with which information is processed. Finally, anxiety is mediated, in this model, by a variety of individual difference factors including, but not limited to, constitutional factors, personal coping skills, perceived self-efficacy, and one's habitual mode of what is been termed "self presentation."

Ingram and Kendall's description of anxiety corresponds well to clinical observations of the diverse nature of anxiety symptoms in a given individual. Their model provides a useful framework for distinguishing the specific features of anxiety, the broader functional limitations imposed by psychopathology, and a variety of mediating/predisposing factors.

## Future Orientation and Anxiety

Of all the symptoms of anxiety, fear of the future is perhaps the most interesting. Anxious individuals *expect* bad things to happen to them, even though most of their predictions are never borne out. Despite the common-sense evidence that the past is the best predictor of the future, many chronically anxious individuals believe that the more time that elapses without a catastrophe, the more likely one is to occur in the immediate future. Thus, they experience increasing tension as more time elapses without something untoward happening. Their catastropic predictions are seldom, if ever, realized because of they are extremely exaggerated. A music student, for example, became convinced that she would have a heart attack while playing onstage during one of many recitals she was required to give. Her assessment partly stemmed from a belief that tachycardia meant that a heart attack was imminent. With each succeeding successful performance, her anxiety *increased* because she was so convinced of the inevitability of her prediction.

The significance of this future orientation is especially important when one considers the therapeutic implications. It is well known that active rehearsal and visualization of anticipated stressors is part of the "work of worry" of people confronting stressful events. In a study of parachute jumpers psychologists Seymour Epstein and Walter Fenz found that novice and experienced parachutists differed less in the degree of anxiety than in its timing.[10] Anticipatory anxiety peaked for the experienced parachutists well in advance of the jump, while the novices were immobilized by anxiety when it was most critical not to be overwhelmed with anxiety—at the moment they were to leave the plane.

We conducted a similar study using experienced and inexperienced musicians, who were asked to retrospectively assess their anxiety at three different points leading to an important performance and during the performance itself.[11] Consistent with the data reported by Epstein and Fenz, the inexperienced musicians experienced peak anxiety during the performance, when they were least equipped to cope with it. The more experienced musicians, in contrast, felt less anxious during the performance than prior to it. Many of the latter reported anticipating, through visualization and mental rehearsal, the circumstances of the performance and thus worked through the worst of the anxiety in advance.

The threat posed by the prospect of an inherently stressful situation can focus anxiety and channel apprehension. Many anxious individuals seem to benefit from planning and carrying out activities that involve dealing with a stressor. For example, one musician with chronic anxiety found that during the concert season her anxiety was quite low in between performances, but peaked sharply shortly before each engagement. In contrast, she reported moderate, but chronic anxiety during the late spring and summer months when she had few opportunities to perform. She preferred the former situation because of the emotional variety afforded by periods of tension and relaxation and because of the intense relief she experienced after her performances and for long periods of time in between concerts.

## Summary

Our working model of anxiety can be summarized by five statements.

First, anxiety is the most prevalent form of psychological distress, one that accompanies many other psychological and physical conditions.

Second, the clinical manifestations of anxiety show marked variability from one person to another. A working model of anxiety has been described that characterizes the manifestations for a given individual in terms of (a) critical symptoms, (b) common psychopathological characteristics, and (c) individual differences in vulnerability and coping skills.

Third, the expression of anxiety is characterized by symptoms in three broad domains: cognitive, physiological, and behavioral. These factors tend to act in synchrony, particularly when the expression and anxiety reach very high levels.

Fourth, the cognitive factor is especially important in the etiology, mediation, and maintenance of anxiety. A schema concerning risk and danger is common to virtually all anxiety disorders, but a thorough assessment of each individual's cognitive processes is nonetheless important to assess the highly personalized manner in which anxiety expresses itself.

Finally, anxiety needs to be appreciated for its adaptive, as well as maladaptive, qualities. Foremost among these is its function as a warning system, which can motivate effective coping responses rather than reflexive avoidant behavior.

In sum, anxiety in its many manifestations may be quite appropriate and adaptive. Given the many psychological and physical threats that abound in our daily lives, anxiety may be trying to tell us something about the nature of modern life—if we would only take the time to listen.

Many performers seek some basic rules for dealing with anxiety that can be put into practice directly. In general, we caution against thinking that any type of anxiety, can be easily and simply treated. However, certain therapeutic strategies may be immediately useful for the performer willing to spend some time working with them. One such technique described by Aaron Beck and Steven Emery, concerns "becoming aware of anxiety."[12]

The word AWARE is an acronym for five fundamental components of learning to cope with anxiety. In order, these components are: *a*ccepting anxiety as a natural part of being human; *w*atching one's anxiety and learning to pay attention to its effects; learning to *a*ct with anxiety by realizing that it need not prevent us from doing something demanding; *r*epeating the first three steps when one is vulnerable to anxiety until the effect is minimized; and *ex*pecting that because it is a natural part of being a performer. The list below outlines each of these five points in greater detail.

> *A*ccept anxiety as a natural response to stressful events.
> *W*atch how your anxiety comes and goes. Remind yourself that intense anxiety will diminish with time. By watching your anxiety, you can put a little distance between yourself and its effects.
> *A*ct with anxiety. Remember that it's possible to function while you feel anxious. Try to be tolerant of yourself when you feel this way. Many things we do are frightening or risky, and you may have good reasons to feel anxious. Just remember that you can cope with many things even when you feel anxious; it needn't get the better of you.
> *R*epeat the first three steps as many times needed until the effects of anxiety begin to diminish. This may require considerable patience; your anxiety didn't develop overnight and isn't likely to diminish especially quickly either.
> *E*xpect anxiety; as part of the human condition, it is something all of us must deal with. It does come and go. Try to view anxiety as something you can live with, rather than as a sign that something is wrong with you.
> —*Beck and Emery, 1985*

If you can take these concepts to heart, you will gain a new perspective when you feel anxious that you could not achieve by denying or trying to eliminate it.

# Getting Help for Stress
# and Anxiety

*This performance's problem should always be the next performance's insight.*

          —*Anton Weinberg, Unfinished Sentences*

**O**ne of the most important aspects of our approach to performance anxiety is that many of the details of developing an effective approach are left up to the performer. It is tempting to tell performers that anxiety can be successfully treated using one technique or another, but we strongly believe that the best approach is based on self-assessment and personal problem solving. No one knows your limits and capabilities as a performer better than you do, although other people, such as teachers or peers, may be able to evaluate your musical capabilities more objectively. However, for several reasons, an objective assessment of one's musical capabilities is not necessarily the most useful or even accurate source of information that can be obtained. First, performers normally learn a "stage presence" that can mask their feelings. As a result, it may be possible for them to be musically expressive while feeling psychologically distressed. Another problem with "objective" assessments is that they must rely on the end product of one's musical efforts and generally can't take into account what has been done to achieve the effects. This is perhaps best exemplified by auditions in which performers are impersonally ushered into a room and asked to play for a committee of judges whom they have never met but who determine the performers' suitability based solely on the quality of the music. A French horn player auditioning for a summer engagement in a regional orchestra experienced the ultimate in impersonal auditions. His audition consisted of entering a room that contained a chair, a tape recorder, and a metronome. He was instructed (via the recorder) to play for a period of time along with the metronome; at no point did he have any contact with the audition committee. Some may view this process as a way to obtain the most objective assessment possible of musical skills, but to this player the experience brought home how little of himself he was personally able to communicate to the audition committee. The dissociation between the personal qualities of performers and their music clearly illustrated by this example underscores the need for performers to realize that objectivity alone can never capture the quality of music or the process by which it was created.

We have found that many performers who seek psychological help expect to be subjected to a merciless dissection of their musical performance skills. They may imagine the therapist to be someone who observes them without regard for the musical qualities of what they are doing. Such an attitude is counterproductive. It should be a therapist's intention to encourage performers to become therapists in their own right by learning to observe, modify, and change their performance practices as needs or problems dictate. We agree that there are limits to how far one can analyze musical expressiveness, but we feel that some performers are unnecessarily negative about what can be accomplished by this approach. Adopting an analytic attitude toward the performance of music in no way detracts from the quality of that music, provided the performer is able to keep things in perspective. Our approach to performance problems is to encourage the performer to actively collaborate with the therapist, rather than remaining solely the object of the therapist's attention. When the performer and therapist can enter into a collaborative working relationship, it is possible to deal with a wide range of musical performance problems very effectively.

We hope that such experiences as that of the horn player are not common, thought it seems that every seasoned veteran has comparable stories. Although it might seem that being treated so impersonally would have deleterious effects, many performers can put things in perspective and retain a sense of personal integrity even as their skills are subjected to objective criticism. However, in doing so, almost of necessity, performers begin to build a psychological wall between themselves, the music, and the audience, whether critics or friends. Psychologists refer to this process as "dissociation," which means fragmenting, or splitting off, elements of consciousness into isolated compartments. The dissociation of most performers is mild and wouldn't be considered a clinical problem, but the effects are perceptible and can cause the performers to feel isolated because no one else can understand their point of view. How many performers, in response to the comment, "You looked so relaxed and confident up there!" would respond with something like, "If you only knew how I *felt!*"?

It may be that a certain amount of dissociation (perhaps "distancing" would be a better word) is inevitable for the performer to retain a sense of personal integrity. This may be especially true for performers who have chosen careers in a field where opportunities are few, standards are extremely high, and criteria for judging excellence often ambiguous. Even those who have found a niche in the musical world are subjected to greater public scrutiny than most other professionals because of the highly public nature of their art.

The successful performer is probably someone who has developed the capacity to effectively evaluate feedback from others, while at the same time retaining a perspective that facilitates informed judgments about one's own best interests. You are your own best expert because you are in the best position to assess how well your private thoughts and feelings correspond to the feedback you get from others. You might think of this as becoming self-center*ing,* (as opposed to being self-centered).

Although many (if not most) teachers of musicians are aware of the importance of self-centering, a tradition in musical education makes it natural for performers to view their teachers as the ultimate authorities on their performance skills (if not their personal qualities as well). In our experience, many musicians at the conclusion of a performance are conditioned to immediately seek feedback and validation from those in attendance. "How did I do?" they ask, often without realizing that they themselves may be in the best position to pass judgment.

How is it possible to cultivate a relationship with performers that is supportive and encourages self-exploration through accurate self-assessment and effective problem-solving? This task is not easy, and is made especially troublesome because many performers are habitually excessively self-critical. "I'll look like a fool," "I can't make a mistake or play less than perfectly," or "I must be crazy to be nervous about playing this piece" are common types of comments made by many performers. Such comments invite a reassuring response that, to the performer, might convey validation—such as, "Don't worry about playing the piece perfectly—we'll understand." But such a reassuring comment can be interpreted in two ways. On the one hand, it might mean that the other person is supportive of the performer's *effort* and is not concerned about the outcome. But it might also indicate a lack of very high expectations of the performer. Such inherently ambiguous statements may be difficult to interpret, and can leave the performer more confused than before. Using self-criticism as a way to "fish" for compliments can often have unanticipated results.

There are other reasons for being critical of one's musical skills. It's one way of anticipating criticisms that others may make, thereby "beating them to the punch." "I know—the slow movement of the Beethoven didn't have much rhythmic pulse," was the first comment a student made to her teacher after playing a sonata during a performance class. She responded to an anticipated criticism only to find that her teacher was quite complimentary about her performance. In making this statement, the student also conveyed the impression that she was able to simultaneously play and critique her own playing—an extremely difficult task.

Negative self-criticism may, of course, reflect an accurate evaluation of one's capabilities, an attitude that is especially prevalent in musical training, where performance standards are very high. Musicians frequently find their performances judged by minute details that they may feel unable to detect, let alone correct. As their technical expertise increases, their skills are subjected to even more rigorous scrutiny. It is not surprising that many performers develop increasingly negative self-assessments of their capabilities, even though by more objective standards their skills are actually improving.[1]

Achieving an effective working relationship with a performer, particularly when one is a therapist rather than a teacher, takes considerable sensitivity. Let us examine some of the factors that seem to bear on this issue in order to try to establish some basic guidelines for helping performers become more comfortable in working with others to accurately assess their own musical capabilities.

First, performers are generally extremely sensitive to judgments by others. Motives for performing in public often center on gaining approval from others, but, conversely, feature an intense fear and expectation of criticism. This attitude has much in common with an external *locus of control,* in which individuals defer to others for judgments of their worth and competence. With respect to the therapeutic relationship, this tendency means that the performer is likely to see the therapist as a source of praise and validation as well as of criticism, which he or she has come to expect from teachers and coaches. As a result, the therapist's feedback to the client will probably be construed as either praise or criticsm. In other words, the therapist may find it difficult to communicate in a manner that would be perceived as nonjudgmental. Thus, it can be challenging to establish a collaborative working relationship in which both performer and therapist take active roles in critiquing the target behavior. It is often necessary for the therapist to promote a more active client involvement so that therapy can progress past the point of being perceived as just another source of praise or criticism.

Measures that can enhance this type of therapeutic relationship include, first, teaching self-assessment skills so that the performer can begin to develop sensitivity to his or her own capabilities. Self-rating scales such as the Beck Anxiety Scale and Beck Depression Inventory are useful because they are brief and straightforward to interpret. Explaining their use and providing direct feedback to the client is helpful in cultivating his or her capacity to assess and differentiate personal states in terms other than polar opposites, such as "good" or "bad," which are often among a performer's self-referential statements.

Second, providing objective feedback can strengthen the therapeutic relationship. For example, audio-and/or videotape can serve as a source of data to which both performer and therapist can respond consistently. This is especially helpful when assessing performances in which intense physical activation frequently colors the performer's subjective impressions so that he or she may perceive things far differently than those in attendance. Performers prone to anxiety, for example, often focus on its all-encompassing, intense sensations, despite assertions from others that they looked calm. Video and, to a lesser degree, audio feedback can help a client develop a broader perspective on the manifestations of their anxiety. Moreover, a review of such material usually takes place when the performer is less activated and consequently has lower sensory acuity and hypervigilance. In this case, analytic perceptions are likely to be quite different than during the performance. Overall, the thrust of this aspect of the therapeutic relationship is to help the performer develop accurate self-assessment skills as a means of learning to trust his or her own perceptions and sensations.

Highly respected teachers and coaches often acquire the status of a "guru" with whom the performer strongly identified. This style of relationship has several costs and benefits. On the positive, pragmatic side, working with an acknowledged authority often ensures artistic progress and may enhance career development through a combination of the highly refined skills a performer may acquire and the network of professional contacts that such an authority has access to. On the negative side, guru-like teachers are frequently seen as possessing far-reaching powers and knowledge that invite blind faith in their advice. In therapeutic consultations, a performer previously exposed to such individuals may be predisposed to react to a therapist in any of several ways. One is to transfer the guru's qualities to the therapist. In this way, a performer seeking psychological help can reassure him- or herself that treatment is a credible enterprise. The effect is heightened to the degree that the teacher endorses the performer's preconceptions. Therapists who attempt to appraise performers of these notions may initially have a difficult time establishing credibility and a good working relationship.

Some potential clients devalue therapy because they feel that their "guru" has taught them everything they need. Why seek treatment? In some instances teachers will react negatively to a performer's request to seek therapy because they feel that therapy is useless for dealing with what they perceive as musical problems. In such situations, the performer may doubt his or her own perceptions, in the same way that child who is told "you're not afraid" by a parent may deny or relabel inner feelings to be more in line with the adult's interpretation.

In dealing with this aspect of the therapeutic relationship, it is important to keep three things in mind. First, the therapist needs to provide a setting in which the performer's conflicting feelings can be openly explored. Second, by learning of the performer's past relationships with teachers, the therapist can clearly show that therapy is different and how it differs. Third, by encouraging self-exploration and self-monotoring, the therapist can help the performer more effectively develop self-perceptions that are independent of others' evaluations.

A third factor affecting the therapeutic relationship is expectations of therapy. Performers who seek assistance for problems like stage fright are often either unsure of how therapy can help or have preconceptions about their need for treatment. Frequently, performers—like many people with psychologial distress—avoid seeking help because of certain misperceptions about therapy. For example, a common fear among performers is that they may be deeply psychologically disturbed as a result of, or as indicated by, their anxiety. This belief is usually a symptom of the common danger/fear thinking of anxious individuals, not an accurate depiction of their state. Second, performers may perceive therapy as another performance, in which significant expectations—by the therapist rather than by the audience—are imposed on them. This perception affects many different facets of therapy, but the key lies in the tendency of such clients to perceive the therapist as another one of the judges, ajudicators, and critics to whom they have been exposed for years. The heightened self-consciousness engendered by this state of mind is obviously counterproductive. First, self-consciousness can significantly inhibit self-disclosure of information that the client feels reflects poorly on him- or herself. Second, it frequently adds to anxiety as the client searches for "right" thing to say. Third, it minimizes spontaneous expression in the same way anxiety causes musicians to give careful, over-controlled musical performances.

The therapeutic relationship can also be impeded by the tendency of many performers to focus on their experience without reflecting on and evaluating its relation to their personal lives. This problem is not unique to performers, but is intensified somewhat because self-criticism and self-awareness are often viewed as counterproductive to effective performing. Performers are taught to be analytical about their music, but seldom about themselves in relation to the music. In some instances, they are unwilling to seek help for anxiety because it will raise—and reify—problems they are only dimly aware of except at a purely symptomatic level. Denial of anxiety takes many forms, but underlying many of these is a tendency to avoid in-depth personal reflection and analysis of contributory factors.

On the other hand, a number of performers' characteristics can enhance the establishment of a psychotherapeutic relationship. First among these is that most musicians have already experienced close collaborative relationships with teachers and coaches and are therefore accustomed to this style of working relationship. If these relationships have been adaptive and helpful, the transfer of attitudes and styles of relating to therapy can be highly productive.[2]

Second, performers—effective ones—work hard and are used to the idea that much progress in music is accomplished outside of a lesson. It is generally easy to engage performers in therapy by making the same point: consultation sessions should help them work through problems and issues that they work on every day.

Third, performers can frequently take advantage of modes of expression and communication that are not routinely available to clients whose communication is exclusively verbal. Emotional responses to music are often very close to the surface, and singing or playing an instrument frequently triggers psychologically significant responses—both positive and negative—that might not be amenable to verbal expression.[3] The ability of a performer to move between modes of communication in this manner is a valuable tool that can help client and therapist clarify and deal with problems.

Fourth, musical skills are founded, to a great degree, on inductive thought. Learning a piece of music is generally undertaken from a component level, beginning with notes and other elemental building blocks. Musical insight and understanding only develops once the performer has assimilated the technical elements of a piece, which at the outset are the object of conscious attention, but which subsequently fade into the background as new, more abstract musical concepts become the focus.

In an analogous way, cognitive therapy proceeds inductively, beginning with an elemental analysis of symptomatic behavior that provides clues to deeper beliefs and attitudes.[4] This shared feature of musical performance and psychotherapy can be drawn upon in establishing a working therapeutic relationship, and examples from each realm can help the performer perceive the similarities between developing musical understanding and self-understanding.

Performers and those who work with them—in particular, teachers and coaches—can also develop collaborative, therapeutically effective relationships that can help mitigate anxiety and other stressors related to performing. To do so, however, requires rethinking the typical student–teacher relationship in the direction of a more cooperative working relationship. It may be argued that this type of relationship is more easily established when the musician works with someone outside the musical field, such as a psychotherapist, but in our opinion teachers and performers, by working together, can often solve many of the performance problems related to anxiety.

In our discussion of a collaborative therapeutic relationship, we should also include some recommendations for performers. If you feel that this approach to performance anxiety is a valid one, you may have to change some traditional attitudes toward teachers and others. Paramount among these is the idea that someone else—a teacher or a therapist—can tell you what is needed to solve your problem. In fact, the more active you are in your own "treatment," the better the results will be. In other words, there is a great deal you can do in collaboration with others to get at the root of your problem. In the following paragraphs, we describe an optimal approach for a performer requesting help for performance anxiety. This approach requires you to become actively involved in the treatment program because the more you invest in learning about the problem, the more able you will be to develop effective ways of helping yourself. Of course, your therapist or teacher does not sit and do nothing; his or her role may be more like that of an athletic coach whose job is to help you acquire and practice various skills.

As a musician, you may have grown accustomed to treating teachers as omniscient people who can solve almost any problem, musical or not. But just as there are different opinions on how best to interpret a piece of music, there are many different ways of learning to cope with anxiety and stress. Based on our experience working with teachers, students, and performers, we feel that you can make the most headway on these problems by working with someone who is not dogmatic, someone who is sufficiently flexible to work with you collaboratively. Keep in mind that the manifestations of anxiety are much less discernible to the observer than is the music, which can be heard by any listener. The experience of anxiety is highly personal, so a teacher or therapist has to rely on you—the performer—to describe it accurately, without making light of its impact or exaggerating its intensity. You should become an active collaborator in your own treatment, providing information, looking for clues, experimenting with various techniques, reporting on the results, and, ultimately, determining what approaches work best for you.

As psychotherapists, our primary concern is that you become actively involved in dealing with the many stresses and sources of anxiety to which you are prone. We are well aware that becoming a performer is a long and arduous journey and that problems can develop at many points along the way. We also believe that, as a performer, you are the person best equipped to investigate your problems and to help develop solutions.

It should be obvious to you by now that getting help for performance anxiety entails more than simply showing up for therapy sessions. Therapy is much like studying with a music teacher: lessons usually involve going over material the student has been working on and introducing new music to be prepared in subsequent practice sessions. Working on anxiety benefits from a similar approach. Here are some specific tips on how to get the most out of therapy. Keep in mind that this approach demands that you take an active role in planning and carrying out your own treatment.[5]

1. *Have a specific idea of something to work on in your sessions.* Are there technical aspects of your playing that anxiety interferes with? Are you focused more on the people in the audience than on the music? Do you find it difficult to play a piece from memory? By focusing on specific skills you'd like to acquire, you'll be able to make better progress than if you approach therapy with the general intention of just being less anxious. Reducing anxiety is generally best accomplished by developing skills that increase self-confidence and make it easier and more fulfilling for you to perform. By working with your therapist to identify the necessary skills, you'll take a positive step to maximize the benefits from your therapy sessions.

2. *Be direct with your therapist in talking about your anxiety.* Therapists are used to the idea that people have difficulties adjust-

ing to the demands in their lives, and they certainly do not expect clients to have solved all their problems. Seeing a therapist is different from performing in public, though many performers feel self-conscious, almost like they're onstage, during therapy sessions. Therapy should be one place where you can openly and honestly discuss and work on your performance problems. Thinking of therapy as a resource available for your benefit is a good approach. If you are direct and do not downplay your problems, you and your therapist will be able to more clearly understand what's likely to be helpful than if you avoid or minimize the distressing issues.

3. *Be willing to change.* Reducing performance anxiety will inevitably involve some changes on your part. For example, you may have to develop new ways of thinking about anxiety and your reaction to it. You may need to create new practice or rehearsal strategies to help you cope with the demands of a live performance. You may have to change your physical responses to the stresses of a performance by practicing new breathing techniques or learning to relax muscles that have been chronically tense. Therapy cannot change the demands made of you as a performer, but it can help you change your responses to performing.

Being willing to change means keeping an open mind about doing things differently and being willing to spend some time to make the changes stick. The process is like learning to play an unfamiliar style of music, like moving from the baroque to an impressionistic idiom. Even though both styles have certain common features, you have to make many changes in your accustomed patterns. Similarly, with therapy, change—for example, in your style of thinking—may require you to develop a new perspective, which will need practice and rehearsal before it can become a part of your repertoire.

4. *Discuss things and ask questions of the therapist.* Consider therapeutic suggestions as just that—ideas to be tried, experimented with, and perhaps modified—not as orders. Be sure that you understand what's being proposed and that you have a good idea of how to proceed. If, for instance, your therapist and you decide that it would be helpful for you to play for a fellow student in between lessons, work out the details ahead of time. When will it take place? Who will I play for? What music will I use? Where would be the most advantageous place to play? By working out such details,

you'll find it much easier to carry out therapeutic recommendations than if you had simply agreed in principle to a general plan.

5. *Learn to be your own therapist/coach/teacher.* Much of what you accomplish in therapy takes place outside the therapy session. Moreover, treatment of performance anxiety tends to be short-term, so you'll be working on your own once your treatment has been completed. One of the goals of therapy is to provide you with the knowledge and skills to become aware of the nature of your anxiety and to cope with it.

A good question to ask yourself when you're working on a problem is, "If I were helping another performer with this problem, what would I recommend?" Putting yourself in the role of a therapist/coach/teacher can create some distance between yourself and the problem. That kind of perspective can contribute to developing solutions that you might otherwise overlook.

6. *Set realistic short- and long-range goals.* What are your aspirations as a performer? Are you focused only on an upcoming end-of-semester jury? Do you aspire to become a symphonic musician or a soloist? Is your goal to enjoy performing more? There's a direct relationship between our goals and how much anxiety we experience. For instance, if your goal is to play a piece of music with perfect technical accuracy for a master class, you're likely to feel much more tension than if your intention is to learn something new about interpretation from your teacher.

Having realistic goals is also a good way of keeping anxiety in perspective. By focusing on an achievable objective, you are likely to feel less buffeted by tension and anxiety than if you're simply attempting to get through one performance after another with no particular aim.

7. *Experiment, take notes, be innovative, follow your hunches.* Most of your gains from therapy are likely to come from your own efforts to develop strategies for dealing with your anxiety. The process is much like that of a scientist conducting an experiment, in which many different ways of attacking the problem are tried before an effective solution is reached. By adopting this role, you can distance yourself from the anxiety and thereby make it less overwhelming. Try to be open to the experience of anxiety—take specific note of how it makes you feel, what you think about, how

you act. By treating anxiety in this manner, you'll be better able to develop ideas about coping with its unpleasant aspects.

One example of how the problem-solving approach advocated here dovetails nicely with musical instrumentation technology is shown in a MIDI-based performance analysis, which concludes this chapter. Recent advances in musical instrument technology provide performers, particularly keyboard players, with some potentially helpful tools for dealing with performance-related problems. In particular, MIDI technology is an especially interesting development and can be put to good use by keyboard performers. MIDI stands for *Musical Instrument Digital Interface,* an electronic system for translating notes played on a suitably equipped keyboard into computerized digital representations. The characteristics of the music, including pitch, volume, and timbre, are all digitally encoded and stored in a computer for later retrieval and analysis.

Figure 6–1 graphically depicts two performances of a section of an organ fugue by Buxtehude that were made under different conditions. Each graph shows the individual notes played by the instrumentalist. In the top figure is a sample played by a musician sight reading this section of the fugue. The passage consists of a series of descending and ascending notes approximately at intervals of a sixth, played by both right and left hands. To the left of the graph the pitch of each note is indicated. The duration of a note is signified by the length of the mark, in horizontal units, on the graph. Notes held for a relatively long time appear elongated; in contrast, notes played relatively quickly appear as small dots. By looking at this figure, we can immediately see what notes were played and how long each note was held. Assuming that we know the score on which this rendition was based, we can make a comparison between the notes in the original score and the notes played by the performer. In the first rendition of this passage, the performer, who was sight reading, played relatively slowly, as illustrated by many elongated notes. It is interesting to compare this rendition of the passage with that played after the performer had practiced it. This rendition is depicted in the bottom graph, which shows the notes and their duration more clearly. Notice how the notes are now relatively short, indicating that the piece was played more rapidly. Notice, also, that the relative length of each of the notes is far more constant than in the first rendition. This indicates that the perform-

A. Sight reading

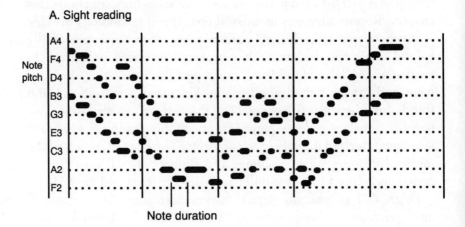

Note pitch

B. Following practice

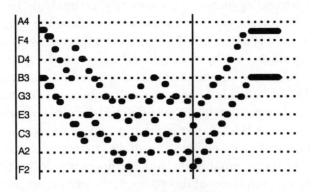

**FIGURE 6–1**
*Passage from Buxtehude's Fugue in G*

ance was relatively smooth and even, and the notes were accorded roughly constant values up to the final note, which was prolonged in accordance with the score.

How might this information be put to good use by a performer? There are several useful applications. First, a graphic record of one's progress can be helpful in assessing how well one has learned a piece of music. A tangible record of one's progress is a very useful way to quantify changes in the performance of a piece over time. Also, performers who have used this sort of information often find it reassuring, from a psychological standpoint, to refer back to accumulated records of their learning, and they derive comfort from seeing the effects of their many hours of practice. These benefits can be especially important as a performance draws near. Some performers, particularly those who lack confidence in their abilities, may begin to feel that their practice has not led to perceptible changes in their playing skill. By going back and literally *looking* at the changes that have taken place as a piece has been learned, they will often feel reassured.

A second important use of the MIDI technology illustrated in this figure is as a means of evaluating one's performance skills on a note by note basis. Having such detailed information available within moments of having played a piece of music can be a powerful tool for they analysis or subsequent development of its technical or interpretive aspects. You may, for example, be interested in the impact of a paticular pattern of fingering on a piece that can only be played very quickly. By making a MIDI recording, the performer can play the piece quickly and then go back and study the individual notes in detail at a much more leisurely pace. The MIDI-based graphic score of the music thus provides the performer with a very detailed, tangible record of his or her development of a piece of music.

Another interesting application of this technology is to analyze selected events during the performance of a piece of music. For example, if a mistake was made, a score such as this makes it possible to go back and study not just the note or notes that were missed, but also the musical events leading up to the error. Most performers are aware that mistakes, or technical errors, often represent the end stages of a process in which motor control may gradually be lost. In the preceding figure, technical mistakes were held to a minimum, largely because the performer in the first read-through played very slowly.

Finally, a MIDI-based analysis of a keyboard passage contains information that is very helpful in assessing the consistency of one's touch. By touch we mean the rate at which keys are depresssed and the degree to which successive notes overlap. In the preceding figure, the notes were played so that they were only very slightly connected, particularly in the first read-through (part A). In part B, there is more space between successive notes, lending a staccato quality to the playing.

For many keyboard performers, MIDI technology can provide an important analytic tool that is particularly helpful in the early stages of learning and perfecting passages of a piece of music that may otherwise be difficult to apprehend and study.[6]

# The Cognitive Side of Performing

*There are no such things as mistakes, only musical misunderstandings.*
*—Anton Weinberg, Unfinished Sentences*

**M**uch of the emphasis in this book is on the ways we think about ourselves and our capabilities as performers. A great deal of evidence shows that our thoughts have a significant impact on how we feel, and this is never more true than when one is talking about performing. However, the connection between thoughts, feelings, and behaviors is not as direct as some people may think, despite the appealing claims of those who advocate such theories as "positive thinking." First, we never observe thoughts directly, and so it's difficult to think of them like concrete objects. However, some basic ideas about thinking can give us clues to how thoughts affect our behavior, including performance skills. Because cognitive factors comprise one of the cornerstones of the approach adopted in this book, we should discuss the issue in some detail and examine some of the most important ways in which thoughts influence behavior. We use a framework provided by psychologist Donald Meichenbaum, who has grouped thought patterns into several convenient categories.[1]

## Thoughts as Automatic Responses

Specific thoughts (or images) may become associated with specific behaviors, so that the occurrence of either tends to bring on the other. For example, one musician found that whenever he began to play a piece of music (whether while practicing or onstage), he was distracted by the thought that he would forget what he was playing at some point. It seemed that the act of beginning to play inevitably caused him to think about this. And, in an interesting reversal of the situation, when he thought of having a memory slip, he felt anxiously compelled to seek out an instrument to play in order to reassure himself that he could remember the music. These two experiences—one of playing, the other of worrying—became so closely and unpleasantly associated that he began to cut back on practicing to avoid worrying about having a memory slip. In the short run, this did help him avoid the troublesome thought; but, of course, he increased the likelihood of his prediction coming true because he had reduced the amount of time he spent fixing a piece of music in memory. The association between worrying about his memory and playing in turn triggered other maladaptive thoughts. He began to criticize himself for having such thoughts, feeling worried that the prediction would come true (though it had not) but angry at himself because of his inability to control his thinking. When he eventually tackled this aspect of a more general problem of playing in public (fear of a memory slip was a minor part of his difficulty), a straightforward solution was developed. He used a technique called "thought stopping," in which he verbalized the command "stop" as soon as he became aware of worrisome thoughts while playing. Drawing conscious attention to the thought gave him a measure of control and prevented it from dominating his awareness as it previously had done. Second, he learned to inhibit the anxious urge to practice compulsively whenever he was struck by a troubling thought. In its place, he developed a structured practice schedule that was regulated by the clock rather than by anxious cognitions. In addition, he learned a simple relaxation technique that helped dissipate the tension caused by his thoughts and that provided a useful alternative to compulsive practicing. Finally, he learned and practiced a series of "self-statements" that constituted a rational way of addressing the underlying problem (since his concern about a memory slip was not particularly far-fetched). In response to fears of a memory lapse, he learned to do two things. First, he tried to focus his response to a specific issue, such as a troublesome measure in a piece. Second, he reassured himself that he would work especially hard on this problem area during his next practice session. By using all of these techniques, he was able to dissociate the fearful thought from his adaptive impulse to practice, which he otherwise enjoyed. The anxiety previously evoked by the obsessive thought was gradually replaced by self-assurance as the thought (which eventually became a "concern" rather than a frightening certainty) became linked with the positive feelings resulting from a good practice session.

## Thoughts and the Anxiety Spiral

Thoughts also come into play in performance situations when they become part of an automatic sequence of anxiety-provoking events that often occur before an event such as a recital or concert. This sequence often has a spiraling effect, in which anxious thoughts trigger defensive behaviors, which heighten apprehension, increase vigilance, promote even more worry, and so on. By the time performers afflicted by this spiral get to the event, they may be so anxious that the prospect of performing becomes completely unnerving. This gradually increasing cycle of anxiety—a mixture of thoughts, feelings, and behaviors—can be so smoothly integrated that one is hardly aware of the step-by-step, incremental pressure.

This problem was reported by Tom, a church organist, who, though he generally enjoyed playing for other people, experienced severe hand and leg tremors whenever he became anxious. At times, the shaking was so pronounced that it caused him to restrike keys unintentionally and, in general, resulted in a loss of muscle control. Because he had had the problem for several years, he had grown to anticipate it, and he worried that the shaking would become so debilitating that he would have to stop playing. With the help of a therapist who worked with him shortly before a major church service, Tom discovered that a vicious cycle of thoughts and behaviors caused his tremor to worsen markedly. As Tom's worry increased, shortly before the beginning of the service, his tremor increased in severity. The more apparent the trembling became, the more he worried that it would prevent him from playing. Moreover, his efforts to stop the tremors by controlling the muscles in his hands and arms only made the problem worse.

Tom was helped by learning how his anxiety gradually increased before a performance and by developing relaxation and concentration-focusing responses that could be applied at successive stages. He learned to detect fleeting muscle tremors before they developed into uncontrollable shaking. He practiced a simple quieting response (momentarily closing his eyes, taking a deep breath, relaxing his muscles, and visualizing a calming image or word) whenever he became aware that a thought or physical sensation was triggering spiraling anxiety. By responding to the early, almost imperceptible signs of an impending episode, he experienced progressively fewer full attacks of the "shakes."

## Errors in Logic

Many anxious performers think about performing in stress-provoking ways that are illogical or erroneous. Anxiety is generally accompanied by a tendency to interpret minor problems as major catastrophes and to anticipate danger where none exists. For example, it's possible to think your way into a state of anxiety by focusing on mistakes in a piece you're preparing for a recital and concluding that you'll never be able to perform it well. There are two errors of reasoning in this statement. The first is that mistakes are necessarily predictive of a bad performance. The second is the assertion that one will never be able to play the piece properly. The first error involves drawing a conclusion based on insufficient or overly selective evidence. The other is the use of a definitive word like "never," which offers little hope for change. This is an example of "absolutistic thinking," and it is very evident in the way one student thought about her upcoming piano performance examination.

"I'm scheduled to play my sophomore exam in three weeks and I just can't play the octave passage in the middle of the Beethoven. I know I'm going to fail." Betsy, an accomplished pianist, had carefully prepared a demanding program and had achieved considerable mastery. Yet her concern, up to the time of the exam, remained focused on a passage in one piece, two measures in length, that she was able to play accurately about seventy percent of the time. In the exam, she played exceptionally well, even though, in her opinion, the octaves were "sloppy." She recognized afterward that she had created unnecessary anxiety for herself by blowing the significance of this detail far out of proportion. More generally, Betsy began to realize that her pattern of motivation amounted to making herself extremely anxious ahead of time. One of the main ways she accomplished this was focusing on troublesome passages as evidence of her pianistic ineptness, thereby ignoring the rest of her playing, which confirmed her ample talents. Made anxious by self-criticism, she then became motivated to practice. Betsy's problem was that she viewed things out of context by magnifying her shortcomings and minimizing her capabilites. Such logical errors are very common among performers, who tend to overemphasize the significance of individual notes within the larger context of an extended piece.

One of the most insidious effects of anxiety is that it can cause us to lose our perspective on things. When we are anxious, we feel the world closing in on us and our attention becomes riveted on a very small number of things. When performing, for example, our attention may be captured by trembling knees or a pounding heart. At such times, it is difficult to step back and put things into perspective. Yet, it is important to do this, at least in some fashion. When we are anxious, nothing seems more important. We may feel that everyone in the audience is acutely aware of our discomfort and very critical of us. In other words, anxiety brings certain elements into focus, but prevents us from seeing the broader picture.

There are a number of ways to deal with this problem, but a very simple way is to think of some sayings, or some ideas, that help you realize that life offers more than stressful performances. Three such sayings are given below as examples.

*A Temptest in a Teapot.* This is a nice saying to remind yourself that anxiety can cause you to become too personally involved in a situation. Conflicts or disagreements between people are a good example of such circumstances. When we feel threatened or upset by someone, it's easy to feel that our existence is being undermined and that we are personally threatened. A sense of perspective can be restored when we recall that conflicts, arguments, and disagreements are as much a natural part of daily life as pleasant exchanges and that personal relationships are usually not established or ended on the basis of a single exchange. By ascribing a realistic degree of importance to events, you will be less likely to overreact to day-to-day situations and to create far-reaching repercussions of conflicts.

*This, Too, Shall Pass.* Anxiety is normally a time-limited emotion. It's impossible to maintain peak tension for more than a short period of time. Sometimes people describe anxiety as a wave that washes over them so forcefully that it is hard to ignore. But waves move on, and so does anxiety. Many people find that they can tolerate the discomfort of anxiety partly because they know it will end. On the other hand, many anxious people cannot let go of their anxiety because they constantly anticipate the next bout of anxiety and dwell on the experience long after it has passed. Accepting the inevitability of anxiety without either anticipating or wallowing in its symptoms is a healthy and adaptive attitude to acquire.

*When You're Up to Your Ass in Alligators, It's Hard to Remember That You Meant to Drain the Swamp.* We often make commitments and take responsibilities without fully realizing what they entail. The further we proceed, the more we are caught in the many difficulties that seem to accompany doing anything worthwhile. It's easy to become discouraged and lose your perspective when this happens. When you feel overwhelmed with responsibilities and problems, remember this saying and (1) focus on what you really have to accomplish (not what you'd like to do or what others think you should do), (2) form a plan to help you resolve the immediate stress, and (3) take some action to simultaneously reduce the immediate source of your distress and bring you closer to your overall goal. Use your anxiety as a cue to get going.

Despite the usefulness of saying such as these, there is an important difference between being able to regain perspective and engaging in what psychologists call rationalization. When we rationalize, we try to explain away problems or discomfort by attributing them to forces outside our control. A performer might rationalize a poor performance, for example, by suggesting that the concert stage was poorly lit, or that the sound system was inadequate, or that the audience was unappreciative. Rationalization is not taking perspective, which does not attempt to explain anything. Rather, perspective taking entails stepping back from a situation and looking at it from a different vantage point. Perspective taking can be useful at different times, during periods of preparation, immediately before a performance, or sometimes even during a performance itself.

The preceding sayings and thoughts may help you keep your perspective. Anxiety can capture our attention and make us feel that everything we do is very urgent. While it is true that we must pay immediate attention to some things (such as an imminent physical risk), most of the time we can afford to pause and think about things before reacting.

When we are anxious, our natural inclination is to do something—anything—to alleviate the acute distress. Anxiety can be so compelling that we do things hastily that we may later regret or that compound the problem. It is important to pay attention to your anxiety without being carried away by it. Use anxiety as a signal to take perspective on your situation, determine an appropriate course of action, and initiate a response to help the problem.

## Irrational Beliefs

The psychologist Albert Ellis is well known for explaining how our irrational beliefs about the world contribute to our feelings about ourselves.[2] Ellis described a set of core beliefs that he believes are characteristic of psychologically troubled individuals. Among them is the belief "I must be approved of by virtually everyone I come into contact with." Such beliefs require some explanation, because we normally tend to deny them, so irrational may they appear at first glance. However, they are often implicit in our behavior. At a conscious, verbal level, we may see things quite differently, but our beliefs direct much of our behavior from an inconspicuous vantage point removed from conscious awareness. Rather than being directly observed, these beliefs can instead be inferred from our behavior and statements. They represent the general rules, or assumptions, on which we base much of our everyday behavior. The beliefs described by Ellis, which make us psychologically unhappy, have several noteworthy features. First, they are absolutistic, in that they put things in definitive, unambiguous terms. "I must be liked by everyone" is an absolutistic phrase because it lays out a clear-cut rule for interacting with others. Second, these beliefs are not spelled out in enough detail to allow us to determine their validity personally. Terse and definitive, such beliefs have an aura of authenticity, but lack grounding in real-world conditions and do not permit exceptions. The idea that one must be liked by *everyone,* for example, is obviously unreasonable, at least in the sense that certain aspects are not clearly spelled out. Who determined that I must be liked by everyone? What consequences will I suffer if someone does not like me? How must I behave to ensure that others will like me? Finally, many of these irrational beliefs reflect preoccupations with how we imagine we must behave so that others will like or accept us. In other words, many of our troublesome beliefs create difficulties because they are erroneous assumptions about how other people think and act. They are often "rules of conduct" that we use in lieu of personal experience with other people.

Because such beliefs can often only be inferred based on our behavior and statements, it can be difficult and time consuming to elucidate them. Moreover, some of our behavior may appear inconsistent with our beliefs. This was true of a violinist who claimed that he very much enjoyed performing but frequently cancelled his engagements because of "subaverage" conditions in halls or conductors who were difficult to get along with. In fact, he feared performing except under highly controlled conditions. An underlying belief that "it's only safe to perform under optimal conditions" appeared to be at the root of his anxiety and markedly limited his time onstage.

These beliefs often can be traced to a few basic sources. First, they may reflect things we have been told and have accepted at face value. Parents, teachers, coaches, and colleagues all have beliefs about how best to perform, and our own views tend to reflect those who have influenced us. Direct experience can also contribute to these beliefs, as when a performer says something like, "I've learned from experience that it's important to make the audience like you." Finally, we may develop adaptive or maladapative beliefs based on what we observe happening to others. However, the source of a belief is probably less important than its influence on our behavior in either a helpful or constricting way.

For example, Beth, a conservatory-trained vocalist, was troubled by inexplicable anxiety that worsened as her successful career developed. Although engaged to sing with increasingly prestigious orchestras and choral groups, she became increasingly apprehensive while preparing for upcoming concerts. Performing before full houses and getting rave reviews, she nevertheless feared that each successful performance made the inevitability of failure more imminent. Rather than gaining confidence from her successful performances, Beth became increasingly anxious about eventual inevitable failure. The basis for her seemingly unwarranted anxiety was a variant of the old adage "sunshine follows rain," which was reinterpreted as "rain follows sunshine." Beth had been raised by a single father who, although initially successful in his career, struggled with chronic alcoholism and was barely able to make ends meet. Her mother, a woman of considerable musical talent, died when Beth was three. Based on these experiences, Beth had developed a deep-seated pessimism and she believed that such things as fame, prestige, and physical health were but a transient prelude to failure. Thus, her musical successes were diluted by her expectation of subsequent failure. As a result, the more she performed successfully, the greater became her fear of catastrophic failure. Beth's pessimistic belief in the inevitability of failure lay at the base of her fear of success.

## Thinking and Problem-Solving

When confronted with musical problems, we try to come up with workable solutions.[3] Sometimes, however, our ability to analyze and solve a problem effectively is curtailed because we don't consider it in detail. Particularly when one is under time pressure, it can be difficult to step back and put problems into proper perspective. In this case, we look for short-term solutions that provide only symptomatic relief without touching the underlying issues.

Ben, for example, who was preparing a difficult piece for a recital, became increasingly anxious that one movement was not yielding to his normal practice techniques. The passage consisted of a series of very rapid chords played with the left hand in combination with slower, more sustained chords played using the right hand and pedal. The passage was a significant challenge to Ben, who was sufficiently talented to be able to learn most new music very quickly. Normally, he approached music as a whole, studying its structure and trying to understand how the notes and chord progressions fit together. With most music, he was able to play the notes slowly initially and then acquire speed as the patterns gradually fell into place. His musical scores were seldom marked with fingerings or notations like those of most of his classmates, and he was somewhat disdainful of musicians who struggled to work out the music note by note.

Ben's first attempt to solve the problem of the unyielding passage was not particularly successful. He decided that to "go for the sound" and ignore specific notes, which were inevitably left behind at the tempo required. Time after time he went through the passage, varying the tempo and trying to achieve an overall effect that proved elusive. His difficulties arouse mainly because he had not taken enough time to evaluate the problem and deal with it in detail. Any thoughts of examining his problem in detail were quickly dismissed because Ben felt he did not have enough time to learn the music note by note. He found the process of imagining himself performing the music effectively more reassuring than the prospect of sitting down and learning it. After struggling for several days, Ben abruptly abandoned the piece and, even though he was under extreme time pressure, made a last-minute substitution in his program.

Like Ben, many of us retain our ineffectual problem-solving skills, even when confronted with evidence that the old ways don't work well. In fact, we often redouble our efforts to make problems yield to our preferred ways of solving them, because we are convinced that time and intense effort will ensure success. But such an approach is often compulsive in that it makes us feel that we are doing something about the problem when we may be reinforcing it through mindless repetition—and making ourselves more tense and anxious in the process.

Effective problem solving can be outlined in a few basic steps. First, define the problem in manageable, realistic terms. The way you frame a problem at the outset will greatly affect your motivation and ability to deal with it. Be as specific as you can. "I'll never be able to play this piece, even though my recital is in three weeks" sounds like an insurmountable problem, whereas "I still can't play measure X up to the tempo of the rest of the piece" provides a much clearer indication of what needs to be done. Second, take some time to consider realistic options, even though you may be tempted to use a "tried and true" solution. Is slow practice the only way to master a technically difficult passage? Why not play the notes using dotted rhythms to create syncopation, so that half the notes will be played rapidly, the others more slowly? What about working out fingering problems first, even if this seems needlessly time consuming? What about studying the score away from your instrument, visualizing in detail the placement of each finger on the keys or the muscles used elsewhere in the body to produce the sound? Just as there are virtually unlimited ways of conceptualizing problems, there are equal numbers of potential solutions.

After his recital, Ben came back to the piece and explored the problem in greater detail. He realized that (a) his fingerings, while practical while playing slowly, would not work effectively as the tempo increased; (b) he resisted taking the time to work out fingerings because he took pride in playing most scores at sight; and (c) he had never before played a piece by this particular composer. Eventually, the insights he gained by working out the problem in detail helped him formulate a plan for learning the recalcitrant passage more effectively than would otherwise have been the case.

## Thoughts and Coping Skills

When considered in broader terms than just solving problems, the way we think about things often holds clues to how we cope with stressful situations generally.[4] Coping skills encompass a wide range of behaviors that help cut down the amount of stress and anxiety we feel. Some performers' coping style is designed to avoid stressful situations altogether, though this usually creates more problems than it solves. Avoiding practice because it creates anxiety about an upcoming recital is a good example of this maladaptive style. Avoidant behavior may serve the immediate purpose of making us feel momentarily less anxious, but it is obviously counterproductive in the long run. There are other styles of coping skills, which work with varying degrees of success, depending on the individual and the circumstances. Some performers, for instance, cope with stress by using drugs or alcohol to make them forget, at least temporarily, about their intense anxiety. Still others simply deny that they are under stress and hope that a positive attitude can overcome the tension.

For example, when Kathy, a skillful violinist, was asked how she coped with her anxiety before a performance, she confided, "I tell myself over and over again, 'You can do it, you can do it' I *never* let myself have any negative thoughts, because if I did, then something really bad might happen." Her response had been somewhat helpful, but at the cost of denying the reality of her anxiety.

Kathy's style of coping with performance stress was to try to block the threatening feelings. Doing so requires conscious effort and considerable mental energy; even if one succeeds in subduing the threatening feelings temporarily, they may be expressed less directly through such things as loss of sleep or physical ailments. This coping style has the further disadvantage of involving conscious, repetitive self-statements, which may distract one from the music being performed. Nonetheless, denying one's anxiety and trying to think positively about performing are advocated by many as a means of getting "psyched up" for a performance, despite their lack of advantages over any other such technique.

As an alternative to this style, consider learning to accept and monitor stress and anxiety, rather than denying it. A related idea is that, although perhaps inevitable, stress does not have to be avoided at all costs, provided it does not exceed certain limits. A coping style that emphasizes working productively when under stress is an attractive alternative to expending one's energy denying stress and related feelings of anxiety.

## Thoughts and Defense Mechanisms

The term "defense mechanism," derived from Freudian psychology, refers to psychological strategies we use to keep ourselves from being overwhelmed by anxiety.[5] Defense mechanisms help us avoid excessive anxiety by minimizing our awareness or otherwise distorting our perception of the associated feelings. Defense mechanisms protect us from anxiety created by psychological conflicts that threaten to upset our equilibrium. Among the most common defense mechanisms are *repression* and *denial* (in which anxious feelings are blocked from conscious awareness) and *projection* (in which we attribute to other people feelings that are too threatening to admit to in ourselves).

Although defense mechanisms can provide relief from anxiety, they often make us feel unnecessarily psychologically constricted. To the degree that our behavior reflects the effects of defense mechanisms, we tend to be cautious in what we do and incapable of spontaneous behavior.

For example, "They're out to get me" was Charles's assessment of his jury committee before his end-of-semester examination. Scholastically a borderline student, he was on the verge of expulsion and had been given one more chance by the faculty to demonstrate that he could prepare and perform a modest repertoire. He was so absorbed in projecting his anger and hostility onto the committee that he failed to acknowledge his own role in his predicament. He believed that his musical skills were obvious, and he balked at having to prove to others what he knew to be true about himself. His anger also surfaced in therapy, although each succeeding eruption was more closely directed at the true source of his problems: himself. He had ignored numerous opportunities to develop as a musician while in a haze of drugs and chemical substances upon which he was psychologically dependent. Eventually, he mobilized his considerable anger effectively and began a long, arduous reversal that resulted in his reinstatment into the program months later.

## Thought Patterns and Performance Skills

Although you may not be aware of them, extraneous thoughts probably run through your mind while you play. Internal comments such as the following can influence your concentration as you perform:

> "*Deep breath . . . How am I doing? . . . Got through that one. . . . Did I lock the car? . . . Get ready for the octaves. . . . I love it! . . . What do they think? . . . I always miss that arpeggio—damn! . . . Hope I get home in time for* Star Trek. *. . . Take it slower. . . . Easy does it. . . . "*

These fragmentary thoughts occurred to one performer while playing a passage of music during a practice performance. This information was obtained by making a tape recording of the performance. The passage was then played back, and the performer stopped the tape whenever he recalled having had a specific thought. The thought was written down and the tape restarted and played to the next point at which the performer recalled a particular thought. This very interesting exercise can be practiced easily by any performer, with nothing more sophisticated than a cassette recorder. This exercise can help develop an awareness that, even though you feel that you are engrossed in a piece of music, the experience may trigger thoughts or ideas that have very little to do with the expressive aspects of the music. In this example, many of the thoughts are somewhat anxious and could easily distract the performer. In our experience, performers who experience stage fright are very prone to such distracting thoughts. Trying to focus on the music as much as possible, without being distracted by extraneous thoughts, is a reasonable goal, but in practice can be difficult, because most of us find it hard to limit our conscious attention to just one single activity. Moreover, some interesting research in psychology suggests that the portions of the brain that regulate our responses to music and to speech are in very different regions. This finding implies that it may be possible for the brain to engage in the two activities at once—verbal and musical performing.

If distracting thoughts are a problem for you as a performer, try as a first step, to become aware of what thoughts run through your mind as you play. It's a good idea to observe yourself on several different occasions, sometimes with different pieces of music, sometimes with different pieces of music, sometimes with the same music played several times. You may find certain thoughts occurring again and again, highlighting a particular theme. Or, you may find ideas occurring more randomly, with no apparent pattern. Either way, such thoughts can easily divert your attention away from the music.

As a long-term goal, try to integrate your thinking with your musical expression. The goal should not be to eliminate thinking while performing, but to bring your thinking into line with your musical intentions. You might use several techniques to achieve this effect. First, spend some time listening to the music and developing attractive images. By practicing these images, thoughts, and ideas, you may find it easier to associate them with the music as you perform it. Second, spend some time listening to the music when you are very relaxed. When we are tense and anxious, our thoughts speed up, and so many performers find, as they prepare to perform, that their activation is accompanied by barely controllable thoughts. If you can experience the music while relaxed, you can often minimize the number and intrusiveness of otherwise distracting thoughts. Third, spend some time studying the musical score and looking for the points that may trigger particular thoughts. For example, a technically demanding passage may cause anticipatory thoughts, such as, "Uh-oh, here comes that passage again!" While such a thought may usefully warn you of the difficult passage, it can also make you react in such a way that you are not well equipped to deal with the passage when it comes. By studying the score and trying to anticipate the musical challenges ahead of time, you can reduce the chances of a negative or catastrophic reaction, at least in terms of your thoughts, at the time of performance. Finally, you might want to try several techniques that can help dissipate unpleasant, repetitive, intrusive thoughts. We've already mentioned "thought stopping," which requires that you alert yourself in some way whenever you become aware of a bothersome thought and to terminate it. You might say "Stop!" to yourself; or you might place an elastic band around your wrist and snap it lightly whenever you become aware of an intrusive thought. You might also consider creating an interference effect while you are playing or performing by counting to yourself, saying a word or several words out loud, or doing something else to disrupt the flow of the bothersome thoughts. Initially, such activity will probably interfere with the fluency of your playing, but eventually you will probably be able to control both your thinking and your playing, so that neither interferes with the other and instead compliment each other.

## Summary

We have considered a variety of ways in which thoughts can affect our feelings and behavior. In talking with musicians, we are struck by how often they have only a limited understanding of the many ways in which thinking influences behavior. Many musicians endorse the benefits of positive thinking, which we discussed as one cognitive coping style, but fail to consider the many other ways in which thinking styles and musical performance skills are related.

Many of the psychological difficulties experienced by performers stem, at least partly, from the way they evaluate their situation. All of us engage in self talk, the inner dialogue of thoughts that runs through our minds most of the time and frequently distracts us. Self talk—whether related to a coping strategy, an underlying belief about the world, a problem-solving skill, or a defense mechanism—is an inevitable companion to most forms of deliberate behavior. Only on those comparatively rare occasions when we are so absorbed in what we are doing that we cease to be self-conscious do we find such thoughts fading into the darker recesses of awareness. Often described as "peak" or "flow" experiences, these occasions involve personal involvement that is not impeded by self-consciousness or anxiety.

Most of the rest of the time, we are aware of what we are doing and constantly think about what is going on. This is especially true of performers, who are capable of making music while thinking about what they are doing. Such an experience is common because music and thoughts, or inner speech are independent aspects of consciousness. An important aspect of developing effective performance skills is to gain a clear understanding of the relationship between thoughts and music and how this relationship changes when we are practicing, rehearsing, performing, or just thinking about musical images. Perhaps you have identified with some of the musicians described in this chapter whose ways of thinking about performing affected how comfortable they felt and how well they were able to perform. In each instance, as music attention was focused on their way of thinking about the music and its performance as on the purely musical and technical aspects of performing. While effective performance skills obviously are dependent on sound musical skills, the cognitive dimension has considerable potential for helping musicians realistically appraise and effectively cope with the demands of performing.

# Basic Stress Management Skills

*Nunc, vero inter saxum et locum durum sum. ("Now, I am really be-*
*tween a rock and a hard place!")*

—Henry Beard

Tom: *A twenty-one-year-old violinist, Tom was preparing for*
*his junior recital in two months, the thought of which made*
*him feel excessively tense. "I know I've just got to relax," he*
*said empathically, "otherwise there's no way I'll be able to play*
*well." Tom's way of assessing his situation simply added to his*
*pressures. He saw relaxing as something he* had *to do, as an*
*obligation, in addition to everything else he was trying to cope*
*with as he prepared for the recital.*

*Fortunately, Tom was somewhat aware of his tendencies*
*toward compulsive activity and came to appreciate some of the*
*broader aspects of the situation. He said that a teacher had*
*told him that he "just needed to relax," and that he was simply*
*following orders. However, this advice made him even more*
*anxious than before. And, paradoxically, some of the sensa-*
*tions of being relaxed could make Tom anxious. Clearly, there*
*was far more to his situation than relaxation training alone*
*could alleviate.*

*First, Tom experimented with becoming aware of the pro-*
*cess of relaxation, using the "quieting response," which has*
*four basic steps:*

1. *Taking a deep breath.*
2. *Closing one's eyes.*
3. *Letting go of muscle tension.*

*4. Forming a pleasant, relaxing image.*

*This technique was presented to Tom as an experiment for him to play with, modify, and develop for his own use. He decided for step 4, for instance, to visualize the opening phrases of a Chopin nocturne that he had been attracted to as a child. Beginning in this manner helped Tom learn about relaxing in a nonthreatening and manageable way.*

Tom needed to learn that his way of *approaching* music and relaxation—and, indeed, many of his day-to-day activities—was the real culprit. In his usual approach, relaxation training would have become a substitute for compulsive practicing and wouldn't significantly have altered the tension and energy that motivated his behavior. His problem was compounded by the relatively short time until his recital, which added to his pressures and made his need to relax seem even more pressing.

There is an important difference between learning to feel comfortable as a performer and going through the motions of exercises and activities that are supposed to make you relax. Tom's initial approach to the problems posed by his anticipatory anxiety favored the latter, and the prospect of relaxing was itself threatening to him. He practiced the violin in a similar way—he was technically competent without, however, allowing himself to be involved in the music. Relaxation, like playing, evoked compulsive responses that were not conducive to either activity. Just as he could spend hours repeatedly playing passages to "perfect" them, he could have become caught up in the technical aspects of relaxation training and never fully appreciated its effects.

Our discussion of stress and anxiety management techniques begins with Tom's story because we want to make two points. First, as in music, relaxation technique alone is not everything. We have no magic formulas to ensure you will feel relaxed while performing. No one relaxation technique is best suited to every performer, any more than there is a single best way to strike a key on a piano keyboard.

Second, learning relaxation and other stress management procedures may or may not be helpful, depending on the way they are approached. For example, if you are very busily preparing for a performance, and have to take the time to learn and practice a new skill (whether it's relaxation or anything else), you'll probably find yourself more, rather than less, anxious than when you decided to seek help. Like musical skills, techniques to help you cope effectively with stress and tension are best cultivated in a relatively tension-free atmosphere. Three weeks before an important performance is not the best time to learn a skill such as progressive relaxation. If you are considering learning some of the skills described in this book, try to do so when you will not feel pressed by time to short-cut the process of learning the procedures and coming to experience their full effects. We take it for granted that music we are to perform is best learned long before the performance itself. The same logic holds for the stress management procedures discussed in the remainder of this chapter.

Three specific techniques to deal with anxiety are very commonly recommended: Relaxation, mental imagery, and cognitive monitoring.[1] To these we would add a group of techniques that are most applicable when you begin to work on a new piece of music and that can help you recognize how the music affects your thoughts, feelings, and behavior. Each of these therapeutic activities involves basic skills that need to be practiced before you can experience any real benefits. We begin by considering basic relaxation skills, and then turn our attention successively to mental imagery, cognitive restructuring, and learning strategies.

## Relaxation and the Quieting Response

Relaxation is an elusive concept, especially when applied to musical performance skills.[2] Feeling relaxed while performing is very different from the relaxation of meditation, for example, or daydreaming. Some performers fear being too relaxed on stage because they feel that such a state inhibits optimal performance. Our assessment of the potential benefits of relaxation stresses three factors. First, daily systematic practice of relaxation skills can help lower a performer's overall level of tension and thereby create a greater tolerance for the stress and tension that may be experienced onstage. Second, relaxation techniques can help retrain otherwise tense muscle groups that interfere with the fluid movements required for an effective performance. Third, relaxation exercises can, after some time, be used to develop effective antidotes to tension, apprehension, or anxiety, which tend to ebb and flow over time as one is preparing for or involved in a performance.

Let's consider some of the basic techniques that have proven effective for many people. One of the simplest and most basic relaxation technique is the quieting response described by Charles Stroebel.[3] The quieting response is a relatively brief exercise that, with practice, can be used in a variety of situations that evoke excessive tension or anxiety. There are four basic steps:

1. Begin by taking a deep, relaxing breath.
2. Allow your eyes to slowly close.
3. Allow yourself to "let go" of excess muscle tension.
4. Contemplate a pleasant, relaxing image.

These steps in the quieting response can be carried out in a short time, if necessary—even in a few seconds. The quieting response is intended to help you counteract momentary tension or anxiety by producing a competing state of relaxation. It's useful in many situations, such as when you're waiting to go onstage, immediately prior to playing or singing; or in response to anxious thoughts that tend to increase tension.

Although the quieting response appears simple, each of the four steps should be learned carefully so that they promote a relaxed state. Just telling yourself to relax will not necessarily have this effect and frequently adds to tension. Perhaps you have been nervous while performing and had a teacher or coach suddenly tell you to *relax*. If you're like most people, the sudden interruption of your concentration, the fact you're seemingly being ordered to do something, and the necessity of figuring out what you must do to become relaxed can make you completely lose your composure and tense up.

Whatever form of relaxation you choose, try to approach it with the attitude of allowing, rather than forcing yourself to relax. As a performer, you have no doubt acquired the ability to control the muscles needed to play your instrument, mainly as the result of intentional, repetitive practice. Likewise, relaxation training involves practice, but in this case the emphasis is on letting go of muscular tension. A basic rule in relaxation training is that the more conscious effort you invest, the less likely you are to achieve the desired effect.[4] Let's see how this idea might affect the quieting response.

### Deep Breathing

Taking a deep breath can be done in many different ways. We suggest that, like a good singer, you learn basic diaphragmatic breathing techniques. Taking a deep breath involves feeling that your lungs are expanding in several directions simultaneously—up and down, front and back.[5] The analogy of blowing up a round balloon in the abdominal area might be helpful. The rate at which you breathe is important, and you will have to experiment to determine what speed is most comfortable for you. Try for a slow, relaxed pace that allows you ample time to fill your lungs with air; then exhale equally slowly. Counting while you inhale and exhale can be helpful, and you can vary the count as you practice. Try different rates of counting (beginning, perhaps, with one count every two or three seconds) until you achieve a comfortable cadence.

When practicing basic breathing techniques, most people quickly discover that they have far greater lung capacity than they usually use. This is especially evident when exhaling, a fact that can be easily demonstrated in the following way. Take a deep breath, hold it for a few seconds, and then release it. As the air rushes out of your lungs, you will come to a point at which it would be natural to inhale the next breath. When you reach this point, however, continue pushing air out of your lungs until the resistance you feel becomes somewhat uncomfortable. This secondary exhalation will probably take almost as much time as the primary exhalation after which you would normally take another breath. Experiment with these and other aspects of breathing and practice the exercises until you are able to breathe deeply without having to divert your conscious attention to the task.

### Closing Your Eyes

It may be tempting to overlook such a simple act, but each step in the process of relaxing will have greatest effect if carried out in a relaxed manner. There are many ways to close your eyes, but not all of them will promote relaxation. Closing your eyes can be done forcefully, so that your whole face becomes a mask of tension, or tentatively, so that the muscles around the eyes begin to quiver erratically. You can close your eyes quickly or slowly, as well. In short, this seemingly insignificant phase of the quieting response should not be overlooked.

This step illustrates an interesting point about learning to relax. When most people are told to relax (or, tell themselves to relax), their tension tends to increase. When responding to instructions, we often react as if given a military order, no matter what we've been asked to do. "Close your eyes" has the sound of a command, which can interfere with achieving the effect. Focusing on the sensations themselves, rather than the desired goal, brings about relaxation. Each step along the way should involve a sense of being relaxed. Try for a relative absense of effortful activity and a corresponding sense of ease.

Here are some ideas about how to close your eyes. First, spend some time experimenting with the muscles that control your eyes and eyelids. How independently of one another do they move? Slowly close your eyelids, and see if you notice that anything else is happening. Do your eyes feel as though they are rotating down or in another direction? Do you feel muscular tension in the eye socket that seems to spread over an area beyond the eyelid itself? How about the muscles under your eyebrows or around the eye? If you experiment, you will discover that you can almost block your vision by lowering your eyebrows and raising your cheeks at the same time, without lowering your eyelids.

The point of all of this has much in common with a comment of the pianist Vladimir Horowitz. An interviewer asked him to describe the most difficult music he had ever played. Horowitz replied, "the C major scale." Horowitz then elaborated on the intricacies of playing a single note, conveying an appreciation for the significance of the minute musical details that are the basis of musical expressiveness. Applying Horowitz's meaning to relaxation, we begin to realize that effective relaxation, like musical expressiveness, is mainly a matter of attending to small details. As the overall visual effect of a painting stems from the coherence of many individual brushstrokes, the process of relaxing is as the result of a great many minutely detailed actions.

As you experiment, you will find an effective means of closing your eyes, provided that you are not too rushed to achieve the desired effect. Here are some additional suggestions that you may find helpful.

1. Using the rhythm of your breathing as a guide, move your eyelids up and down at a relatively constant rate. Open your eyelids as you inhale, close them as you exhale. When you become comfortable with this process, reverse it a few times until you acquire a sense of synchrony between your breathing and the movement of your eyelids.

2. Hold one hand just a little above eye level, then slowly allow it to lower. Follow the movement of your hand with your eyes. Then raise and lower your hand, all the while following its movement with your eyes. When this routine feels smooth and comfortable, follow the movement of your hand with a corresponding up-and-down movement of your eyelids.

As you learn about the many different muscles involved in this simple exercise, consider some additional factors. Can you move your eyes and eylids independently of one another? With practice, could you raise one eyelid while closing the other? Could you learn other things about your eyes and how they move? Taking some time to explore the complex world of your eyes and their environment is an effective way of understanding a few of the many subtle effects that combine to determine how relaxed or tense we feel. With experience, you can cultivate this phase of the quieting response in a manner that contributes perceptibly to your overall relaxation.

## Allow Tension to Leave Your Body

Most musicians are well accustomed to the effort required to develop performance skills. Pianists, for example, used to practicing technical exercises such as those of C. L. Hanon or Carl Czerny probably can recall attacking these exercises in ways that may have been counterproductive. One such student recounted with pride that, through sheer force of will and endless repetition, he was able to play the entire set of Hanon exercises in less than the recommended time (one hour). However, his efforts probably resulted in an excessively effortful style of playing, despite whatever limited benefits he may have obtained in terms of playing quickly.

If your style of performing is so effortful, you may become frustrated when you first experiment with the third step in the quieting response. Letting go of tension entails allowing it to diminish without using conscious, deliberate force. Letting go means taking advantage of the natural tendency of muscles to return to a relaxed condition when they are no longer distended by tension. Like a rubber band, which requires some effort to be stretched almost to the breaking point but none whatsoever to be returned to its resting state, some of your tense muscles (the most common physical symptom of tension) only need to be released, not forced, to become relaxed. Experience this by slowly clenching your hand into a fist. Continue squeezing for a few seconds, increasing the tension in your fingers. You will find that you can let go of most of the tension by simply releasing your hand. Try this exercise in different ways, including (a) an abrupt release, (b) a gradual release, and (c) a step-by-step release, in which you let go of a small amount of tension, then hold; then release a bit more, then hold; and so on. Once you develop a sense of how this feels, you could try the same procedure on different sets of muscles, alternately tensing and releasing them. You might also experiment with releasing general muscular tension by curling up into a ball (like a diver doing a somersault), and then releasing the tension in any of the ways just described.

In talking about letting go of tension, we're not being precise. Obviously, you can't release all of the tension in your body, even if you are lying down and completely supported on a flat surface. Many of the muscles in the body are in dynamic opposition to one another, so relaxing one causes tension in another. Try this simple exercise to demonstrate this principle to yourself. Extend your arm in front of you, with your wrist straight. Now flex your wrist, moving your hand up and down. Place the fingers of your other hand on your forearm so that your index finger rests on the top and the thumb on the bottom. As you flex your wrist, you should be able to feel corresponding changes in the tension of the muscles under your fingertips. Raising your wrist causes muscles on the top to contract and tense, while those below become relaxed. Lowering the wrist has the opposite effect. It's difficult to find a position in which both sets of muscles are completely relaxed.

Thus, letting go of tension in your body is not entirely possible, because some sets of muscles increase in tension when others relax.

However, it is possible to achieve a state in which you have minimized excessive, useless tension.

## Forming a Pleasant Image

When you come to the step in this exercise that calls for a relaxing image, it is most important for you to choose something that you personally find relaxing. Although people tend to think in terms of visual imagery, most musicians can form detailed auditory images as well, and these can certainly achieve the same effect. Images are discussed in detail in the next section, so we'll deal with them only briefly here. It is a good idea to give yourself some time to cultivate the image (or images) to be used in this phase of the quieting response, because imagery has a very powerful effect on tension. After reflection, you may find yourself drawn to a memory, a painting, a word, or a phrase. Perhaps you invariably associate a segment of a piece of music with feelings of well-being, like the musician described at the opening of this chapter. Whatever you settle on (and you may find that your relaxing image should change occasionally), keep the following three suggestions in mind as you incorporate it into the quieting response:

1. Cultivate as vivid and focused an image as possible.
2. Stay with the image for a measurable period of time.
3. Practice the image so it's readily available to you.

When putting the four stages of the quieting response together, you may be surprised to find that the entire exercise eventually can take a relatively short time. It might seem from this account to require considerable time, but this is because we have described the process in great detail. Just as when you practice a new piece of music, learning a procedure like the quieting response is more time-consuming than carrying it out. However, the importance of "rehearsal" can't be overemphasized. If you spend the necessary time at the beginning experimenting with, refining, and becoming comfortable with the response, you will experience more perceptible effects in the end than if you were to practice the steps hurriedly or forcefully. Just as, when learning a piece of music, you incorporate the individual musical elements such as the notes into patterns you don't have to think about, so practicing the quieting response to the point where the four stages become almost automatic allows you to derive its benefits without much conscious effort.

The quieting response is a good starting point for basic stress management techniques. It provides you with some general principles of relaxation, is relatively easy to learn, and can be used in situations where more sustained relaxation may not be feasable. We suggest that you keep notes on your progress if you practice the quieting response and that you approach it, as you would a new piece of music, thoughtfully and carefully.

## Progressive Relaxation Techniques

A relaxation technique that goes further than the quieting response is "progressive relaxation," which is based on the work of the physician Edmund Jacobson. In his work, Jacobson came to believe that many of the patients referred to him for supposed medical complaints were actually suffering from chronic tension and anxiety.[6] Of all of the current relaxation techniques, none has received more attention than progressive relaxation. As the name implies, the procedures employed in progressive relaxation are intended to help the person relax gradually. There are many variations of progressive relaxation techniques, which differ in the time needed to learn the procedures and to achieve relaxation. As with music, the more time you devote to this activity, the greater the potential benefits.

Several other considerations should also be mentioned at the outset. First, if possible, strive to learn progressive relaxation techniques when you are not unduly preoccupied or distressed by other things. Relaxation techniques are best learned when you are able to focus your attention and do not feel distracted. Second, relaxation techniques do not guarantee that you will never feel anxious or apprehensive once you have learned to relax. One of the main benefits of relaxation training is that it can help you feel relaxed, for at least brief periods, when you may need a break from tense situations. For example, if you tend to feel tense most of the day, one or two sessions of progressive relaxation to punctuate your tension may help reduce its overall level. Obviously, it is not feasible to practice progressive relaxation onstage. Progressive relaxation should be considered as a technique to help you achieve an overall reduction in your level of tension. This overall reduction may, in turn, make you feel more comfortable when you are in a performance situation. Now, let's look at the procedure.

The best way to begin progressive relaxation exercises (or any other form of relaxation) is to sit quietly for a few moments and allow your body to calm itself. You might start by attending to your breathing. Most of us breathe rather shallowly and rapidly, so that we use very little of our total lung capacity. A good starting point for progressive relaxation is taking a series of deep breaths, pacing yourself as you go. You may want to count silently to yourself in a cadence, such as four counts in, and four out, at about one count per second. Experiment until you find a rhythm for breathing that allows you to breath deeply and fully, without strain.

Another important condition for beginning a relaxation session is reducing the stimulation you are exposed to. One of the simplest ways is to close your eyes, but, as we have just seen, there are different ways of achieving this result. Closing your eyes might seem simple, but remember that progressive relaxation stresses gradual relaxation. Therefore, try to allow your eyes to close, as if your eyelids were being slowly and gently pulled down by gravity. You may find it helpful to hold one finger horizontally in front of your eyes and then gradually move the finger down, following it with the line of your eyelid. Practice this technique until you can achieve a slow, relaxed eye closure.

Once you have mastered these conditions—breathing regularly and closing your eyes—you are ready to begin the progressive relaxation procedure. The essence of progressive relaxation involves alternately tensing and releasing a number of the specific muscle sets throughout the body. You begin with the muscles at one end of the body, usually the feet. Once the muscles in the feet have been relaxed by alternately tensing and releasing them, you move on to the next higher set. Continue this progression until you have tensed and relaxed the main muscle sets in your entire body.

Several things can be learned from progressive relaxation. First, this technique helps you isolate the sensations of different sets of muscles throughout your body. Second, it helps you learn what tension, as well as relaxation, feels like in these muscles. Third, it helps you control muscles that you previously may not have even been aware of. Finally, and perhaps most importantly, progressive relaxation techniques can help you become relaxed.

Inducing relaxation can proceed from the point at which you have minimized external stimulation, achieved regular, relaxed breathing, and gradually allowed your eyes to close. At this point, you can turn your attention inwardly to the sensations of various parts of your body. Here we'll describe a basic procedure in which you begin alternately tensing and releasing muscle sets with the feet. First, turn your attention inward and sense the muscles in your feet. Once you can attend to these sensations, begin the exercise by slowly tensing the toes of one foot, curling them up and creating a sense of tension. Tense these muscles slowly and deliberately, perhaps using a silent count as you do so. When you have achieved moderate tension—that is, perceptible, but not physically painful— hold your toes in this position for several seconds and then gradually release the tension. You will notice that the toes return to their normal position and that there is a perceptible feeling of relaxation in the corresponding muscles. Next, try to identify the muscles in your ankle that control the movement of your foot. There are a number of muscles in this area, but see if you can isolate one or two. As before, begin by slowly tensing these muscles. The easiest way is to tense your foot so that the the toes are drawn up toward the front of the leg. Do this slowly and gradually, so that you feel a rise in muscle tension in the ankle. As before, maintain the tension in this area for two or three seconds, then gradually allow the foot to return to its normal resting point. Now repeat the same procedure with the other foot.

Continue in this manner to the muscles in your calf, around your knee, and in your thigh, first in one leg and then in the other. Tense each muscle set, hold it for a few seconds, and then release the tension. When you have finished this phase of the exercise, you will have alternately tensed and released most of the major muscle sets in the lower part of your body.

Continue moving upward and become aware of the muscles in the lower part of your belly, the abdominal area. These muscles are often very tense in performers, who find it difficult to breathe deeply as a result. It is especially important to alternately tense and release these muscles. Continuing to move upward, repeat the procedure for the muscles in the chest, which help support the upper body. And although they do not control breathing when they are tense, effective breathing can be inhibited. It is important, therefore, to become aware of tension levels in the chest area and to learn to deeply relax them.

The muscles of the shoulders are also an important source of tension. Many performers elevate their shoulders as they become progressively tense, and you may already know what it feels like to be tense in these areas. The task now is to relax the muscles. Alternately tense and release the muscles on both the right and left side, until you have achieved a perceptible and comfortable state of relaxation. Continue by moving down each arm from the shoulder, tensing and releasing the upper arm, elbow area, and forearm of each arm in succession. Finally, clench and unclench your fist in the same way that you did your toes at the beginning of this exercise.

The head and neck comprise the final area to be relaxed. Beginning with the back of the neck, try to identify the muscles in this area that help support the head. Tense and then release these muscles. Then turn your attention to the muscles of your face. Although this might feel odd, contort your face into a frown, bring your eyebrows down, and move the lower part of your mouth up, as if you were trying to swallow your eyebrows. This rather ridiculous image does convey a means of inducing tension in these facial muscles. As before, hold the tension for a few seconds and then release it. Finally, tense and release the muscles of your forehead.

The preceding description, although abbreviated, will give you a general idea of how progressive relaxation proceeds. We cannot, however, overemphasize the importance of pacing the exercise so that you carry it out in a slow, relaxed, and deliberate manner. As you begin practicing this exercise, start with only a few muscles sets at a time, rather than trying to work through the entire exercise at once. Remember that you are learning a new skill and—like any other skill—it takes time to perfect.

As you become increasingly comfortable with this procedure, you will more easily become relaxed with a minimum of effort. When you begin learning this technique, allocate at least two periods a day, at least twenty minutes each, to experiment and practice. As you experiment, you will find ways of modifying the procedure to make it especially helpful for you. Try it at different times of the day; vary the cadence of your breathing; do the relaxation exercise in different areas of your body; in general, try to tailor the procedures to help you achieve the maximum benefit.

Relaxation training is one of the most important and fundamental skills in stress and anxiety management. The time you invest in learning relaxation techniques, even though it may be considerable at first, will be amply rewarded if you persist. Relaxation training also helps lay the foundation for other stress management techniques. You will see, for example, that the discussion of imagery in the next section presupposes that you are already somewhat familiar with relaxation.

## Imagery

As part of their practice routines, many performers use mental rehearsal—forming images in their minds of the performance and how they hope to perform. Mental rehearsal techniques are only one way to prepare for a performance that can be undertaken away from the instrument. Other common, related techniques include motivational strategies like giving oneself "pep talks," mentally reviewing the musical score, and working out detailed plans for the performance and the events surrounding it.

Yet the use of such mental strategies in advance of a performance is often hit-or-miss, depending mainly on the effectiveness with which such techniques are employed. Some performers, for example, distract themselves or otherwise interfere with effective preparation because of the way they approach mental rehearsal. A cartoon by Gary Larson captioned "Roger screws up" shows an unfortunate cymbal player who's obviously been telling himself, "This time I won't screw up, I won't, I won't . . ." since well before the performance began—oblivious to the fact that he's holding only one cymbal! This illustrates that, to be effective, mental rehearsal (a) needs to be done in combination with proper practice and preparation, and (b) should focus on a more positive aspect of the performance rather than on just "not screwing up."

The effectiveness of mental rehearsal techniques has been demonstrated quite successfully in studies of athletes. Basketball players, for example, show improved free-throw shooting percentages when they engage in mental rehearsal prior to the act of shooting the ball. The benefit of this technique has been found to lie somewhere in between live practice and no practice at all.

The effectiveness of mental rehearsal techniques, therefore, depends partly on the degree to which they are incorporated into active practicing, preparing, and performing. They can not substitute for other forms of preparation, but they do provide an extra margin of security because they can reinforce learning. One advantage of such techniques is that they make it possible to visualize an ideal performance of a work—even if this level of accomplishment cannot actually be achieved. The performer can imagine, for instance, playing a technically demanding passage in a musically sensitive manner, free of technical limitations or mechanical errors. The effect of such an image can be similar to that of attending a performance by an artist whose interpretation of a piece evokes such a powerful overall image that it can, at least temporarily, elevate the level of one's playing. Active rehearsal, particularly when frequent and systematic, can help achieve and sustain such an effect.

An important distinction should be made between the idea that "practice makes perfect" and "practice makes *permanent*."[7] Practice of any sort, including mental rehearsal, helps a performer develop consistent behavior, but does not guarantee "perfection." Imagining oneself playing a piece perfectly does not guarantee that one can do so in reality any more than systematic, live rehearsal, but it does help ensure that the piece will be played to the best of the performer's capabilities. Students who frequently lament "I practiced this piece for hours and *thought* I could play it perfectly!" are missing the point: they're aiming for an idealized goal, perfection, rather than for refinement of their individual skills. Similarly, believing that mental rehearsal of a flawless performance will ensure its realization is unrealistic. The purpose of mental rehearsal is to set new images for performing that serve as goals to be gradually achieved through the refinement of one's techniques. Mental practice should be viewed as a useful tool, not a magical technique that ensures a flawless performance.

Like any tool, mental rehearsal profits from being used effectively. Certain features of mental rehearsal appear to maximize its effectiveness, just as some ways of practicing a piece of music are more effective than others. It's especially important to realize that the amount of time one spends in active or mental rehearsal is not the best predictor of success—far more important is how you practice. Recent work by a number of psychologists has provided evidence that several specific factors enhance the effectiveness of mental rehearsal.

For years, Psychologist Martin Seligman has investigated the causes and manifestations of psychological depression. He coined the term "learned helplessness" to characterize the attitude of people who have developed a passive, hopeless, and pessimistic approach to the world as part of their depression.[8] More recently, he has shifted his focus to the opposite situation, to people whose active, optimistic stance toward life appears to make them especially successful in coping with everyday events. Seligman has found that a basic optimism—expecting a favorable outcome from your efforts—is an important aspect of planning and visualizing things before doing them. An optimistic attitude does not guarantee success, of course, but, rather reflects an outlook that allows for less-than-optimal results while also predisposing the individual toward favorable outcomes. According to Seligman, effective responses to many stressful situations—such as those encountered by performers—result from a combination of optimism, ability, and motivation.

What does this have to do with mental rehearsal? Seligman's findings suggest that positive mental images before a performance will have a more beneficial effect on the performance than pessimistic mental imagery. A performer who anticipates failure and danger in a forthcoming recital is less likely to do well than someone whose preparatory mental rehearsal is based on greater optimism.

Aside from optimism, performers would do well to keep in mind several other aspects of effective mental imagery. These include six helpful suggestions by Buffington.[9]

1. Stress accuracy in mental—as well as actual—practice. When you mentally rehearse a piece of music, work out a detailed image of how you expect the music to sound and what you must do to achieve the desired effect. It's a good idea to write down the features of your imagery exercise, so that you can make your mental practice consistent from one time to the next. Make sure that your imagery corresponds to the physical activity in a live performance, otherwise you may work at cross-purposes and/or detract from the overall effect.

2. Along with imagining yourself performing, build in some positive images that emphasize your capabilities and skills. For example, you might develop a visual image of yourself onstage before a

live audience. As you imagine this scene in detail, accompany it with statements like "I know I can do this." With continued association, such images will help you develop a sense of security.

3. Cultivate an attitude that puts problems and difficulties in perspective, without denying their reality. Seligman has identified three important aspects of such realistic optimism: (1) most problems are temporary, (2) specific problems, such as a troublesome measure that doesn't seem to yield to practice, in no way guarantee general failure, and (3) most people have more control over situations than they suppose. A balanced attitude can help you anticipate and visualize problems in advance and aid in generating feasible solutions.

4. Learn to focus your imagery on performing itself, so that you can eventually screen out less-relevant factors. Being task oriented in your mental imagery means that you focus on hearing yourself play the first few notes of a piece in your mind, rather than on how the audience might react or how long you expect to be onstage. If you are a pianist and are attuned to visual images, practicing visualizing your hands as they play a passage will probably be of greater help than visualizing in detail how you will appear to the audience. Picture the score in detail; try to visualize even ledger lines and notes from your vantage point at the keyboard. The more you are able to visualize yourself in the performance situation, the better you will be able to simulate the feelings and events that you will eventually experience.

5. Make your mental rehearsals (as well as your live rehearsals) correspond as closely as possible to the circumstances of the performance. For example, practice at the same time of day you expect to perform. Mental rehearsal is especially helpful when you don't have access to your instrument—it can be done virtually anywhere. Try to simulate the physical state that you expect in the performance during some of your mental rehearsal sessions. The point is to create an overall effect that emulates the conditions under which you will actually perform.

6. Give the practice and refinement of mental rehearsal a chance to develop its effect. This skill requires rehearsal, and may not work especially effectively the first few times you try it. Pay attention to the circumstances under which you practice. Just as active practice profits from minimal distractions, mental rehearsal is likely to be

most effective under relatively tranquil conditions. Even if you are unable to control the external environment to achieve this effect, you can often achieve inner tranquility through deep breathing and other relaxation techniques.

Mental rehearsal and imagery can be very useful tools for many performers. Research has shown that they can augment the effects of live practice and have the added benefit of being available when one does not have access to an instrument. Used in conjunction with breathing and relaxation techniques, mental practice can help develop an association between feeling relaxed and what one does. These techniques belongs in the repertoire of preparatory techniques of every performer.

To give you a clearer idea of how to use these procedures, try the following self-assessment exercise, which is based on imagining the audience. The purpose of this exercise is to help you learn how you might respond to different types of audiences. This is a "guided imagery" exercise, in which you will be asked to visualize certain scenes in great detail while in a state of relaxed concentration. It can be too distracting to undertake the exercise while reading the instructions, so you should familiarize yourself with the sequence of images before beginning.

Begin with the quieting response to achieve a state of relaxation. (It will be helpful if you have already practiced the quieting response, but if you are unfamiliar with this procedure, refer to page 171). In a state of deep relaxation, you should feel relaxed, yet alert and capable of noticing what is going on in different areas of your body.

The exercise consists of developing a succession of detailed images of different types of audiences and checking to see how you respond to each. There is no need to develop all four images in a single session, nor is it essential to limit yourself to those suggested here. But here are four situations that you may find interesting to begin with:

1. By yourself in a practice room.
2. In a studio during a lesson or coaching session.
3. Before an audience of friends and colleagues.
4. Before a large audience of strangers.

Assume that you are performing music that poses significant challenges to your skills and powers of concentration.

As you introduce and develop each image in detail, see what you notice about your physical responses. These reactions may be very slight, almost imperceptible. They may catch you by surprise, like a muscle twitch you have never experienced before, and may interrupt the image you are developing and cause you to become distracted. You may want to alter them immediately, but as much as possible, maintain your focus on the image while you become aware of the variety of ways in which you are responding to the image.

Don't be surprised if this procedure seems difficult at first. It is not easy to attend to more than one thing at a time. What you're doing is like keeping your eyes on a distant island while standing on the deck of a moving boat. You can keep the island in view even as you are aware of the motion of the boat, the feel of the wind on your face, the warmth of the sun, and the shifting tension in your legs as you maintain your balance. In the same way, when experimenting with each of these images, fix them clearly in your mind, like the island, while becoming aware of how you are reacting.

When you have completed the exercise and returned to your normal awareness, consider how you responded to each image. Note the various sensations you experienced and be especially attentive to those involving apprehension, anxiety, or fear. Describe them to yourself; check them in detail; see how they relate to your feelings in comparable real situations. Be especially attentive to signs of stress in situations where you think of yourself as comfortable—for example, when practicing alone or working with a trusted teacher or coach.

## Cognitive Restructuring

The way we think about things largely determines how we feel, and if this statement seems to imply that thoughts direct our feelings, then we should hasten to add that the reverse can hold true as well. Whichever way you look at it, thoughts ("cognitions") play a significant role in how we feel, so that an analysis of the way we think about things is essential for effective stress and anxiety management.

It's one thing to say that cognitions are important determinants of feelings, but quite another to understand the implications of this connection for anxiety. First, we should clarify what we mean by "cognitions." In part, as mentioned elsewhere, we are referring to the stream of mental activity that takes place during most of our waking hours. Sometimes thoughts are very perceptible, but at other times they seem muted and in the background. This flow of mental activity is something that we can become aware of by consciously deciding to focus on it, but tapping this stream of consciousness can present you with a welter of images and impressions that appear to have little logic. However, if you pay attention to these mental events, you are likely to discover that certain themes recur. Moreover, you will probably find yourself affected by them in some fashion. These are the raw materials that we refer to when we speak of "thoughts" or "cognitions".

But thinking is more than this stream of mental events. Our thoughts reflect deeply seated attitudes and beliefs of which we may be only minimally aware. These attitudes and beliefs, however, play a significant role in the degree of our stress or anxiety.

Thoughts like the following are commonly reported by performers. Most of them seem to be linked to certain attitudes that have been formed during years of practicing and performing:

> *Practice makes perfect.*
> *You're only as good as your* next *performance.*
> *There's no way I'll be able to memorize everything in time!*
> *I just know that* everyone *heard the mistake in the Beethoven!*
> *I can't stand the thought of letting everyone down if I play*
>  *poorly.*
> *I should be able to play better than Steve. He only started*
>  *playing three years ago, and besides that, he* never *practices.*
> *My whole career hinges on this one performance.*

Suppose that a performer is thinking about an upcoming performance. Even while practicing he will probably become aware of a stream of thoughts flowing through his mind. Perhaps, on reflection, he becomes aware of the following thoughts: "I don't know if I'll have this piece ready in time." "This is a very difficult piece to play, I'm not sure why I decided to perform it in the first place." "I'm sure there are going to be a lot of people present at the performance who will know this music, and who will be likely to criticize my playing of it." While each of these thoughts conveys specific ideas about the performance, collectively they reflect a broader attitude toward performing. This individual's underlying attitude, as shown by these thoughts, manifests insecurity. Expressed as a single statement of attitude, it might be, "I'm skeptical about my ability to cope with the demands of public performance." Such an attitude, distilled from individual thoughts, is very close to the "raw data" that we refer to when we talk about "cognitive restructuring."

Once we have linked our thoughts and feelings and illuminated the relationship between them and our underlying beliefs and attitudes, how do we change maladaptive attitudes toward performing? Let's consider in some detail some basic ideas on how to proceed with this activity. The technique we are discussing, "cognitive restructuring," is a process by which maladaptive thoughts and attitudes are brought to conscious awareness, tested to determine their accuracy, and then either challenged, revised, or altered as needed. This process can be broken down into the following four basic steps. *Step one* is becoming aware of thoughts and feelings, and, more generally, our interpretations of ongoing events. This process is termed "self-monitoring." You can engage in self-monitoring in a number of ways. Self-monitoring can involve nothing more than making a list of thoughts as they occur to you. To facilitate this, you might keep a notebook and pencil at hand so that you can record your thoughts from time to time. We especially recommend that you do this when you are either practicing or preparing for a performance, so that you can become aware of the nature of this mental activity. *Step two* is to gather information related to these thoughts and attitudes. To return to our earlier example, a performer who feels unequal to the task of performing would be asked to provide some evidence underlying this conclusion. Like a scientist testing a theory, the performer is asked to supply data that supports the accuracy of the underlying thought or attitude. This data-gathering stage is vital, because it helps establish the basic impressions we form about ourselves. Its important to note here that cognitive restructuring involves more than just replacing maladaptive thoughts with more positive variants. The procedure involves testing one's personal assumptions to determine which are accurate and which are not. So this second step of gathering information about the basis of one's thoughts is essential to the process of dealing with the cognitive component of anxiety.

*Step three* involves analyzing the data you have obtained and determining how well it fits with how you view yourself. Anxious or highly stressed people often interpret things that happen to them in distorted ways. For example, performers with perfectionist attitudes toward performing but little self-confidence may selectively look for evidence that reinforces their poor self-image. During a practice session, such performers may become preoccupied with one note out of thousands in a piece of music that they just can't seem to play accurately or musically. During a rehearsal, they may focus on what they perceive as critical comments by those in attendance, completely ignoring positive feedback. In this phase of cognitive restructuring, the performer begins to examine the ways in which thought patterns affect one's self-image.

*Step four* entails making changes in dysfunctional attitudes so that they fit more closely with the information that has been collected. For example, a performer who believes, "I just can't play from memory," may, after examining this belief, find that it is not entirely true. Instead, it may be more accurate to rephrase this as follows: "Unless I have prepared extremely well and am comfortable with the audience, playing this particular piece from memory is very challenging." Thus, many of our beliefs are shorthand ways of making statements about ourselves that need to be elaborated in greater detail. This telegraphic style of thinking reflects the fact that our beliefs and attitudes are often summarized impressions, based on a great deal of information, not all of which is completely consistent. Cognitive restructuring, as described here, provides an understanding of how thoughts which can be observed through "self-monitoring," can affect feelings, and may, moreover, reflect underlying beliefs that may have to change as you become increasingly comfortable in performing.

Many of the maladaptive attitudes that performers have about themselves and their performance capabilities are based on more than personal experience. In particular, many musicians have been told "truisms" about music by parents, teachers, and others. Some of these ideas were listed earlier (p. 18), and we suggest that you consider them in detail. Look for examples of thoughts or ideas you believe are unquestionably accurate and which have played a role in shaping your development as a musician and a performer. The simple question to ask about each of these is, "Is this true of myself?" When you can identify and articulate your beliefs about yourself and what it means to perform, you will made substantial steps toward managing your anxiety effectively.

If the way you think about performing is creating problems, here are some additional ways of working on the thoughts, attitudes, and underlying beliefs that can affect your feeling when you perform.[10]

1. *Identify the troublesome thoughts.* Keep a list; write them down; look for patterns that repeat themselves. Recognize that your thoughts are not the same as reality, that they reflect your analysis of what happens to you.

Consider the experience of a flautist who was intensely anxious at the prospect of an upcoming orchestral concert in which she had to play a brief solo. Upon reflection, she noticed that any mention of the concert triggered "butterflies" in her stomach and the associated thought, "I can *never* get through the performance without something bad happening." This thought, in turn, made her so uneasy that she would find some sort of diversion to distract her. It was so highly integrated with her feelings and behavior that she was not really aware of thinking anything in particular. Rather, when she felt apprehensive, she would quickly distract herself from anything related to the concert in a reflexive way.

Her apprehension appeared to be intensified by the automatic thought that she would inevitably fail, yet she was hardly aware of such thoughts until she began to actively keep track of them. By doing this, she accomplished two things. First, she learned to distinguish between "reality" and her interpretation of it. Imagining a catastrophy at the casual mention of her concert reflected an interpretive distortion of what was only a remote possibility. Second, she learned to interrupt the smooth chain of associations between events she perceived, her interpretations of these events, and her consequent responses. This understanding eventually helped minimize her anxious thoughts, which were out of proportion to the actual threat posed by the concert.

2. *Examine the evidence* underlying your thoughts and beliefs; collect some actual data. A pianist in her third year of college became increasingly inhibited about playing in public. She reported thinking, "I look foolish to everyone in the audience. I just know they're aware how anxious I am when I play, and I'm sure they

talk about me all the time." This student had, on many occasions, experienced intense anxiety, which was manifested in profuse sweating, trembling, and blushing. In a group with other performers, she was able to gain an accurate perspective on how people in the audience perceived her. Yes, people were occasionally aware that she blushed; no, they were not aware that she was sweating or shaking. Her intense experience of these symptoms made her assume that they were obvious to everyone else. People who heard her play talked afterwards about the intensity and musicality of her playing, but they did not mention what was to her the most visible feature of her performing—the symptoms of her anxiety.

3. *Conduct experiments* to test your thoughts and related ideas. Look for opportunities to perform in which you can try out different ways of coping with your apprehensions. Arrange a series of practice performances for groups of different size and composition so that you can learn how you are likely to be affected by different audiences. While preparing for his senior recital, one student, who had previously performed as infrequently as possible, realized that he had very little idea about how he might respond to playing a recital he knew many of his classmates would dread. He arranged a series of run-throughs, each scheduled a day or two ahead of time, and played for listeners whom he viewed as authoritative and knowledgable to evaluate his reactions to the performance environment. He found, on the positive side, that live performances increased his level of alertness—a natural effect of the arousal that most performers experience. On the other hand, he found that his finger dexterity was somewhat inhibited by a pronounced hand tremor, although with each succeeding performance the tremor diminished slightly. When he gave the actual recital, he was not only aware of how he would respond, but he had "damped out" some of the signs of arousal engendered by the performance situation.

4. Finally instead of constantly criticizing yourself, perhaps you might try to *talk with yourself* as you would to a friend with a similar problem.

## Low-Stress Practice

When beginning to practice a new piece of music, it's important to be attentive to subtle indications of excessive muscular and psychological tension. There is a perceptible difference between relaxed, yet focused concentration, and effortful, strained attention to a task, which taxes one's capabilities. Tension of the latter sort is an uneconomical and unnecessary investment of physical and mental energy. Several factors can contribute to excessive levels of tension, including:

1. A tempo beyond one's level of skill.
2. Unnecessary muscular tension, such as grimaces or postural anomalies, that has little to do, either motorically or artistically, with musical playing.
3. Excessive self-talk, which divert's one's attention from playing. For example, reactions to technically difficult passages often include thoughts like "I can *never* play this" or "I *have* to learn this in order to *get through* this piece," which tend to heighten frustration instead of enhancing learning.

Such tensions are perhaps natural when one is confronted by challenging music; however, if they persist while the music is being rehearsed, they can cause several problems for the performer. First, they represent competing information (like static on a telephone line) that diverts one's attention from learning. Second, tension may become associated with specific passage to the point that is likely to be automatically evoked by the performance of the music.

When a piece is being learned, these residual levels of tension can accumulate to the point that they may interfere with a smooth, relaxed performance. Sensitivity to these subtle feelings requires the performer to pay attention to internal cues and sensations reflecting the cognitive and muscular correlates of tension. The primary purpose of this suggestion is to ensure that the piece is learned and practiced with minimal muscular and psychological tension. Practicing in a relaxed, yet focused manner is a good way to achieve this purpose.

The following exercise can help you become aware of subtle sources of tension. Try to wear loose-fitting, comfortable clothes that don't restrict body movement or inhibit sensation.

Begin by sitting in a chair in which you would feel comfortable practicing and learning music. If you are a keyboard player, sit comfortably on the bench. Have your instrument available, but don't do anything with it. Take two or three minutes to sit quietly, gradually turning your attention inwardly to the feelings and sensations created by the way you're sitting. Orient yourself to internal, rather than external, sensations. These preparations should help you become aware of how the various parts of your body feel as you prepare to learn new music. Proceed by shifting your attention to areas where muscular tension is especially likely to accumulate. How much tension do you feel in your neck and shoulders? Is there more tension in these areas than is needed to support your head and to sit upright? If so, try to release the excess tension, perhaps by alternately tensing and relaxing the muscles a few times. You may find other ways to release the tension, so experiment until you've found something that works. Turn your attention to the lower back area and take stock of how tense the muscles there feel. Once again, are you aware of excess tension—more than you need to sit comfortably? Continue in this fashion for a few minutes, gently adjusting the way you're sitting to minimize excessive muscular tension.

Now take a few minutes to focus on inner sensations other than those from your muscles. Can you detect your heartbeat? Can you become aware of how deeply you're breathing? Do you notice any other sensations related to your physical state? As with muscle tension, we often expend more energy than is necessary to achieve a particular effect. Your breathing, for instance, may be relatively rapid and shallow, as if you were gearing up for an athletic event or were frightened by something. Check the sensations of the more peripheral parts of your body, like fingers and toes. Can you detect anything particular, for example, like whether they are relatively cold or warm? Excessive tension is usually manifested by feelings of coldness and, perhaps, less sensitivity. Sitting quietly for a few minutes will probably cause a feeling of warmth to develop, so relax while this process is going on.

Now turn your attention for a few minutes to the thoughts and images in your mind, without trying to focus on any one in particular. See if you can "watch" your thoughts as they ebb and flow, allowing them to run freely. As with the other sensations, you may find that, as you sit quietly for a few minutes, the number and vividness of your thoughts and images may diminish or increase. Allow this to happen naturally, without trying to force anything.

When you have spent some time directing your attention to the sensations and images from within, slowly begin to turn your attention toward your instrument, still without playing. Gradually bring it into focus, noticing its many features and qualities. As you do, check yourself inwardly for changes in any of the areas you've been reflecting on: posture and muscular tension, other physical sensations, or mental images and thoughts.

Now turn to the music that you are studying, and again try to detect changes in posture, internal sensations, or thoughts. As you scan the music in anticipation of playing, see how you feel. Are you more tense? Do you experience even a minute increase in tension or apprehension, or subtle changes in how you are sitting? Do you feel a sudden, yet subtle, rush of adrenalin as your system gears up for action? When you have checked out these feelings for a few minutes, gently bring yourself back to your customary state of wakefulness and alertness.

This exercise provides some indication of the diversity of the physical, cognitive, and behavioral sensations that are frequently taken for granted or overlooked when one's attention focused on playing music. To the extent that you can feel such subtle pleasant or unpleasant sensations, you're becoming aware of nonmusical phenomena that may have become associated with the music you are learning. The goal of all this is to help you develop behavioral, mental, and physical patterns that are condusive to learning and that you wish to associate with the music. Practicing when you are excessively mentally or physically tense makes these states more likely to recur when the music is performed later. In other words, we learn a great deal more than simply the music we're practicing: feelings and sensations that become associated with the music can be evoked when the music is later recreated during a performance.

We have considered a number of techniques routinely used by psychologists to help people who experience distressful tension and anxiety. Beyond these are many other techniques that you might wish to consider, though a detailed consideration of them is beyond the scope of this book.

# Anxiety and Stress in Perspective

Throughout this book are many suggestions for ways to deal with the stresses and strains of performing. If you take the time to read the whole book and try out these ideas, you will find that, over time, they can help you become comfortable with performing. However, it is also useful to have a more integrative view of musical performance anxiety, its effects, and what can be done to alleviate the resultant distress. This chapter reviews some practical basic ideas about performance anxiety and what you can do to deal with its effects.

It's helpful to remember that musical performance anxiety is a very common "occupational hazard" for all musicians. We usually associate it with solo performing, but many other musicians, including ensemble players, have to deal with significant levels of anxiety. Even conductors, as well as performers, may encounter the problem as well. Although conductors may not seem as obviously involved in actually playing as are performers, their role can, nonetheless, be extremely trying. The basic lesson here is that really no one involved in musical performance activities is immune from anxiety or stress. In fact, one especially helpful perspective on performance anxiety is found in the book, *Conducting Techniques,* by Brock McElheran.

A point made by McElheran, with which we wholeheartedly agree, is that training and talent are useless if a performer is too apprehensive to use these skills in public, and in his brief book McElheran elegantly summarizes some basic suggestions about anxiety management that we feel are extremely useful. Of course, there are many other such resources for performers and a wealth of materials on performance anxiety which we encourage you to explore. You will find that each author may have a slightly different perspective on the problem, but that certain underlying ideas keep recurring. Here are some practical suggestions about managing anxiety advocated by McEhleran.

1. Be thoroughly prepared. Remember that none of the techniques in this book will be of much help if you don't have a solid musical foundation.
2. Play well within the boundaries of your technical skills. Many performers try to play in public their most difficult pieces, leaving themselves little reserve to cope with the demands on a performer in a live performance. Pieces that you struggle with in the comparative safety of the practice room are not good candidates for the stage.
3. Keep in mind that most performers have to contend with anxiety. Many famous musicians, athletes, and others in the public eye have to deal with the same fear and apprehension as the neophyte perfomer. If you feel anxious, remember that you are in good company. Perhaps this will help put things in perspective the  next time you're standing backstage and feel like running out of the concert hall and never coming back!
4. Maintain your normal routine when preparing a performance. Although it may be necessary to allow extra time for practice, it's also important not to neglect one's regular activities. Some musicians become so preoccupied with performing that their lives become essentially one dimensional.
5. Consider the question "What am I really afraid of?" Perhaps you could imagine some worst-case scenarios, such as a totally disastrous performance in which you flee the stage as members of the audience laugh hysterically or demand their money back! Although such an outcome is extremely unlikely, being able to visualize such a ridiculous scenario, and then perhaps laugh at it, can help you admit to yourself fears that you would much rather

not think about. It's also a way to acknowledge that you, like everyone, can make mistakes. The simple act of contemplating the worst can sometimes restore a sense of perspective and even inject humor into otherwise deeply foreboding anxieties.

6. Try to put your life, including performing into proper perspective. So what if you have a bad performance? Is it really the end of the world? Does it mean you will never perform again in the future?

7. Try to overlook minor errors when you perform; they "come with the territory." If you listen to commercial performances as points of comparison, remember that studio recordings are extensively edited to eliminate mistakes in the final version, unlike live performances. It's also important to keep in mind that listeners are more interested in the *overall* impressions created by music than they are in note-perfect performances.

8. Treat performing as an opportunity rather than as a death sentence. Your self-talk should emphasize that you *choose* to perform—no one can force you to go on stage against your will. You might play amateur psychologist with yourself by thinking of someone else who would gladly take your place should you decide to back out of a performance.

9. Act calmly, even if you feel nervous or upset. The more you dwell on feeling anxious, the more you become preoccupied with it, the worse you will feel. The converse of this holds true as well. Remember that the focus of your attention should be on communicating musical ideas, not anxious feelings.

10. Learn not to be surprised or dismayed if you feel tense or if you feel somewhat apprehensive before or during a performance. Remember that such feelings are natural, and try not to worry about them too much. During a performance, try to forget about yourself and the audience and simply get lost in the music. See if you can experience some of the pleasure you are undoubtedly giving to your listeners. Worrying about the audience, the reactions of critics, or sweaty palms only detracts from the enjoyment

of becoming immersed in the music. The more you're able to concentrate exclusively on the musical expression, the less likely you are to feel anxious. Try to make performing something that *everyone* can enjoy. (Adapted from McElhern, *Conducting Technique*)

Consider any of these ideas as suggestions that may be of help in your particular situation. Try to read as much as you can about what other musicians, performers, and authors say about stress, anxiety, and performing. Talk with your friends and colleagues about your experiences as performers, and be willing to share both the good and bad memories. In other words, take an active approach to the problem of anxiety—don't let it ruin your life. Let's now take one last look at anxiety, how it affects performers, and how you can begin to cope with it.

## How Anxiety Expresses Itself

As you know by now, anxiety is expressed in three ways. First, anxious people report persistent frightening thoughts. Such thoughts, a manifestation of "self-talk," tend to persist despite our best efforts to dispel them. Sometimes they are expressed as mental images, or frightening, worrisome mental pictures we like to characterize as "gremlins," which can divert one's attention from the music. Second, anxiety may take the form of physical sensations, such as sweating, trembling, or nausea. These sensations are part of an inborn response system that helps us deal with risk or danger. This response is innate and really can't be eliminated. Rather, you can learn to expect these feelings, so that they become less distressing than if you believe that they indicate something is wrong with you. The third major component of anxiety, the behavioral factor, involves the urge to run away or hide from the source of one's fears. For performers, this tendency often takes the form of avoiding practicing, because the mere thought about a forthcoming performance may evoke distressful anxiety.

## How Anxiety Can Affect Us

The effects of anxiety and, more generally, the emotional states of performers, should be considered from three temporal vantage points: in advance of, during, and after a performance. Before a performance, anxiety may be expressed in anticipatory, catastrophic thoughts—expecting that the worst will happen. "Expecting the worst" may mean different things to different people; but expectations may vary anywhere from having a minor memory slip to actually dying on stage.[1] Pre-performance anxiety may have other effects, such as causing one to practice too much and too hard, or too little. Over practice often results from extreme anxiety linked to a lack of self-confidence. While there is nothing wrong with in-depth preparation—and a successful performance may take many months of preparation—some performers overdo it. A major risk in practicing too much is that it may make one vulnerable to physical impairments, such as "overuse syndromes." On the other hand, anxiety sometimes leads performers to avoid practicing. In this case, thoughts of an impending performance evoke so much trepidation that the performer avoids the anxiety by staying away from the practice room. Although such behavior seems to make little objective sense, to an anxious person, almost anything associated with the performance triggers anxiety, and is to be avoided. In the long run, such a strategy is obviously not helpful, because failure to practice or prepare properly may bring about the catastrophic outcome that the anxious performer anticipates.

The effects of anxiety may be manifest in several ways during a performance as well. First, anxiety inhibits spontaneity and makes performers play cautiously, with a minimum of musical expression. Anxious performers seem intent on avoiding mistakes, rather than accepting that errors are often inevitable byproducts of musical expressiveness. Anxious performers tend to play very cautiously and exert excessive conscious control over their performing. In doing so, they actually *increase* the likelihood that they will make technical errors. A second effect of anxiety during a performance is that it calls attention to itself in a most distracting way. Not only do you experience the symptoms of anxiety, but you also begin to think about them, diverting your attention from your music. This quality of anxiety is related to its role as a protective, innate defensive response to perceived danger, and it is difficult to ignore. Of course, performances do not usually pose physical risks, but our biological systems can be "fooled" into this threat response. Fortunately, the more one performs, the more the intensity of these symptoms tends to diminish. Moreover, the symptoms also become easier to ignore, because with experience one comes to realize that this warning signal is a "false alarm," that does not signify real danger. The final point to make about anxiety during a performance is that it is often a source of embarrassment to the performer. Some performers sweat profusely, tremble visibly, or show other signs of anxiety that they feel will be cause for ridicule or criticism by those in the audience. Furthermore, many performers are embarrassed to admit to anxiety, as if to do so is a sign that they are less capable performers than those who do not feel anxious. We can summarize all this by noting that anxiety during a performance increases self-consciousness and diverts one's attention away from the music.

The period of time *after* a performance is marked by a sense of relief and fatigue, a natural consequence of the enormous amount of energy expended during the performance. Although we do not usually think of this phase as involving anxiety, many performers experience depression or tension at the conclusion of what others may have perceived as a highly successful performance. This emotional rollercoaster often catches performers by surprise because its natural to anticipate the aftermath of such an event as a time to take pride in one's accomplishments. Nonetheless, depression, apathy, tension, or anxiety are predictable responses to the end of a long process in which one has invested so much. If you consider the performance as a whole, this gradual expenditure of energy is visible well before the performance begins. Most performers feel highly "charged up" before beginning to play and then become progressively less tense as the performance progresses. By the end, the marked expenditure of both physical and mental energy can leave a performer drained and limp from exhaustion.

## What Anxiety Represents

The feelings and symptoms of anxiety are caused by a natural state of activation, which is the body's way of preparing to deal with danger. Throughout this book, we have emphasized that anxiety is a normal response, not a sign of psychological pathology. However, we are well aware that anxiety can sometimes get out of hand, and it can be difficult to reconcile the fact that something so distressful can really serve any useful purpose.

The imprecise way we use the term "anxiety" in everyday speech probably contributes to the confusion about what it really represents. To begin with, it's important to consider separately the sensations of activation from the thoughts and ideas that accompany this state.[2] From our perspective, the essence of anxiety is found in the unrealistically fearful *interpretation* of a physical state that is quite normal. In other words, anxious people tend to associate risk and danger with the sensations of physical activation. It is as if their internal warning system is too sensitive, like an automobile alarm that is triggered by an accidental bump, rather than by a deliberate attempt to break into the car.

Anxiety may also represent a response to memories of past performance experiences that overloaded one's musical skills. Many musicians have a history of playing music beyond their technical or musical capabilities. When they attempt to do so in performance situations where the audience may be critical or judgmental, (such as a college faculty jury or recital), they may have little margin for error. Anxious performers often show a pattern of selecting music that, while not beyond their capabilities, is really only playable under conditions where there is little stress or pressure. The anxiety they feel during a performance is a warning signal telling them that they are on the verge of overtaxing, or overloading, their reservoir of coping skills.[3]

## Factors Related to Performance Anxiety

A number of factors bear on the amount of anxiety you may feel as a performer. Throughout this book we have discussed many of these, but here, in summary, are five of the major ones. First, consider your musical repertoire. Is it comfortably within your musical and technical capabilities? Is it music that *you* enjoy playing? Is it on the other hand music that you feel you *ought* to play? It is helpful to be able to clarify your various motives for selecting particular music. Whenever you perform, try to select music that you find personally meaningful and enjoyable. Nothing is more difficult for a performer than attempting to be artistically expressive while playing music that evokes no personal feelings or meaning.

Second, consider your style of learning, preparation, and practice. How do you learn a new piece of music? Do you take the piece apart, note by note, and work out the fingerings carefully before attempting to play the whole piece? What is your style of practice? Do you tend to repeat a piece of music without trying to make each repetition somewhat better or different than the previous one? More generally, what are the circumstances under which you are most likely to learn something? Do you work best under pressure? If you do, perhaps you have never given yourself the chance to learn something with the luxury of time on your side. Part of becoming comfortable as a performer involves knowing as much as possible about how you can best learn what will later be performed.

A third factor to consider is your past experiences as a performer. Do you have pleasant or unpleasant memories? Are you aware of how well your own assessments of your performing have matched those of others who heard you play? Remember that performers tend to be self-critical, and often belittle their accomplishments, even when by other standards they have done well. In reviewing your past experiences as a performer, try to obtain a balanced view of your successes and failures. Anxiety is significantly related to consistently negative assessments of how one has performed. If you can find even a bit of positive evidence, you are likely to feel more self-confident in the future. Clearly, the way we interpret the past markedly affects our prospects for coping with future performance challenges. It's not really a matter of the number of performances you have given, so much as what you have learned from them. While we do recommend performing frequently to minimize anxiety, its equally important to learn something new from each performance, hopefully something positive enough to make you eagerly anticipate the next opportunity. Simply going through the motions of one performance after another is not likely to be beneficial in the long run.

Another factor that influences performance anxiety is one's personality and temperament. Consider what you're like as a person. Do you enjoy performing? Perhaps you are normally somewhat shy and introverted, but you really blossom on stage. On the other hand, you may be very musically gifted, but nonetheless feel extremely self-conscious about performing. People differ in terms of how responsive they are to performance situations. We mentioned earlier that some people seem to have an unusually sensitive "trigger mechanism" that causes the alarm bells of anxiety to go off much more readily than for others. If you are such a highly sensitive individual, you may find it especially challenging to become reasonably comfortable in performance situations. It's important to take into account your personality, general behavioral traits and tendencies, and temperament, as you sort out the factors that contribute to your personal attitudes and feelings about performing.

A fifth important factor related to performance anxiety concerns relationships in your social and musical environment, including those with teachers, parents, friends, colleagues, and even audiences. Although it's common to think of performing as a highly individualized activity, music is a medium whose main purpose is to communicate to others. If you feel anxious while performing, examine how you feel in other situations that may not be such obvious sources of anxiety. For example, how do you feel before or during lessons or coaching sessions? Does your breathing change, or do your hands sweat when you play for a coach or a teacher? Do other social circumstances make you feel anxious? Relationships with others may influence the music you select to perform, the conditions under which performances take place, and your reasons for performing. It's a good idea to give some thought to how socially oriented you are as a performer and as a person. The more you find that you truly enjoy music and take pleasure in sharing it with other people, the less likely it is that anxiety will impede performing.

## Coming to Terms with Anxiety

You will find many suggestions throughout this book on how you can deal with the effects of anxiety and stress as a performer. However, as a summary, we would like to make three overall suggestions.

### Step One: Become Aware of Your Anxiety

At the outset, the most important step in dealing with anxiety is becoming aware of its effects on you.[4] You may wonder why we suggest this, since you probably feel that it's hard to ignore the signs of anxiety. From a therapeutic standpoint, becoming aware of anxiety is really a process of self-discovery that requires some introspection. Lets review once again the basic steps in coming to grips with anxiety by becoming AWARE of it.[5] The A stands for *a*ccepting anxiety—viewing anxiety as a natural phenomenon that we needn't be afraid of. The W stands for *w*atching—becoming aware of and observing your anxiety. What are your specific symptoms? Do they include a dry mouth or sweaty palms? Feelings of panic or fear? People tend to experience anxiety in a uniquely personal way, and what may be troublesome to one person may not bother somebody else. Learning to observe anxiety can help you put it at a safe distance where it is not as likely to overwhelm you. The next letter A, reminds us to go ahead and *a*ct even though we may be feeling anxious. Stress and anxiety are a part of life for performers and everyone else. Try to give yourself permission to perform even though you feel anxious, keeping in mind that nearly every personal challenge poses certain risks along with rewards. Experienced and inexperienced performers alike—along with athletes, doctors, mountain climbers, and others who face daily challenges—all have to contend with anxiety. From this vantage point, you're in good company. It's a myth to think that accomplished performers are immune to anxiety. They *are* comparatively successful at keeping anxiety in proper perspective. Being anxious need not diminish your capabilities as a performer unless you become so preoccupied with it that you cannot focus on the music. In sum, this aspect of dealing with anxiety emphasizes the importance of learning to perform even though you feel anxious. The R in AWARE refers to *r*epeating the first three steps when you feel anxious. It means methodically practicing accepting, observing, and acting with anxiety until you eventually learn to respond almost reflexively. We can't overemphasize the importance of repeating these steps as often as needed, for the simple reason that learning to cope with anxiety takes a lot of practice. It helps if you can adopt a tolerant attitude toward anxiety, perhaps even use it to your advantage, rather than try to eliminate it from the experience as a performer. Related to this, the E in "AWARE" stands for *e*xpect, a reminder that anxiety "comes with the territory" of performing and does not signify anything abnormal. We are not saying this to be pessimistic, but rather to point out that most performers experience anxiety and eventually learn to cope with it.

You can do other things as well to become more attuned to anxiety and its effects. Recall, for instance, our earlier comments about learning, preparing, and practicing. Are they associated with anxiety? Does your practicing have an anxious, driven quality to it? Do you often repeat a piece of music or a passage without thinking about what you are doing? Do you practice with the attitude of a young child, thinking "If I play this piece ten times, it will be perfect!"? If so, you may be setting the stage for bouts of anxiety later on, for this is not an especially realistic sentiment. It's a good idea to try out a variety of techniques to increase your awareness of anxiety until you find something especially helpful. Experiment using the self-rating forms found throughout the book; make audio or videotapes of practice performances; ask others to listen to you perform and then provide detailed feedback. Schedule practice performances ahead of time so that you can practice waiting to perform. Finally—and perhaps most important—remember that effective practice is a mind*ful,* not mind*less* activity. Practice doesn't automatically "make perfect" so much as it makes *permanent* the results of your efforts. Casual practice, unthinking repetition, and, more generally, going through the motions of practicing are all likely to contribute to uncertain learning that will eventually affect your playing with a sense of tension that tends to precipitate anxiety.

As you practice becoming AWARE of anxiety, listen carefully to the many inner messages reflected in your thoughts, feelings, and behavior. Keep in mind that performing involves a special state of *activation* similar to, but not identical with, anxiety. The more you practice performing using the techniques described in this book, the more confident you will feel in keeping anxiety in proper perspective.

## Step Two: Skills Training

Once you learn to observe the various facets of anxiety, the next step in dealing with it is to develop some specific skills that will help you cope with anxiety effectively.[6] Throughout this book are discussions of techniques that include relaxation, imagery, and cognitive strategies, any of which can help deal with the effects of anxiety. We recommend that you study them carefully because, like new music, they cannot be practiced and learned overnight. Learning stress management skills is best done when you have time for practice and experimentation. Lets briefly review some of the basic ideas of relaxation, imagery, and cognitive restructuring so that you'll have an idea of where to begin this process.

First, make every effort to develop at least one reliable relaxation technique.[7] Whether you decide on the quieting response, meditation, progressive muscle relaxation, or some other technique, work with just one until you really feel comfortable with it. Try it out under different circumstances; experiment with it even when you are not feeling particularly tense. See how effective it is when you *are* under stress, and "fine tune" it for maximum effect. Eventually, it should help you regulate your physical and mental responses to otherwise highly stressful situations. During a performance, you may not necessarily want to feel completely relaxed, but rather achieve a state of "controlled activation" that enhances, rather than hinders, musical expressiveness. Knowing how to relax when you are learning music is important as well because you can incorporate the technique into a piece from the beginning, so that it becomes an integral component. Conversely, if your practicing is tense, rushed, and distracted, you will tend to evoke such qualities later on when you perform. Clearly, your frame of mind while practicing and learning is very likely to effect how you later feel when you perform.

Second, develop a capacity for mental imagery, a technique that is very useful at virtually every state of practice, preparation, and performing.[8] The ability to visualize music in great detail can improve the ease and dexterity with which it is performed. The imagery you find most helpful may have to be determined by trial and error. Although visual imagery is most often recommended, many musicians prefer to develop auditory or tactile modalities. Perhaps you could use all three to form a very detailed composite of performing. Whichever you choose, remember that the power of imagery depends on systematic practice.

The following narrative is an example of a combined relaxation and imagery exercise that one performer found particularly helpful. It begins with a reminder that, whenever you feel anxious, you can take some direct steps to prevent yourself from feeling overwhelmed.

First, breathe deeply and fully; sit comfortably so that you can breathe comfortably and easily; then take some deep breaths. Count to yourself, if you like, as you inhale and exhale. Begin by counting to three; (inhale) . . . 2 . . . 3 . . . (exhale) . . . 2 . . . 3. Allow yourself to become caught up in the rhythm of your breathing. Do whatever you can to relax your muscles so your breathing becomes deep and relaxed.

Second, allow your eyes to close gradually as you begin to relax. Allow tension to gradually evaporate as you close your eyes and begin to relax. Although it's not necessary, closing your eyes provides one way of diminishing the amount of external stimulation.

As you establish a pattern of deep, relaxed breathing, and as you gradually focus more on becoming relaxed, you may want to think of a word, a phrase, or an image that has a comfortable, relaxing quality. Repeat this to yourself in a relaxed way. Words like "peaceful," "relaxed," "calm," and "tranquil" may have a soothing effect, but many other words and images can have an equally relaxing effect. Perhaps you would like to imagine yourself in a peaceful Irish meadow, watching the sun rise over some green rolling hills, hearing the sound of birds in the distance as they awaken early in the morning. A mist hangs over a valley not far from you, and you can dimly see a herd of cows slowly moving from a barn to a field shrouded in mist . . .

Allow yourself to experience the sensations that accompany relaxation and be aware that you can affect the degree to which you can evoke them. You are in control, and can change the images, and your state of relaxation, smoothly and effortlessly.

As you become more deeply relaxed, you may become aware of muscle tension in different parts of your body. Slowly and gently, see if you can work some of the tension out so that the muscles in these areas begin to relax. You may find it helpful to momentarily tense the muscles, and then release. Alternate tensing and releasing until you begin to experience an absence of tension.

Experiment with different images and breathing patterns until you find one that really makes a difference in how you feel. Then focus on relaxing and visualize a soothing image that allows you to let go without feeling anxious or worried.

When you have spent some time in this state and feel that you'd like to return to full alertness, allow yourself to emerge gently and gradually. There's no need to rush. Take time to gradually bring yourself to full awareness, slowly opening your eyes and allowing whatever images you've been playing with to diminish, just like you imagined the cows in the meadow slowly and gradually moving into the mist of the Irish morning . . .

There are several notable features of this narrative. First, notice that it is highly personalized. This person found the image of an Irish meadow at sunrise to be very relaxing. Likewise, you can spend some time developing pictures and images you personally find relaxing, and then incorporate them into your own personal narratives. Exercises like this can take varying amounts of time, but we suggest that you not rush things. Try to find a time when you are not unduly pressured and do not have to hurry off to an appointment. Just as performers find it difficult to practice under time pressure, relaxation and imagery exercises will be most satisfying when you have time to devote your full attention to them.

This narrative uses both relaxation training and imagery. Notice how it begins with instructions to breathe deeply and fully, followed by closing the eyes to enhance the relaxation effect. Next, an image is developed to further enhance relaxation. By combining these three elements—breathing, turning inwardly, and then visualizing a relaxing image, you can experience a state of relaxation that is an effective antidote to the many sounds of stress associated with either the anticipation or reality of a performance.

The third skill we recommend learning is becoming aware of, and modifying thought patterns that contribute to your performance anxiety. It might seem odd to characterize this as a skill, but the capacity to become aware of maladaptive cognitive activity, like learning to relax or cultivate mental imagery, requires time and practice.[9] This is something that psychotherapists routinely teach their clients, and there is no reason for performers to neglect this aspect of coping with anxiety. Becoming aware of your thought processes may make you aware of how much other people affect your thinking. For example, a performer, who kept track of her thoughts while practicing became aware that much of what passed through her mind reflected the demands and impositions of other people. She became aware that both as a musician and a person, much of her behavior was governed by the expectations of other people. Her thoughts were filled with "shoulds" and "ought to's", a clear indiction that she was spending much of her time trying to meet the expectations of others.

*Step Three: Putting Skills into Practice*

Once you learn to become aware of anxiety and have acquired some skills to help you counteract its effects, the last, and perhaps most important step is to put it all into practice. This process is similar to a musician learning and practicing a piece of music before performing it. Stress coping skills need to be practiced when we are not under pressure to perform, they eventually have to be put into practice under circumstances that are extremely trying at best. How should they be done? Throughout this book, we have emphasized the importance of *gradual* exposure to performance situations, whether you are playing or just practicing relaxation skills. It's better to approach stressful performance situations gradually than in an all-or-none manner. All too often, performers feel that the best way to come to grips with performing is to expose themselves to extremely challenging situations. This idea is maladaptive for several of reasons, not the least of which is that such experiences may go awry because they apply psychological pressures that may seem overwhelming at the time of a performance. In contrast, gradual exposure to increasingly stressful performances via practice performances allows one to gradually and comfortably implement both the musical and relaxation skills you have been developing. If you are frightened at the prospect of playing before a large audience, begin by playing for two or three people and then progress to, perhaps, a half-dozen familiar individuals.

Our basic recommendation is that you find ways to try your newfound skills in performance situations that do not overtax your capabilities. It's best to learn music and perform it in circumstances that are not overwhelming, particularly at first, when you are still coming to terms with the music. Psychological skills such as relaxation, imagery, and cognitive monitoring are best practiced and implemented when you can devote your full attention to them. Later on, as you become comfortable with the process of relaxing, you will find it possible to utilize these skills at will, even during an anxiety-laden performance. Before getting to this stage, however, you must learn the techniques to the point where they are almost reflexive.

The preceding material is a distillation of the basic ideas about stress and anxiety found throughout this book. We hope it will enable you to begin to acquire the skills necessary to make headway against anxiety and its effects in performance contexts.

We believe that a certain amount of stress and anxiety come with the territory of being human as well as with being a performer. Even if you are a relatively stress-free performer, you will still encounter many psychological challenges in other areas of your life. We close, therefore, by presenting some basic principles of psychological well-being for your consideration. These ideas are directed toward you as a person, as much as a performer:

Cultivate a view of the world that is clear and relatively undistorted.

Learn to effectively analyze and cope with the challenges of everyday life.

Be flexible in the face of change and stress; a sense of humor helps, as well.

Be aware that most physically and psychologically draining conflicts can be effectively addressed by taking direct responsibility for your own behavior and the decisions that need to be made.

Maintain a positive personal identity that incorporates a sense of self worth, whatever your skills as a performer may be.

Learn to form mutually satisfying interpersonal relationships in which you give of yourself—and your talents— to others.

Try to relax and enjoy life despite its inevitable stresses and anxieties.

We hope that you will find the ideas presented in this book helpful in coping with the stressors associated with performing. Ultimately, you will probably gain the greatest benefit by adopting our ideas to your own personal situation through trial-and-error experimentation, as we have advocated throughout the book. We don't pretend to have all the answers to performance problems, but instead have tried to provide you with a perspective from which you can effectively evaluate your own skills, capabilities, and shortcomings as a performer and develop effective strategies for change and development. Good luck!

# Notes

## Chapter 1

1. Benjamin Bloom has edited a helpful book called *Developing Talent in Young People* (New York: Ballantine, 1985), which explores the development of exceptional attainments in arts, sciences, and other professions. The book presents an integrative model of how aptitude, motivation, family structure, and educational experiences significantly interact to promote professional expertise. Bloom's ideas are developed through a series of personal histories of highly gifted and accomplished individuals.
2. These and other motivational factors concerning performing are discussed in the context of an analysis of factors contributing to musical performance anxiety in D.O. Fogel, "Toward Effective Treatment for Musical Performance Anxiety, *Psychotherapy: Theory, Research, and Practice* 19 (1982): 368–75.
3. A contemporary perspective on anxiety, which considers the role of self-absorption is found in R.E. Ingram and P.C. Kendall, "The Cognitive Side of Anxiety," *Cognitive Therapy Research* 11 (1987): 523–36.
4. Complete absorption in playing or performing is a state that performers actively strive for, but don't always attain. This state appears to be related to what psychologist Abraham Maslow termed "peak" experiences in his consideration of "self actualization." More recently, this phenomenon—also referred to as "flow"—has been the object of considerable scientific study. The topic discussed in detail in M. Csikszentmihalyi, *Flow: The Psychology of Optimal Experience* (New York: Harper Perennial, 1990).
5. The psychological aspects of musical perception have received a great deal of attention over the years. More recently, however, psychologists have turned their attention to a broader range of topics, including performing, composition and improvisation, because of the curent interest in the cognitive aspects of musical and other phenomena. The following references provide detailed analyses of these and related topics: D. Deutsch, *The Psychology of Music* (New York: Academic Press, 1982); J.A. Sloboda, *The Cognitive Psychology of Music* (Oxford: Clarendon Press, 1985); J.A., Sloboda, *Generative Processes in Music: The Psychology of Performance, Improvisation, and Composition* (Oxford: Clarendon Press, 1988).
6. Hundreds of articles and books deal with various aspects of musical performance skills and a review of them is beyond the scope of this book. However, several books in particular have achieved widespread recognition as being

especially helpful in addressing psychological aspects of musical performance skills, though no single article or book can be said to offer *the* definitive analysis. The treatment of specific performance problems needs to be tailored to the individual. What may prove effective for one performer may have little effect on another. The following books present a spectrum of practical approaches to the psychology of musical performance that may help particular performers. See R. Caldwell, *The Performer Prepares* (Dallas, Texas: PST Publishers, 1990); B. Green, *The Inner Game of Music* (Garden City, N.Y.: Anchor Press, 1986; F. Wilson *Tone Deaf and All Thumbs?* (New York: Viking Press, 1986); E. Ristad *Soprano on Her Head* (Moab, Ut.: Real People Press, 1982).

# Chapter 2

1. See, for example, A. Brandfonbrener, "An Overview of the Medical Problems of Musicians," *Journal of American College Health* 34(1986): 165–69. The author, Dr. Alice Brandfonbrener, is a pioneer in the field of Arts Medicine, which in recent years has brought to the attention of health care professionals the stresses—both medical and psychological—to which performers are prone.
2. Recent interest in the medical and psychological stresses of performing is reflected in the establishment of a new scientific journal, *Medical Problems of Performing Artists,* published by Hanley and Belfus Publishers, Philadelphia. Published quarterly, MPPA is a forum for health care providers, performing artists, and individuals in related fields to consider a wide range of topics concerning the physical and psychological health of performers.
3. The topic of stress has generated a voluminous literature in both psychology and medicine. Much of the impetus for current interest in this area, however, stems from the work of Hans Selye, who formulated a model of stress that emphasized the body's considerable, though not unlimited capacity to absorb, the impact of stressful events. According to Selye, when we are subjected to chronic, unremitting stress, our natural recuperative powers are diminished by the absence of stress-free periods, when recovery and compensation would normally occurs. For a discussion of these and related issues, refer to H. Selye, *Stress in Health and Disease* (Reading, Mass.: Butterworth Publishers, 1976).
4. The influence of Donald Meichnbaum's work on cognitive therapy and stress management is evident throughout this book. Two excellent books that provide detailed explanations of his approach are especially recommended *Stress Inoculation Training* (New York: Pergamon Press, 1985 and *Cognitive Behavior Modification* (New York: Plenum Press, 1977).
5. The concept of self-assessment, which is critical to the area of cognitive behavior modification, has been discussed in detail by many different authors. Albert Ellis was among the first to clearly articulate the importance of understanding how "self-talk" (internal dialogues we constantly carry on within

214 •   *Notes from the Green Room*

ourselves) influences behavior and feelings. See, for example, A. Ellis, *Reason and Emotion in Psychotherapy* (New York: Stuart, 1962). Arnold Lazarus, another cognitive-behavioral psychologist, has also emphasized the importance of self-assessment in the somewhat broader context of the BASIC ID, which is introduced in chapter 3. For further consideration of Lazarus's approach to assessment and related intervention strategies, see his book, *The Practice of MultiModal Therapy* (Baltimore: Johns Hopkins University Press, 1989).

6. Stress management skills have been discussed by many different authors in response to the pioneering work of Hans Selye some years ago. These skills are especially helpful to people in occupations where chronic tension and anxiety are inevitable, as is the case for many professional performers. Increasingly, the focus of work in this area has been on helping people develop healthful lifestyles that minimize the risks of physical and psychological impairments. Although there are many helpful and practical references on this topic, we especially recommend Martha Davis, Elizabeth Eshelman, and Matthew McKay, *The Relaxation and Stress Reduction Workbook,* 3rd ed. (Oakland, Calif.: New Harbinger Publications, 1988). A major work in the health and wellness field, particularly with respect to mind/body relationships, is *Mind as Healer, Mind as Slayer,* by Kenneth Pelletier, (New York: Dela/Seymour Lawrence, 1977). The interested reader might consult many additional resources, including H. Benson, *The Relaxation Response* (New York: Avon Books, 1976), R. Woolfolk and P. Lehrer, *Principles of Stress Management* (New York: Guilford, 1984), P.L. Rice, *Stress and Health: Principles and Practice for Coping and Wellness* (Pacific Grove, Calif.: Brooks/Cole, 1987), and N. Cousins, *Head First: The Biology of Hope* (New York: E.P. Dutton, 1989).

7. Just as the musically uninitiated are often surprised to learn of the enormous diversity of musical styles, anyone investigating relaxation training is faced with diverse options. Relaxation training may seem simple, even trivial, but it has been investigated and practiced from many different conceptual vantage points. In their book *Principles of Stress Mangement* (New York: Guilford, 1984), editors Richard Woolfolk and Paul Lehrer have assembled a scholarly review of many of the most commonly used relaxation training and stress management procedures.

8. The term "inoculation" in the context of anxiety has an obvious connection with the corresponding medical term. In both instances, it refers to exposing an individual to the weakened form of a pathogenic entity (a virus, for example, or an anxiety-arousing situation) to promote the activation of innate defenses, such as the immune system or psychological coping responses. The term "stress inoculation", therefore, refers to a therapeutic approach of subjecting clients to stressful situations that stimulte, but do not overwhelm, coping responses. Psychologist Seymour Epstein has argued that there is an innate "stress inoculation response" through which we naturally deal with anticipated stressors via mental imagery, almost in a form of rehearsal. See S. Epstein, "Natural Healing Processes of the Mind, in *Stress Reduction and*

*Prevention,* eds. D. Meichenbaum and M.E. Jaremko (New York: Plenum, 1983), 39–66.

9. The technique of *graded exposure* has a long history of clinical applications. It is based on the simple proposition that gradual, controlled exposure to a fear-arousing situation provides the individual with an opportunity to activate coping responses without being overwhelmed. Historically, it has much in common with Joseph Wolpe's procedure for treating anxiety, Systematic Desensitization, in which mental images of feared objects or situations are sequentially presented in order of increasing anxiety provocation. Each in turn is visualized while the client is in a relaxed state. Gradual exposure to anxiety-provoking situations appears to be highly effective in helping people develop a sense of mastery and confidence. See J. Wolpe, *The Practice of Behavior Therapy* (New York: Pergamon Press, 1982) for a detailed consideration of these therapeutic principles.

    Several studies have reported on the positive effects of graded exposure and desensitization in the treatment of stage fright. A case study that illustrates the basic principles of this technique may be found in G.R. Norton, L. MacLean, and E. Wachna, "The Use of Cognitive Desensitization and Self-Directed Mastery Training for Treating Stage Fright," *Cognitive Therapy and Research* 1, (1978): 61–64.

10. For a very readable and useful overview of mental imagery, see Arnold Lazarus, *In the Mind's Eye* (New York: Rawson, 1978).

11. Stress inoculation and related techniques have achieved widespread acceptance as effective psychological interventions. For a comprehensive review of these and related procedures, see D. Meichenbaum and M.E. Jaremko, eds., *Stress Reduction and Prevention* (New York: Plenum Press, 1983).

12. The idea that learning to cope with anxiety involves trial-and-error experimentation is emphasized throughout the book. We feel it is very important for performers to become actively involved in the treatment of their particular problems. We believe this is best achieved through a collaborative working relationship, rather than one in which the therapist dictates the course of treatment. For example, consider the suggestion that a performer practice deep breathing. Even though breathing is a perfectly normal activity, there are many ways of doing it. "Taking a deep breath" entails many variations in timing, depth, and regularity, and only through a process of experimentation can a person best determine their natural pattern and how best to achieve a comfortble rate of inhalation and exhalation.

    Relaxation is another area that invites experimentation. No one can really tell someone else how to relax, other than to talk in general terms about letting go of tension. An elusive state, relaxation often occurs only after we have tried, without success several different approaches, only to find ourselves in the desired state without knowing exactly how we got there. To reenter that state later on may entail going through a process that only gradually becomes systematized through practice and experimentation.

13. Thought stopping is a technique for terminating unpleasant thought as soon as we become aware of them. It can be especially helpful in dealing with

obsessions, which are very persistent, stereotypic, and troublesome thoughts. One procedure for interrupting the flow of obsessional thoughts is to shout (and, later, subvocalize) "Stop!" upon becoming aware of their occurrence. Another equally disruptive behavior involves snapping a rubber band conveniently kept on the wrist for such occasions. Many behavioral therapists have written about thought stopping, among them Arnold Lazarus, in *Behavior Therapy and Beyond* (New York: McGraw Hill, 1971).

# Chapter 3

1. This chapter applies Arnold Lazarus' model of "Multimodal Therapy" to the area of musical performance skills. Lazarus has published widely on this and related topics, but provides an excellent summary of the basic model in his recent book, *The Practice of Multimodal Therapy,* mentioned earlier.
2. Ibid.
3. Assessment, or evaluation, is an essential element of therapeutic treatment. It is often tempting to make changes without a careful evaluation of prevailing conditions—for example, when, after a stressful performance, a musician abruptly concludes "I'll *never* play Beethoven again—I just don't have a feel for his music!" The situation is likely to involve a variety of hidden factors that, when taken into account, might dictate a previously unanticipated course of action. However, many performers object having attention directed to their problems, fearing that doing so will only make things worse. We believe that attending to and taking note of the behaviors, thoughts, and feelings that accompany stress and anxiety comprise the most effective first step in bringing about lasting change. While this sort of self-monitoring can admittedly be uncomfortable at times, it aids in the process of coming to terms with reality—with what *is,* rather than what we often fantasize to be the case. In his recent book *Full Catastrophe Living* (New York: Delta, 1990), Jon Kabat-Zinn, provides a powerful rationale for learning to accept ourselves as we are as an important initial step in learning to honestly confront stress and anxiety.
4. The importance of movement and postural factors in stress has been addressed by numerous authors and clinicians, paramount among them, perhaps, being the members of the Alexander school. Also of interest in this regard is the movement-oriented educational system developed by Dr. Moshe Feldenkrais, which has achieved widespread popularity in general stress management, sports psychology, and rehabilitation medicine. A useful set of exercises has been developed and made available on audiotape by Mark Reese and David Zemach-Bersin. The program, called *Relaxercise,* is available through Sensory Motor Learning System, P.O. Box 5674, Berkeley, CA, 94705.
5. Although normally avoided at all cost, mistakes objectively represent an important source of information and feedback. Anton Weinberg's delightful little book *Unfinished Sentences* (Bloomington, Ind.: Pixel Place, 1988) contains the quote that opens one of our chapters: "There are no such things as mis-

takes, only musical misunderstandings" (p. 13). All too often, efforts are made to eradicate mistakes without adequately considering either their meaning or derivation.

6. It is worth pointing out that technical mistakes can serve as a vehicle for much more profound analyses of musical performance skills than might be suspected. The situation is analogous to mistakes in childrens' speech, which—although quickly corrected by irritated parents and impatient teachers—provided the raw material for linguist Noam Chomsky's generative theory of linguistic grammar. An illuminating discussion of some of the parallels between musical and linguistic grammar, in which errors figure prominently, is John Sloboda, *The Musical Mind.*

7. The terminology used to discuss emotional states can be confusing at times. In particular, the terms *mood* and *affect* are frequently used interchangeably, despite referring to different phenomena. In musical terms, mood is often used with reference to the emotional tone of a composition or perhaps of a particular musical style. Affect, on the other hand, often refers to the performer's emotional expression during a performance.

   In a psychological context, both terms are used with reference to the individual; mood describes a prevailing emotional tone, whereas affect refers to more variable feelings that are usually—but not always—concordant with mood. In meteorological terms, it might be helpful to think of mood and affect as analogous to, respectively, "climate" and "weather."

8. *Temperament* has been extensively studied by developmental psychologists and pediatricians. Characteristic patterns of activity, emotionality, social tendencies, and overall responsiveness to the environment consistently distinguish children from birth onward, according to research that began with a longitudinal study of children from birth to adulthood by Herbert Birch, Stella Chess, and Alexander Thomas. See, for example, their article, "The Origins of Personality," *Scientific American* 223 (1970): 2102–9.

9. The idea that anxiety has adaptive qualities, notably as a "warning signal," is an important therapeutic idea that is helpful in counteracting the belief of many performers that to be anxious is to be crazy or somehow abnormal. A good discussion of this aspect of anxiety can be found in the introductory chapter of Aaron Beck and Steven Emery, *Anxiety Disorders and Phobias: A Cognitive Perspective* (New York: Basic Books, 1985).

10. Emotions are powerful cues in determining our preferences for music. Most of us seem to have instinctual reactions to much of what we hear, and nearly everyone has had the experience of being pulled into a piece of music by its appeal to the emotions, with little or nothing else to identify it. See Leonard Meyer, *Emotions and Meaning in Music* (Chicago: University of Chicago Press, 1956) and David Hargreaves, *The Developmental Psychology of Music* (New York: Cambridge University Press, 1986) for extensive analyses of the role of emotions in shaping our preferences for and understanding of musical phenomena.

11. The autonomic nervous system (ANS), a part of the central nervous system, regulates the level of activation we experience. It is divided into two parts, the

sympathetic and parasympathetic systems, which maintain a state of balance reflecting the prevailing activation state. Normally, intense anxiety, usually accompanied by a high arousal level, reflects heightened activaton of the sympathetic nervous system, which functions as the body's alarm system. Activation of the parasympathetic system, on the other hand, is associated with lower levels of activation and arousal.

12. The concept of time is integral to an appreciation of music and has been the focus of philosophers, psychologists, and musicians for years. An intriguing consideration of some of the experiental aspects of time may be found in Robert Grudin, *Time and the Art of Living* (New York: Ticknor and Fields, 1982).

13. The capacity of mental imagery to evoke realistic enactments of real-world events is well known. Imagery is a time-honored psychotherapeutic technique espoused by Arnold Lazarus *(In the Mind's Eye)* and others, and has also made inroads into the popular press. (See for example, P.W. Buffington, "Picture Perfect," *Sky* 8 (1989): 74–78.

14. David Reubart, pianist and author, has explored the many facets of performing under stress (such as playing from memory) in his book, *Anxiety and Musical Performance* (New York: DaCapo Press, 1985).

15. See Ingram and Kendall "The Cognitive Side of Anxiety," for a discussion of how anxiety shares common characteristics with other forms of psychological distress but possesses unique attributes as well.

16. The concept of self-talk is basic to the cognitive-behavioral framework to which we ascribe, and owes much to the work of the psychologist Albert Ellis. For a somewhat abbreviated consideration of this and relatd concepts, refer to A. Ellis, "The Basic Clinical Theory of Rational-Emotive Therapy," in *Handbook of Rational-Emotive Therapy,* A. Ellis and R. Grieger, eds. (New York: Springer, 1977).

17. If we reflect for a moment, most of us will realize that words like *should, ought to,* and *must* figure prominently in our vocabularies. Much of what we do seems to be driven by the sense of obligation reflected in these words, as in: "I *should* practice" or "I *ought* to learn this piece." Psychoanalyst Karen Horney has written an illuminating article on this topic called "Tyranny of the 'Should'," in her book *The Neurotic Personality of Our Time.*

18. One aspect of anxiety that bears some mention concerns interpersonal preferences and the degree to which we feel comfortable with the people who provide a social context for making music. Ensembly musicians probably have to deal with these issues more than soloists, but all performers share their music with *someone,* whether the audience in a packed house or a few friends in casual surroundings. Some performers actively avoid people, and clinical experience tells us that hours spent in practice rooms sometimes constitute a defense aginst contact with other people.

Another aspect of interpersonal issues concerns the relationship between social interactions and musical preferences. See V.J. Konecni, "Social Interaction and Musical Preference," In *The Psychology of Music,* D. Deutsch, ed. (New York: Academic Press, 1982) for a discussion of the theory that responses to aesthetic phenomena are part of a larger process that regulates moods, emotions, and interpersonal behaviors, According to Konecni, our sensitivities to aesthetic experiences interact with our social environment so that our feelings and moods are undergoing constant revision.

19. The use of beta-blockers drugs in the treatment of performance anxiety has received considerable attention in recent years. For recent reviews of the topic including detailed discussions of potential risks and benefits, see M. Lader, "B-Adrenoceptor Antagonists in Neuropsychiatry: An update," *Journal of Clinical Psychiatry* 49 (1988): 213–23; P.M. Lehrer, "The Use of Beta Blockers," *New Jersey Medicine* 84 (1987): 27–33; A.S. Nies, "Clinical Pharmacology of Beta-Adrenergic Blockers," *Medical Problems of Performing Artists* (1986): 25–29; R. Noyes, "Beta-Adrenergic Blockers," in *Handbook of anxiety disorders,* C.G. Last and M. Hesen, eds. (New York: Pergamon, 1988), 445–59.

20. Anxiety manifests a range of somatic symptoms that may include dry mouth, sweating, rapid heartbeat, shallow breathing, trembling or shaking, "butterflies," and urinary urgency. Generally, the number of symptoms provides a rough gauge of the overall level of activation, so that people who experience intense panic may report most, if not all, of these sensations.

21. The topic of breathing is very broad and can only be touched on here. However, breathing is fundamentally important for all performers, including those whose instruments do not rely on breath for sound production. Breathing is also an essential element of all relaxation, stress management, and meditation techniques, and so it is important to appreciate it's many facets and how it can become an effective attribute of adaptive performance skills. Within the general realm of clinical psychology, the following two references (both previously cited) may be especially helpful: Davis, Eshelman, and McKay, *The Relaxation and Stress Reduction Workbook* and Kabat-Zinn, *Full Catastrophe Living.* Both present detailed discussions of effective breathing in their broader discussion of the concept of awareness.

22. The distinction between thoracic and diaphragmatic breathing is important. Persons prone to stress and anxiety seem to tend toward the former. Thoracic breathing uses the intercostal muscles in the ribs to expand the chest and is generally not as effective as diaphragmatic breathing. In diaphragmatic breathing, the large internal muscle (the diaphragm) that separates the chest cavity from the lower abdomen is used. At inhalation, the diaphragm distends downward toward the abdomen, creating room for the lungs to expand in the chest cavity. During exhalation, the diaphragm moves upward as air rushes out of the lungs. A simple exercise to determine your own breathing pattern consists of the following steps. First, lie on the floor on your back, resting one hand on your chest and the other on your abdomen. Breath naturally, and watch the motion of your hands. Do both rise and fall? Does one appear to be relatively stationary while the other moves? Most relaxation and stress management techniques advocate the cultivation of diaphragmatic (or, as it is sometimes called, "abdominal") breathing, For a detailed consideration

of how breathing techniques are related to stress and anxiety, see Robert Fried, *The Breath Connection* (New York: Insight Books, 1990).

23. Beck, A.T., and Emery, S., *Anxiety Disorders and Phobias* (New York: Basic Books, 1985).

# Chapter 4

1. The fight or flight reaction is a very primitive response to the perception of danger. It is controlled by the autonomic nervous system (ANS), which mobilizes the body to deal with an imminent threat. Unfortunately, the fight or flight reaction is typically an "all or none" response, so intense that it is difficult to ignore. This primitive response helped to ensure the survival of our ancestors, who faced many physical threats, such as predatory animals, and the reaction triggers a state of physical vitality and strength intended to deal with such dangers. A number of adaptive responses occur as the organism prepares for action, including a shift of blood from the extremities into the body core, interruption of digestive and other processes, and a diversion of energy to large muscle groups. When activated by the perception of a threat that is not physical (such as a large, intimidating audience), the fight or flight response is less adaptive, because it inhibits many of the capabilities needed to perform effectively. Fingers become cold (and less sensitive) as blood shifts centrally, small muscles sets are deactivated in favor of larger ones, and so on. The experience of a full-blown fight or flight reaction can be most unsettling, despite the fact that it is an innate response designed to help protect us from harm.

2. In talking about practice, we do not mean to imply that there is little interest in the topic. A number of pianists report finding books such as W.S. Newman's *The Pianists' Problems*, (New York: Da Capo, 1984) helpful both for learning and practicing new music. We have however noticed a dearth of studies on how to optimize practice strategies, or evidence that one particular practice technique is better than another. The available psychological studies in this area are reviewed in the two previously cited books by John Sloboda, *The Musical Mind* and *Generative Processes in Music.*

3. These two quotes are from John B. Davies, *The Psychology of Music* (Stanford, Calif.: Stanford University Press, 1978), p. 15.

4. The concept of locus of control is frequently invoked in psychology to describe how people vary in terms of whether their behavior is regulated by inner or outer forces. This concept was first explored by the psychologist Herbert Witkin, who studied how we orient ourselves spatially to the visual environment.

5. See Fogel, "Toward Effective Treatment for Music Performance Anxiety" (Ch. 1, note 2).

6. For a discussion of concepts related to "cognitive maps," see John Sloboda's *The Musical Mind,* and *Generative Processes in Music* for an excellent intro-

duction to such diverse musical activities as composing, performing and improvising.

7. There is general agreement that performing from memory is aided to the degree that multiple coding systems are employed. That is, relying on several sources of encoded information—such as visual note images, physical sensations, formal knowledge of the musical structure of a piece, and so forth—will generally enhance musical recall. This apparent effect may be partly due to the confidence that accompanies learning the music exhaustively and investing the requisite time to achieve such comprehensive preparation, but there is little doubt that encoding information in multiple ways enhances recall for other reasons. An interesting discussion of issues related to this topic may be found in Reubart, *Anxiety and Musical Performance* (Ch. 3, note 14).

8. *Letting go* is of central importance not only in making music, but in learning to relax. In both instances, the desired effect appears to be achieved through an absence of voluntary control—it's difficult to make ourselves relax or play well. Such efforts, on the contrary, usually inhibit expressiveness and lend an effortful, stilted quality to our actions. Virtually all relaxation procedures emphasize the importance of learning to let go, much as musicians are instructed to do once they have learned a piece of music and are preparing it for performance.

9. The idea of a *learning curve* is important here with reference to the observation that successive refinements in all skills take proportionately more time to perfect than the basic elements. Learning curve refers to the relationship between the time invested and the percentage of the goal attained. A piece of music may be basically grasped in a short time, and its overall structure comprehended even more quickly, but to proceed from this point to the stage of muscular and cognitive control required for expressive refinement may require weeks, months, or even years. Performance preparations usually focus on the portion of the learning curve where the investment of time may seem to be paying diminishing returns because what is being learned is very subtle. An outside observer may hear little change from one session to the next, but to the performer, each successive refinement adds significantly to the overall quality of the music.

10. *Thought monitoring* has already been discussed in some detail, but we would like to add one additional point. This technique is especially important for musicians to understand because of the ease with which thoughts and music can coexist—and sometimes interfere—with one another. It is comparatively difficult to concentrate on reading a book while thinking about something else because both activities employ a verbal medium. Thought may intrude, but they tend to interrupt the train of reading. On the other hand, it's easy to think while engaged in music, particularly if the music has been rehearsed to the point of being relatively automatic. Because music and language are quite different modalities, we are capable of engaging in their expression simultaneously.

11. There is some research on the effects of audience characteristics on performance quality and anxiety. There seems to be a fine line between being cowed

and being stimulated by an audience; the most seasoned performers, in terms of formal training and experience, respond most positively to audiences. See D.L. Hamann and M. Sobaje, "Anxiety and the College Musician: A Study of Performance Conditions and Subject Variables," *Psychology of Music* 11 (1983): 37–50.

12. The idea of the *musical present* is essential to keep in mind when considering the overall impact of a musical composition on performer or audience. Irrespective of the length of a musical composition, all that is heard at any one moment is a relatively small number of notes, corresponding to the vertical (harmonic) structure of the music. The musical present is the fleeting instant when music is audibly brought to life, only to be replaced in the next instant by the succeeding notes of the composition. Our capacity to apprehend and remember that we hear is comparatively limited, and the coherence of a piece of music is a reflection of our capacity to integrate a sequence of musical moments into a structural entity. This issue is considered in greater detail in John Davies, *The Psychology of Music* (Stanford, Calif.: Stanford University Press, 1978).

13. A formal research study by Margaret Kendrick and her coworkers attests to the efficacy of group-oriented treatment for stage fright. See M.J. Kendrick, K.D. Craig, D.M. Lawson, and P.O. Davidson, "Cognitive and Behavioral Therapy for Muscal Performance Anxiety," *Journal of Consulting and Clinical Psychology* 50 (1982): 353–62.

14. The anxious anticipation of an event is often more stressful than the event itself, and most performers find that their anxiety peaks sometime before the beginning of a piece of music and then tapers off. See P. Salmon, R. Schrodt, and J. Wright, "A Temporal Gradient of Anxiety in a Stressful Performance Context," *Medical Problems of Performing Artists* 4 (1989): 77–80.

15. The intensity of our anxiety often makes it difficult to remember that it is a warning signal, not a catastrophe in its own right. This aspect of anxiety, referred to as *Hoch's Paradox,* is discussed in considerable detail in Beck and Emery, *Anxiety Disorders and Phobias* (Ch. 3 note 9).

16. The disinction between *thoughts* and *reality* is important to keep in mind, although when we are acutely anxious danger seem disconcertingly realistic and imminent. Many relaxation and stress management programs advocate cultivating the capacity to let go of distressful thoughts, partly to provide at least a momentary respite from anxiety. In addition, our ability to let go demonstrates a fundamental point: thoughts come and go independently of "reality," and we do not have to tolerate stressful thoughts as we might have to, for instance, endure a painful operation. For some helpful suggestions on effectively regulating troublesome thoughts see Kabat-Zinn, *Full Catastrophe Living,* note 3, chapter 3. The thought stopping techniques mentioned earlier (see note 13, chapter 2) are helpful in this regard as well.

17. See C. Stanislavski (1948) *An Actor Prepares.* New York: Theater Arts.

# Chapter 5

1. The topic of anxiety has perhaps stimulated more research and clinical activity than any other form of psychological impairment. The concept of anxiety has

undergone significant revision over the years, as research has progressed. Most contemporary perspectives on anxiety usually emphasizes the manner in which it evolves from the interaction of three basic components: *thoughts* of risk or danger; physical *sensations* associated with sympathetic nervous system activation; and *behavior* marked by avoidance of stressful situations.

2. The prevalence of anxiety disorders has been reported in many research studies, among the largest being the Epidemiological Catchment Area (ECA) study. The results were published in the *Archives of General Psychiatry* in August, 1984. The results of the ECA study, which surveyed over 17,000 residents of five large urban areas, showed anxiety to be the most commonly reported psychological impairment, followed by substance abuse and depression.

3. The fight or flight response has been mentioned previously in terms of it's capacity to rapidly cause a state of heightened alertness. Many of the symptoms of anxiety are the same as those of the fight or flight response, thought these are more likely to be prolonged with anxiety. Both the fight or flight response and anxiety are regulated by the sympathetic part of the autonomic nervous system.

4. Again, Hoch's Paradox, according to which something intended is to warn of danger itself becomes the focus of anxious concern, can throw light on the characteristics of intense anxiety (see note 14, chapter 4).

5. The popularity of the three-factor model of anxiety, which stresses the interaction of thoughts, physical sensations, and behaviors, owes much to the work of psychologist Peter Lang. For a representative discussion of his treatment of this topic, see P.J. Lang, G.A. Miller, and D. Levin, "Anxiety and Fear," in, *Consciousness and Self-regulation,* R.J. Davidson, G.E. Schwartz, and D. Shapiro, eds. (New York: Plenum, 1988, 123–51).

6. The term *response synchrony* has been used to explain how different symptoms of anxiety (thoughts, physical sensations, behaviors) interact with one another as a function of the overall level of anxiety. Intense anxiety is marked by high synchrony: all or most symptoms are present to a significant degree. Highly anxious individuals, in other words, are likely to suffer very disturbing thoughts, marked physiological distress, and strong behavioral avoidant tendencies. At lower levels of anxiety, response synchrony decreases. Thus, troublesome thoughts will not necessarily be accompanied by signs of physiological arousal or behavioral avoidance. People with relatively low levels of anxiety tend to have more variable symptoms than individuals who experience the intense anxiety associated with panic attacks. For a further consideration of this issue, see S.J. Rachman and R.I. Hodgson, "Synchrony and Desynchrony in Fear Avoidance," *Behavior Research and Therapy* 12 (1974): 311–18.

7. The inevitability of anxiety as part of human nature is nicely captured in Rollo May's book, *The Meaning of Anxiety* (New York: Washington Square Press, 1977).

8. One of the preeminent features of anxiety is the manner in which it can spiral out of control, beginning with something as seemingly inconsequential as a troublesome thought. Anxiety-prone individuals may progress from this stage

to symptoms of physiological arousal, which in turn reinforce the frightening thoughts, and so forth. Beck and Emery in *Anxiety Disorders and Phobias* (previously cited) discuss this aspect of anxiety in the context of a consideration of how anxiety seems to feed on itself.

9. See Ingram and Kendall, "The Cognitive Side of Anxiety.

10. An early study of the anticipatory aspects of anxiety was carried out by Fenz and Epstein with experienced sport parachute jumpers, who were found to experience maximum distress just before—rather than at the moment of — their jumps. Novices, on the other hand, were more likely to panic when jumping, despite seeming to be relatively calm beforehand. See W.E. Fenz and S. Epstein, "Gradients of Psychological Arousal of Experienced and Novice Parachutists as a Function of an Approaching Jump," *Psychosomatic Medicine* 29 (1967): 33–51.

11. See Salmon, Schrodt, and Wright (1989), "A Temporal Gradient of Anxiety" (Ch. 4, note 14).

12. See Beck and Emery, *Anxiety Disorders and Phobias* (Ch. 3, note 9).

# Chapter 6

1. The concept of self-efficacy is important to mention in this context. Psychologist Albert Bandura has studied how people cope with demands that confront them and has found that believing that one is capable of doing something may be nearly as important as actually having the necessary skills. Self-efficacy is obviously a desirable characteristic for performers; in its absence, they are likely to be troubled by anxious fears about never measuring up, despite possessing the needed capabilities. An early article by Bandura on self-efficacy provides a good overview of this concept. See A. Bandura, "Self-Efficacy: Toward a Unifying Theory of Behavioral Change," *Psychological Review* 84 (2) (1977): 191–215.

2. A good working relationship with a therapist/teacher/coach (or whomever) is crucial to helping performers develop confidence in themselves. Factors that appear to enhance the quality of such relationships include empathy, genuineness, and warmth, according to psychologists like Carl Rogers. See, for example, C. Rogers, *Client-Centered Therapy* Boston: Houghton-Mifflin, 1951). Beyond these characteristics, therapists who work with performers need to be aware of the importance of avoiding the "guru" approach that some teachers and coaches cultivate with their students. Although some performers may derive undeniable benefit from working with such charismatic individuals, we feel that there is also a place for more collaborative client—therapist relationship, in which therapist and performer collectively work to establish a mutually satisfying relationship.

3. It's somewhat ironic that music can be both the source of so much anxiety and yet such pleasure and enjoyment. Performers suffering from stress and anxiety can easily lose sight of the therapeutic qualities of music. We consider

it significant that many anxious performers don't seem to really enjoy music or derive any obvious benefit from it, because they are so focused on note-perfect performances.

4. The cognitive-behavioral approach advocated here uses "induction" as a basic therapeutic process. In this data-oriented approach, the client (the performer) and the therapist work to agree on the nature of particular problems in terms that are as clear as possible. A performer who asserts that he or she is "incompetent," for instance, will be asked to document the assertion. Through an inductive approach, performers and those with whom they work can achieve a greater level of effective collaboration than might otherwise be the case. See chapter 10 of Beck and Emery, *Anxiety Disorders and Phobias* (Ch. 3, note 9) for additional discussion of this idea.

5. The basis for these suggestions on working with a therapist or coach are adapted from an article in the area of sports. See N. Zeitchick, "How to Take a Lesson," *Tennis* 4 (1989): 40–44.

6. Computer technology offers many interesting ways to refine performance skills. See P. Salmon and J. Newmark, "Clinical Applications of MIDI Technology," *Medical Problems of Performing Artists* 4 (1) (1989): 25–31.

# Chapter 7

1. Donald Meichenbaum's work in the area of cognitive-behavioral therapy has been highly influential in shaping current theories and clinical techniques. The idea of exploring differing manifestations of cognitive processes in a variety of musical contexts is based directly on his analyses of how cognitive and behavioral processes interact as described in D. Michenbaum, "Toward a Cognitive Theory of Self-Control," in *Consiousness and Self-Regulation,* vol. 1, G.E. Schwartz and D. Shapiro eds. (New York: Plenum Press, 1976), 223–60; D. Meichenbaum, *Cognitive Behavior Modification*; D. Meichenbaum and M. Genest, "Cognitive Behavior Modification: An Integration of Cognitive and Behavioral Methods," in *Helping People Change,* 2nd ed., F.H. Kanfer and A.P. Goldstein, eds. (New York: Pergamon Press, 1980); and D. Meichenbaum, *Stress Inoculation Training* (Ch. 2, note 4).

2. Psychologist Albert Ellis's work on *irrational beliefs* is one of the cornerstones of an approach to psychotherapy known as "Rational Emotive Therapy" (RET). For a concise review of the underlying principles of this approach, see A. Ellis, "Rational-Emotive Therapy," in R.J. Corsini (ed.), *Current Psychotherapies* (Itasca, Ill.: F.E. Peacock, 1979).

3. The concept of *problem solving* is an important element in the cognitive perspective for working with performers. This approach is very practical, and it focuses on the description, analysis, and amelioration of problematic aspects of performing in straightforward terms. Most of the therapeutic interventions advocated in the work of Meichenbaum (*Stress Inoculation Training,* see note 1, this Ch.) and Beck (*Anxiety Disorders and Phobias,* Ch. 3, note 9) are

based on the idea that reducing performance (or other) problems to manageable components and then developing specific, appropriate coping responses, is an effective means of reducing psychological stress.

4. The concept of *coping* is important in a consideration of cognitive aspects of performance problems. An especially useful discussion of coping responses and how to encourage them can be found in the work of psychologist Arnold Lazarus, who argues that our coping responses depend on a) how we size up a stressful event and; b) how capable we believe we are of dealing with the perceived challenge.

5. *Defense mechanisms,* in the classic Freudian sense of the term, are innate responses to events that threaten the stability of the *ego,* a core component of one's personality. Among the best-known defense mechanisms are *repression* (driving threatening thoughts or images from conscious awareness), *denial* (choosing to ignore significant, yet threatening, information), *projection* (erroneously attributing to others negative qualities to painful to admit to in oneself), and *intellectualization* (responding to events without emotion; cutting off emotional responses).

# Chapter 8

1. For a comprehensive evaluation of a variety of contemporary stress management procedres, see R.L. Woolfolk and P.M. Lehrer, *Principles and Practices of Stress Management* (Ch. 2, note 7).

2. A great many training resources are available for basic relaxation skills. Among the most useful for everday applications is Davis, Eshelman, and McKay, *The Relaxation and Stress Reduction Workbook* (Ch. 2, note 6).

3. The *quieting response,* developed by Dr. Charles Stroebel, is a useful and effective procedure for achieving moment-to-moment relaxation. It can be particularly useful to performers, who can employ the response even in a performance once it has been learned and practiced to the point of being almost reflexive. A helpful description of the *quieting response* may be found in Woolfolk and Lehrer, *Principles and Practice of Stress Management,* cited above.

4. Psychologist Paul Lehrer (personal communication) emphasizes an oft-quoted dictum that "an effort to relax is a failure to relax." This idea is worth keeping in mind, particularly when working with performers, who habitually invest considerable effort and energy in their performance skills. Effective relaxation and musically sensitive performance abilities both seem to benefit markedly when one can let go and allow—rather than force—things to happen.

5. See Kabat-Zinn, *Full Catastrophe Living* (Ch. 3, note 3) and Davis, Eschelman, and McKay, *The Relaxation and Stress Reduction Workbook* (Ch. 2, note 6) for some helpful exercises in basic breathing techniques.

6. One of the best-known forms of relaxation, that of *progressive muscle relaxation* was developed by physician Edmond Jacobson after observing that more

than half of the patients who consulted him for physical complaints were found to have no clearcut medical disorders in need of treatment. Rather, they suffered from a variety of stress-related conditions that were often highly responsive to relaxation techniques, provided the latter were effectively learned and consistently practiced. See, for example, E. Jacobson, *Modern Treatment of Tense Patients* (Springfield, Ill.: Charles Thomas, 1970) for a more detailed understanding of his approach to this aspect of treatment.

7. An interesting twist on the old dictum, "Practice Makes Perfect" proposed by psychologist John Sloboda is that "Practice Makes *Permanent*," conveying the idea that repetitive practice tends to lead to the encoding of whatever we learn, perfect or not. Repetition by itself does not guarantee accuracy. See also Buffington, "Picture Perfect" (Ch. 3, note 13).

8. Psychologist Martin Seligman has spent years studying a phenomenon he termed *learned helplessness,* an extremely apathetic response to unremitting and insurmountable stressors. *Learned helplessness* is characterized by a tendency to perceive one's situation as hopeless, so that there seems no use in trying to cope with it. Performers who persistently subject themselves to auditions, competitions, adjudications, and so on, but seldom are rewarded for their efforts are prime candidates for the depression that frequently accompanies learned helplessness. See M. Seligman, *Helplessness* (San Francisco: W.H. Freeman, 1975).

9. Buffington, "Picture Perfect" (Ch. 3, note 13).

10. For a consideration of how cognitive monitoring can be integrated effectively into treatment, see R. E. McMullin, *Handbook of Cognitive Therapy Techniques* (New York: Norton, 1986). Peter Desberg and George Marsh's *Controlling Stagefright* (Oakland, Calif.: New Harbinger, 1988) focuses on the cognitive aspects of performance anxiety as well, and contains a number of useful self-assessment forms that teachers, clinicians, and performers are all likely to find helpful.

# Chapter 9

1. Kabat-Zinn, *Full Catastrophe Living* (Ch. 3, note 3).

2. For a discussion of the three-factor model with particular emphasis on self-efficacy, see M.G. Craske and K. Craig, "Musical Performance Anxiety: The Three-System Model, and Self-Efficacy Theory," *Behavior Research and Therapy* 22 (1984): 267–80.

3. It is important to keep in mind the various *adaptive* aspects of anxiety and avoid becoming overly focused on its maladaptive side. Most performers have to come to terms with anxiety, to "make friends" with it in a sense. Refer to writers such as Rollo May (*The Meaning of Anxiety,* previously cited) and others with a humanistic or existentialist perspective to gain a broader perspective on anxiety that stresses its inevitability.

4. Awareness training is stressed in many meditative and contemplative techniques

as a means of becoming increasingly focused on oneself or on what one is doing. Athletes benefit from awareness training, as can musicians whose performance skills require the utmost attention and concentration. A helpful overview of awareness training in the context of a broader program of stress management is found in Kabat-Zinn, *Full Catastrophe Living* (Ch. 3, note 3).

5. Beck and Emery, *Anxiety Disorders and Phobias* (Ch. 3, note 9).

6. The idea that coping can be *proactive,* rather than *reactive* is stressed by many cognitive and behavioral psychologists. Proactive coping means anticipating stressors you are likely to face when you can develop effective countermeasures. Meichenbaum's *Stress Inoculation Training,* previously cited, contains a detailed discussion of how to develop anticipatory coping responses. A somewhat briefer description of these techniques is found in a chapter by Meichenbaum in *Stress Reduction and Prevention,* D. Meichenbaum and M.E. Jaremko, eds. (New York: Plenum Press, 1983).

7. See Kabat-Zinn, *Full Catastrophe Living,* and Davis, Eshelman, amd McKay, *The Relaxation and Stress Reduction Workbook,* for additional suggestions on some basic relaxation techniques. A more formal scholarly review of basic relaxation techniques may be found in Woolfolk and Lehrer, *Principles of Stress Management* (Ch. 2, note 7).

8. Arnold Lazarus's *In the Mind's Eye* (Ch. 2, note 10) is a very useful book for an overview of basic imagery techniques and how they can be applied in a variety of therapeutic settings.

9. Cognitive restructuring techniques have been described by many authors, but an especially helpful description of basic procedures is Rian McMullin, *Handbook of Cognitive Therapy Techniques,* published by New Harbinger Press.

# Index